Supercook's

Kitchencraft

Marshall Cavendish London & New York

Edited by Mary Alice Lamberty
House editors: Isabel Moore
and Veronica Sperling

Published by
Marshall Cavendish Books Limited
58 Old Compton Street
London W1V 5PA

© Marshall Cavendish Limited 1977
This volume first published 1977

Printed in Great Britain

ISBN 0 85685 269 4

Introduction

To eat well is a pleasure, to cook well and correctly is an art, and one worth learning.

KITCHENCRAFT is a comprehensive guide to the craft of cooking, invaluable both for the complete beginner and enthusiastic cook who wishes to brush up on technique. It starts with the basics – a well-planned kitchen, useful equipment and sensible storage arrangements are 'musts' for any aspiring Julia Child – then covers the arts of freezing and preserving, including pickle-making, jam- and marmalade-making, as well as bottling.

The necessary foundation for any good cook's repertoire is an understanding of the properties and uses of such staples as flour, sugar, eggs, milk, etc., and the heart of the book opens with an entire chapter on this subject. Basic cooking techniques are not forgotten either, and how to prepare and cook meat, fish, vegetables and fruit forms a comprehensive chapter on its own, complete with easy-reference charts to give a see-at-a-glance view of what to cook, how and for how long. The section concludes with an entire chapter on what are considered to be the traditional crowning glories of any cook – stocks, soups, breads, pastry and cakes. The different methods are all explained in easy-to-follow basic recipes and often accompanied by step-by-step pictures.

KITCHENCRAFT is a 'must' addition to every bookshelf, an invaluable reference volume for every cook.

Contents

Chapter One

Kitchen planning

For cooking to be a pleasure, your kitchen needs to have a pleasant atmosphere and to be well designed. So knowing some basic facts about design will be helpful whether you are planning a completely new kitchen, remodelling an old one or trying to make the best of what already exists.

A kitchen cannot be planned in a vacuum. It must be seen in relation to the rest of the house, to the functions it will serve. Will it be used only for cooking? For cooking plus family meals? For meals with guests? Will it be the centre of family activity, or will it be used by no more than one or two people at a time?

Naturally, the answers to these questions depend in part on the size of the room. Remember that everybody has a tendency to gravitate towards the kitchen, so if possible arrange a place where people won't be in the way.

Having decided how your kitchen will relate to the rest of the house, you will need to make decisions about large appliances and fitments. The two major ones will be split-level cooking versus a conventional stove and the size of the refrigerator (see below for pros and cons). In addition, you must decide whether you want various other items – dishwasher, freezer, waste disposal, microwave oven – now, or in the future. And, will the washing machine and drier be located in the kitchen? And the heating or hot-water supply? All these decisions must be made early since they will require electrical connections, water and waste pipes.

Fortunately, most ready-built kitchen

A well-planned efficient kitchen.

units come in standard sizes. Therefore all you really need to know to start planning is (a) whether to consider standard-size units, and (b) the range and types of units available. If you design and build, or have built, you own units, they can be made to fit the space available.

Having made these basic decisions you are now ready to draw up your kitchen plan. On graph paper using a suitable scale – 1:10 or 1:12 for small and medium-sized kitchens; 1:20 for large – draw a carefully measured outline of your kitchen. Take accurate measurements of walls, windows, doorways, projections and recesses along the walls. Note at the side of the plan, ceiling and sill heights. Plot on the plan the locations of existing services: gas main, waste water pipe to external drain, mains water supply and hot water pipe. Note in the margin whether these can be moved and in what direction.

Next, make cutouts of major appliances, kitchen units, sink unit, table and chairs. Mark what they are in different colours (an edging of colour will make them stand out on the plan). Now you are ready to try out any number of arrangements. If you are undecided about a split-level stove, or uncertain whether an undercounter or larger refrigerator is best, make cutouts for each size and try out both types. And don't be discouraged if the best possible layout for your kitchen is not achieved on the first attempt; only by examining all the alternatives will the best layout be attained.

The most important part of the kitchen is the work centre where meals are prepared, cooked and cleared away. The three major units – sink, stove and refrigerator – should be grouped relatively close together with good work top and

storage space between each to minimize walking and crisscrossing the area. A line drawn connecting these three places forms the *work triangle*. The sum of the sides of the work triangle should be at least 360 centimetres (12 feet) but no more than 660 centimetres (22 feet). A triangle of less than 360 centimetres (12 feet) probably indicates less than adequate working space; more than 660 centimetres (22 feet) that you will have too much walking to do between appliances. A conveniently sized work centre takes up no more than 9 square metres (100 square feet). If your kitchen is larger than this the extra space can be used for a dining area or snack bar for breakfast and family meals. Or it could be a children's play area or separate laundry section.

The shape and size of your kitchen largely determines the overall layout. These generally fall into four distinct types: galley, corridor, L-shaped and U-shaped.

The **Galley Kitchen** has all units along one wall. Provided the maximum distance between the furthest appliances is no more than 360-420 centimetres (12-19 feet), this plan works relatively well, though two or three people in the area simultaneously will cause congestion. Storage and countertops are less abundant than with other shapes. In small flats and bedsitters, the length of the unit can be reduced to about a metre by means of a hob-refrigerator-sink unit, though workspace is nil and storage scanty. Often these units are fitted with doors that incorporate more storage space as well as hide the kitchen when it is not in use.

The **Corridor Kitchen** is a relatively narrow kitchen with a door at each end and enough width for units to run along the facing walls. It is best to have sink and

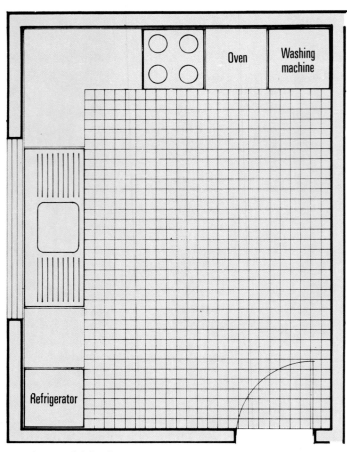

L-shaped kitchen

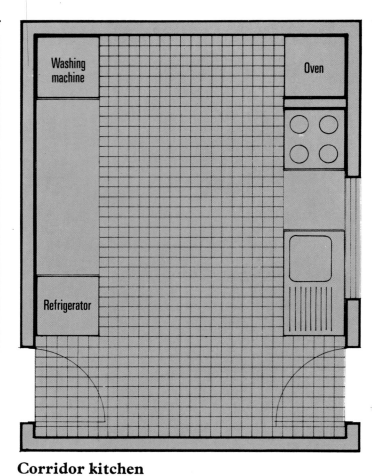

Corridor kitchen

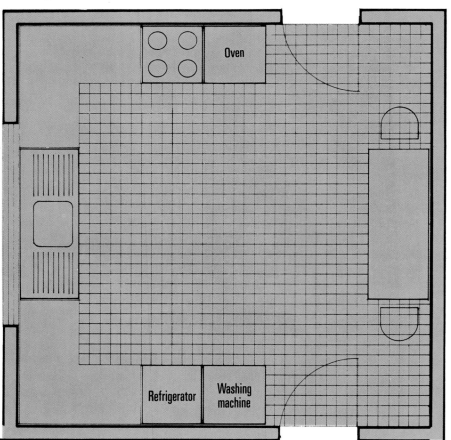

U-shaped kitchen

Galley kitchen

stove on the same wall, because carrying hot saucepans across the area can conflict with other people walking through. Place the refrigerator on the opposite wall. The corridor should be at least wide enough to allow cupboard doors to open easily.

The **L-Shaped Kitchen** can have appliances and work surfaces along adjacent walls. This creates an efficient work triangle and leaves a large area of the kitchen free for other uses, such as an eating area or snack bar.

The **U-Shaped Kitchen** gives maximum storage and counter space and minimum walking distances, and is potentially the most efficient in terms of layout. Frequently one side of the U is a double-sided divider separating the cooking and dining areas.

Major Planning Points

Sinks

The sink will probably be the first item to be placed on the floor plan, since its location is likely to be restricted by the position of the existing stack or gulley. Drains are expensive, if not impossible, to move; so you should think twice and get expert advice before contemplating a major change. Usually the sink is placed under a window, which gives good light and often a pleasant view, but a window is not vital and an efficient plan should not be sacrificed just for the sake of having a view. Check that the sill height is a minimum of 84 centimetres (33 inches) to allow the sink unit to fit neatly under it. If possible do not place the sink in a corner where it will be difficult for a second person to help with the washing up and drying.

Many types of sink are available: stainless steel or enamel, single or double units, shallow or deep, with waste disposal unit or without, with no, single or double drainboard. If you have the room, a double sink with two drainboards and swivel mixer tap allows for the most efficient washing up. Dirty dishes on the left if you are right-handed, are washed in the first basin, rinsed in the second and placed in a dishrack on the right drainboard. Do not dismiss the deep sink because most kitchen units have shallow ones. It is especially convenient for washing large saucepans and for soaking (and hiding!) them during meals; on the other hand, it does require more effort to get to things at the bottom.

Stoves

Stoves, especially gas types, are best placed away from windows and doors, because draughts increase fire risks and cause heat loss. Also a wall can be faced with a heat resistant and washable material which can be easily cleaned.

If you re-locate the gas stove, make sure the gas pipe can be brought to the new location without major difficulty. Have the stove attached to the pipe with a flexible hose so that it can be moved out for cleaning.

Be sure there is room to open the oven door conveniently. Note where your chosen model is hinged (most are hinged at the bottom or on the left). A left-hinged oven, for instance, will be more convenient situated at the left end of your plan; if it is placed at the right end, you will always have to walk around the door to get back to your work area. For either a side-hinged or a bottom-hinged door you will need at least 100 centimetres (3½ feet) of space in front of the oven, to allow the cook to stand in front of the open door.

In addition to the stove's location, you will have to decide between gas and electricity, a subject on which many people have strong feelings. Gas cooking has the advantage of rapid regulation of heat whereas, while electricity changes its heat output slowly, it provides a uniform, constant heat. (If a pot boils over on gas you turn off the supply, on electricity you lift the pot off the heat). Since gas is presently cheaper than electricity, a gas stove will be cheaper to run, especially if you also use gas for central heating. It is possible to have both gas and electricity for cooking, especially if you choose a split-level system, for instance a gas hob and an electric oven and grill, or two electric hot plates and two gas burners with either gas or electric oven.

In choosing a stove you will first have to consider the space available – there is a standard-size width plus many non-standard sizes. Second, you will have to decide on the desirability of other features: the size and location of the grill; the number of ovens, the self-cleaning oven; a plate warming drawer or rack; a rotisserie; a fan-assisted oven. The big decision may be between a split-level system and a conventional stove. A split-level system, currently fashionable, has the advantage of an eye level oven and below hob storage for saucepans. A disadvantage in small kitchens is the

reduction of worktop space. Additionally, if hob and oven are far apart, you may find yourself trying to watch something under the grill while finishing off a sauce on the hob.

Refrigerators

Since most refrigerator doors are hinged on the right (although you can order some models with left side hinges), be sure to put your refrigerator at the right end of a row rather than at the left end, otherwise you will always have to reach over or walk around the door. Ideally, the door should be able to open right back so that shelves and trays can be fully removed for washing. In a few models the door need not open this far for removing shelves.

As a general rule the refrigerator should not be placed beside the stove because radiant heat from the oven might heat the refrigerator's casing, causing the motor to work overtime. New refrigerators are supposed to be well enough insulated to withstand the heat but, to be on the safe side, leave a 15 centimetre (6 inch) gap between the two. With a low refrigerator, continue the work surface to cover the gap and use the space for tray storage or hanging tea towels on a pull-out rail. Before you build in a refrigerator find out where and how much ventilation will be needed. Some need the circulation only at the top or bottom, others require the unit to stay several inches away from the wall.

Your biggest decisions will be the size of your refrigerator, and whether it should have a freezer section with a separate door. Although the under-counter unit with small freezer is still considered adequate by many, you will probably find a unit standing 170 centimetres (5½ feet) to 190 centimetres (6¼ feet) including separate freezer section better and less subject to over-stuffing with food. It will allow you to shop weekly, or even less frequently. Single people and working wives especially will benefit from having a large freezer section.

Even if you plan to get a separate deep freezer, you will find a refrigerator-freezer handy. Since the refrigerator is located in the work triangle, things used regularly in small amounts in cooking (stock, parsley stems, other herbs, chopped onion), home-made baby foods, ice-cream, fish fingers, other childrens' food, leftover meats and ice are all available. Also, this is the freezer the family will open and frost up saving you the even harder work of defrosting the bigger unit more frequently.

Study the layout of the refrigerator carefully before you buy. Is the salad crisper a good size for you? Is the egg tray large enough? Do the door shelves suit your needs? Where will you put the milk, taller bottles? Seriously consider getting a self-defrosting model – some have self-defrosting freezers which make life easier.

Most refrigerators are electric, but a few small models are gas. The latter are silent, having no motors to make a noise.

Other large appliances
A deep freezer need not be located in either the work triangle or kitchen, since it is used for long-term storage rather than for frequently used items. Ideally, you will open it once a day or less to remove that day's or the next's food. Your choice will be between front-opening and chest type models. The front-opening freezer is less economical to run because cold air escapes more easily when the door is opened, but it takes up less floor space and contents can be seen more easily. It should be placed in a cool area to keep running costs to a minimum.

A dishwasher is usually located near the sink because it requires both water and waste plumbing. Generally it is built-in, though some can be rolled up to the sink and attached, and others are countertop size. Look for ease of loading, flexibility of positioning glassware and cups, and number of place settings. The larger it is the more useful it will be – remember you do not run it until it is full, which may be once a day or every second or third day.

You will need to know whether your chosen model of dishwasher or washing machine needs both hot and cold water connections or cold water only. If both, check that your hot water supply is adequate and of a suitable type. If only cold water is used, the machine will heat it electrically and is therefore likely to be more expensive to run. On plumbed-in models make sure taps and electricity switch are within easy reach.

Ventilation is the next major problem area to be considered. It's one thing to cook a delicious, pungent-smelling meal but quite another to live with the lingering smell of it through the following hours or even days! Obviously the easiest form of ventilation is an open window, but many kitchens are now built without windows and sometimes (in the middle of winter,

for instance) it is just not convenient or possible to open it even when you have one. The two most popular forms of artificial ventilation are extractor fans, usually placed high up on the window panes (assuming you have one), or a ventilation hood which is fitted on to the top of the stove.

Work surfaces and storage units
Most manufacturers' units are 90 centimetres (36 inches) high, which is considered a good all-purpose height for the average-sized woman. (Some units can be found to suit shorter or taller people). In actual fact various tasks require different work heights: 90 centimetres (36 inches) for the sink, 75-80 centimetres (29-31 inches) for mixing (lower for pastry rolling) and 80-90 (31-36 inches) for cooking, though the lower height becomes dangerous with small children around. But against these ideals must be balanced the desirability of a continuous work surface which is more flexible to use and easier to keep clean. In a corridor or U-shaped kitchen one area might be designed at a lower height to accommodate preparation tasks.

On your floor plan be sure to place work surfaces beside the stove (or hob), sink and tall refrigerator. Note these minimum requirements: 45-60 centimetres (18-24 inches) on the latch side of the refrigerator; 60-90 centimetres (24-36 inches) on each side of the sink for washing and food preparation; and 60 centimetres (24 inches) on one side of the stove and 30 centimetres (12 inches) on the other if the stove is at the end of a row. In addition, try to fit in a 90 centimetre (36 inch) mixing area plus a similarly sized serving space near the stove.

Where a worktop serves two uses, take the larger dimension and add 30 centimetres (12 inches). Thus, for example, a stove and sink on the same wall would be separated by 120 centimetres (48 inches) of counterspace.

Most kitchen unit manufacturers supply work surfaces of any length required, so bridge over low refrigerators, dishwashers, washing machines and driers.

Most surfaces, being laminated plastic, will be spoiled by contact with pans straight from the oven. A built-in marble slab, wooden chopping board or a ceramic tile area will take care of this problem.

Storage units are of three basic sorts.

Under work-surface cupboards are at least 60 centimetres (24 inches) deep. Wall-hung cupboards are shallower (45 centimetres [18 inches]) and should start no more than 150 centimetres (5 feet) above the floor, or 60 centimetres (24 inches) above the counter top. They should either reach the ceiling or have false fronts (or sliding doors if space is short) to fill in between top and ceiling. Exposed cupboard tops accumulate terrible amounts of greasy dust. Tall units are as deep as undercounter units and are used for larders, general shelved storage and brooms. If your plan allows, one or two would be useful. See pages 17 to 18 for a more detailed assessment of storage.

Heating
At the floor plan stage remember to consider how you will heat the kitchen and where you will put the heating unit. In a small kitchen an infra-red wall heater or an electric blower heater may be adequate and most economical of space. In a larger room you will probably want more heat, preferably at the non-cooking end. Skirting-board heating along one wall might be adequate or perhaps an extra tall but narrow radiator. Try not to have table seating tight against a radiator, or you will have constant complaints.

Electricity
Once your floor plan is in order you are ready to design your electrical layout. This consists of two parts: power points and lighting. Be generous with both.

You will need one power point for each built-in (present or potential) electrical appliance (stove, wall oven, refrigerator, waste disposal, dishwasher, ventilation hood over cooker, washing machine and clothes drier). In addition each work area should have a double power point to take care of small appliances (mixer, coffee mill, blender, kettle, radio) which are likely to be used in several different locations. Be sure the rest of the kitchen is adequately supplied.

Make sure all power points for large appliances are accessible – a power point at skirting board level behind a dishwasher or washing machine is not reachable. Also avoid low-level power points for the refrigerator and freezer, because it is all too easy for a toddler to turn them off without anybody noticing.

Good lighting is essential even during the day. And except in small kitchens you

will have at least two areas with different lighting requirements, namely the cooking/preparation section and the eating/living section. In the cooking/food preparation area, fluorescent batten fittings provide a good level of illumination and can be attached neatly under wall hung cupboards to light work surfaces where good illumination is most needed. Since these light sources are between you and your work rather than behind you, you will not be working in your own shadow. These should switch on independently of all other lights.

This part of the kitchen will also need an overhead light for general illumination so you can see into cupboards. This could be either fluorescent or incandescent (tungsten), and should switch on and off independently of both undercounter and eating area lighting – in an eat-in kitchen there is great advantage in turning off the cooking-area lights when the meal is served!

Since fluorescent lighting is rather harsh for general illumination, you may decide on tungsten lighting for the eating area. But whatever your choice, put the lights for the two areas on separate on/off switches and be sure a switch is beside each kitchen door. Remember a light can be controlled by two switches. Thus you may want a light switch by the back outside door and another by the door to

A streamlined L-shaped kitchen.

the hall or dining room. This will allow you to enter a dark kitchen, light it, walk through and switch off the light as you leave by the other door. Locate switches on the latch side of the door frame not behind the door on the hinge side.

Fluorescent lights are more economical than other types if you remember not to switch on and off frequently. This is because the starter (which also burns out before the tube) uses a lot of power. So 'save electricity, switch it off' does not apply. Unless you will be out of the kitchen for more than an hour, don't bother to switch off.

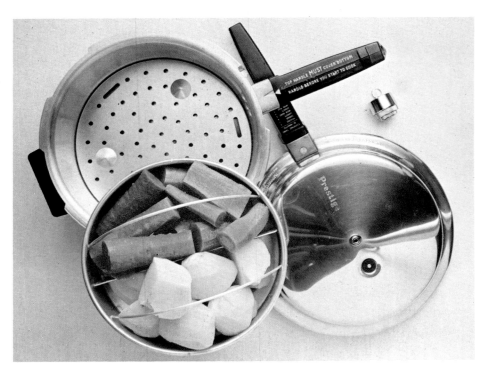

Flooring

Floor finishes need to be abrasion resistant, since they have to stand up to heavy wear. Unglazed ceramic floor tiles are attractive, durable, easily kept clean and not hard on the feet. Be sure to select the nonslip type. They are best laid on a concrete floor. Timber floors can be sealed and polished or covered with sealed cork floor tiles, vinyl tiles or vinyl sheet flooring. Also possible are heavy duty, washable, stain-resistant carpet tiles, long popular in North America.

Finally, unless you do everything yourself, you will have to deal with builders, plumbers and electricians. You will probably find that the workmen know their jobs and do them well. However, there is usually an intermediary – a contractor or architect – and your ideas and instructions may not always reach the workmen. Therefore, get to know them, respect their craftsmanship but be ready to ask lots of questions. Tell them what you want done and why – do not depend on others to have done this! Point out special features or oddities you want to save or emphasize, so they will treat them carefully. Stick to your original plan unless you have good reason to change it. Remember that changes will be expensive, and that you will be paying for them.

Before the builders arrive double-check the plans (yours, the architect's, or builder's), including all measurements. See that doors and windows are correctly positioned. Check the siting of lights, light switches, power points, water pipes (cold, hot, waste), gas. If you want unusual or specific fitments (windows, doors, lights, cupboards) learn for yourself whether they are available from your local stockist. Too often you are told something is unavailable only at the crisis point (after the hole for the new window is made . . .)

Before the plumbers arrive, make sure the secondary turn-off valves are accessible and that taps for plumbed-in appliances are reachable by a non-athlete. If you do not know, ask the plumber where the mains turn-off is (usually outside the house); this will be your best chance to learn. Also make sure that the cold water pipes are not placed too near the hot water and central-heating pipes, causing the cold water to flow hot for short periods.

Small equipment, storage and maintenance

The choice of large appliances – stove, refrigerator, freezer – has already been discussed; now the decisions concern smaller equipment, storage and maintenance.

Equipment

Having the right tool for the job makes any cook's task easier, quicker and more efficient. However, this does not mean that you should buy gadgets which you will seldom use. Your choice of utensils must depend on the life you lead and your style of eating. Start with a few well-designed tools and collect others when the need arises.

Cookware

The cookware you choose is important, because you will probably use it for many years. Check that saucepans and frying pans balance well both on the stove and in the hand – they should not be too heavy to lift when full. Handles should be well insulated, securely fixed and comfortable to hold. Lids should fit tightly.

Choose a heavy-bottomed pan, since it conducts heat better and prevents sticking and scorching. If you think you will do a lot of oven cooking, get pans with oven-proof handles which can double as casseroles. A non-stick surface is not essential for most uses and requires extra care to avoid scratching. Although matched sets look attractive, unmatched pans suited for different uses are far more practical. Saucepans present a hard choice because each type of metal has advantages and drawbacks.

Tin-lined copper with a heavy bottom is probably the best heat conductor and the quickest to respond to temperature changes, but it is expensive and needs constant attention to keep the copper gleaming. Excessively high heat will cause the tin to melt, and after some years of use, even with the best of care, the pan will have to be re-tinned.

Aluminium has good heat diffusion, but no matter how expensive it will become scratched and pitted. Certain foods, especially acid ones and those containing egg (which becomes discoloured), should not be cooked in aluminium pans.

Stainless steel is a poor heat conductor unless the bottom is made of a combination of metals. But it is long-lasting and durable.

Vitreous enamel on pressed steel or cast iron conducts heat well and the finish is easy to clean. Saucepans are heavy and expensive. Cheap soft enamel pans are unsatisfactory because they tend to be light and thin-bottomed, and they chip easily.

Pyrosil and other glass ceramic saucepans with removable handles are attractive and easy to care for. They are good for boiling and stew-type dishes but sauces tend to burn in them because they retain heat too well. They should not be the only type of pan you own.

Basic needs

To start, a milk pan with pouring lips on each side, two or three saucepans of different sizes, a 23 centimetre (9 inch) frying pan and one or two casseroles should be sufficient. Oval casseroles are practical because they can hold a chicken or whole fish as well as stews and soups. Casserole dishes should not be used on top of the stove if they are labelled *ovenproof* or *heatproof*, because they cannot stand direct heat. If they are called *flameproof*, however, they can be placed over direct heat.

A pressure cooker, although not essential, can be very useful for a busy cook. And with the escalating cost of fuel, it also represents a considerable saving in cooking costs. A roasting pan generally comes with the stove but if you need one, consider getting a large oval baking dish of heavy metal. In addition to poultry and joints, you will find it useful for *gratins* and a variety of other dishes. A roasting pan should fit into the oven easily with space for air circulation all around. It should be of heavy enough metal to put on top of the stove for making gravy. A kettle, deep-frying pan and omelette pan are all good to have but not essential. The kettle should have a comfortable insulated handle and good pouring spout. Choose a strong deep-frying pan with draining basket and lid. Two handles are useful,

since they make it easier to lift when full. An omelette pan should not be too large (18-20 centimetres [7-8 inches] is easiest to handle). It should be of heavy metal and have sloping sides. Use it only for omelettes and crêpes, and sticking will never be a problem. Directions for seasoning and care should come with the pan.

Baking equipment depends on what you are likely to make. Cake tins and baking sheets that nest well take up less storage space. A non-stick finish reduces the difficulty of getting a cake out after baking (as does a loose-bottomed tin), but care must be taken not to mar the finish; never cut pieces from a cake still in this type of tin. A pie plate can be used for both double and single crust pies and tarts, though a flan ring and baking sheet are more usual for single crust pastry.

Basic aids

A selection of good tools will help you to work more efficiently in the kitchen. Most important are knives, for dull or poor ones are slow and frustrating to work with. Choose high-quality ones of stainless or carbon steel. Handles should be comfortable to hold and blades should be riveted to the shank of the handle, so they will not work loose in use.

For your first knives choose from among a large heavy chopping knife, a medium length filleting knife and a vegetable knife. These can be used for almost everything except bread and horizontal cake slicing, so a bread knife should also be given priority. In time a carving knife and fork are useful to have, but a good kitchen knife makes an adequate substitute. Along with your knives be sure to get a knife sharpener or steel, because all knives need frequent sharpening.

A serrated-edge stainless steel knife is useful for foods that are discoloured by other metals. A palette knife is used for

To sharpen a knife, stroke it across the steel from base to top, diagonally.

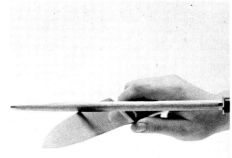

With the same motion, stroke the other side of the edge on the underside.

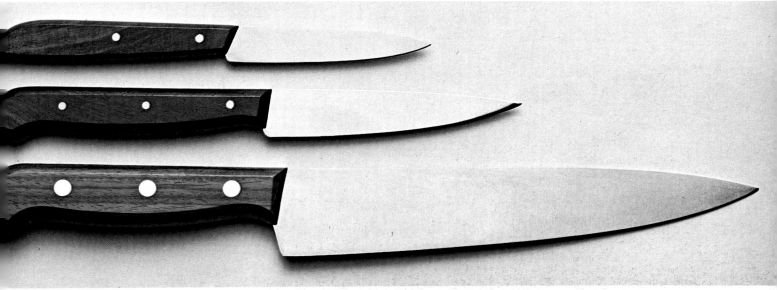

spreading icings and fillings rather than for cutting but if you intend to do a lot of cake-making, it is a very useful investment. Its limber blade means it can double as a spatula and cake server.

A can opener, either hand held, with a key that turns the cutting point, or wall mounted, is an essential kitchen tool.

Get a good corkscrew of either the type wine waiters use or the kind with a round cap which fits the top of the bottle. The latter's advantage is that less muscle power is needed – you simply push down on the two handles and the cork comes up.

A small-size ladle, useful for getting all sorts of liquids out of saucepans, can double as a sauce spoon. A large whisk has more uses than a small one, especially if you do not have either a rotary beater or an electric mixer. A collection of spoons, both metal and wooden, are invaluable. Wooden ones should be made of smooth, close-grained hard wood. Some should be flat bottomed, others without a bowl. There is no substitute for a grater. The four sided type with slicer and coarse, medium and fine graters serves all purposes. Kitchen scissors have many uses, including cutting raw meat such as liver and tender vegetables. The type with a C-shaped piece cut out of each blade slices easily through poultry bones.

Other useful but not essential aids include a vegetable peeler, rolling pin, lemon squeezer and garlic press.

Containers

Cooking cannot be done without a variety of containers. Sieves come in assorted sizes and are either conical or bowl shaped. A bowl-shaped sieve of medium diameter and with a medium mesh is probably the most useful, since it can be used for sieving flours, making purées and straining liquids. Metal mesh is best for most uses, but a nylon mesh prevents fruit and acid or white vegetables from discolouring.

A colander is used to drain vegetables and other bulky items. Metal is preferable to plastic because it can also be used over boiling water as a steamer. A slotted draining spoon is useful, but not essential. Various-sized bowls aid kitchen efficiency; a nest of three covers most needs, but if you can only get one, make it large. The type with a lip makes pouring much easier. A deep bowl is needed for rotary and electric beaters; a wide, flat-bottomed shape is more suitable for a wire whisk. Ceramic, glass or metal bowls are superior to plastics, since they have a greater range of uses. Often plastic bowls cannot be used with boiling water, nor can they be kept 100 per cent grease-free, and therefore they are unsuitable for whisking egg whites. Four to six small bowls or ramekins, preferably ovenproof so they can serve general cooking purposes, are useful for holding small prepared items, such as mashed garlic, chopped parsley, melted butter and lemon peel and juice, until they are needed. Other miscellaneous items necessary in the practical kitchen include measuring spoons, a measuring jug for liquids and a scale. Scales can be of the spring-balance type (either wall hung or free standing) or of the separate weight balance type. Properly used, the latter are more accurate, though the spring-type is acceptable for cooking too.

A chopping board at least 20 by 30 centimetres (8 by 12 inches), and preferably a little bigger is a must. A fine-grained hardwood will last for years. Some boards are made of formica or other plastics, but these become marked and rough with continuous use and a wooden board, unlike formica, can be used as a resting place for hot casseroles and pans as well as chopping. Wire cake racks, used primarily to allow air to circulate freely around cakes and biscuits, can also be a resting place for hot pots if they are not too heavy.

Several thick, large pot holders, which can be squares, gloves or the wrap-around two-handed type, are essential. If they have magnets in their handles they will stick to any metal surface, otherwise they should be hung on a hook beside the stove – they are of no use kept far from it!

Get thermometers – meat, deep-fat, sugar – early in your cooking career when you will need them most. A meat thermometer is inserted into the thickest part of a joint to record the internal temperature, which is the best indicator of doneness. Deep-fat and sugar thermometers measure the temperature of liquids.

A carving board with a juice well is not a great luxury because it makes the job so much easier. Make sure it is large enough to hold poultry and large joints of meat.

Electrical aids

In recent years an array of small electrical appliances has appeared on the market. No attempt can be made here to cover them all, and only the more basic and popular are covered, although others, of course, may be invaluable for your particular cooking needs. All should carry the 'kitemark' of the British Electrotechnical Approvals Board, indicating they meet minimum safety standards.

An electric kettle provides the quickest way to boil water and is far more economical than using pan or kettle on top of the stove. Get into the habit of putting no more water than you need in the kettle – heating five pints when you want one

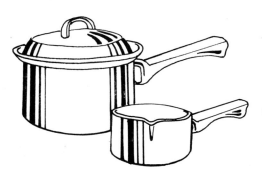 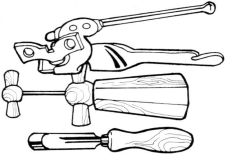 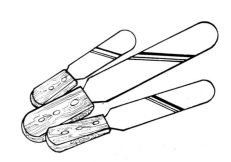

is a terrible waste of money.

Electric mixers are invaluable for creaming butter, whipping eggs, beating doughs and batters and mashing potatoes. Basically there are two types, the table model and the hand-held or portable. Both will do any work normally done by hand with a wooden spoon or whisk. Mixers should have strong motors, yet in the case of the hand models not be too heavy. Varying speeds are an advantage for coping with different jobs, such as stirring, beating and whipping.

Table models are fairly heavy and are best kept on the work surface near a power point. They do not need to be held while in operation, leaving you free to prepare other items.

Portable or hand mixers are not as powerful as table models, but they have the advantage of easy storage in a drawer or cupboard. Some mixers come with one set of beaters which are used for everything; other models come with several types of beaters for different jobs. Bladed beaters are used for creaming and beating, wire ones for whisking and whipping and, sometimes, spiral hooks for combining mixtures such as dough. Extra attachments – blenders, mixers, shredders and juicers – can be bought for some table models. If you think these attachments will be useful, then starting with an appropriate model is a good idea.

A blender can be an attachment to a mixer or bought separately as a free-standing unit. They come in several sizes, and the type you choose depends on your present and foreseeable needs: larger blenders are more convenient for soups and drinks. Blenders will liquidize and purée, and some of the more powerful models will chop and grind as well. If the blender can only be used for liquids, a separate grinder attachment may be necessary for grinding such things as nuts, breadcrumbs and coffee beans.

Grinders and mincers can be attachments on a mixer or independent, free-standing units. A grinder is sometimes an extra unit on a blender, designed to cope with jobs the blender cannot do. It is ideal for pulverizing small amounts of very hard foods such as nuts and coffee beans. A coffee grinder is a specialized form of grinder. Electric mincers perform in the same way as a manual model only more quickly and with less effort. They can be used for mincing cooked or raw meat, poultry and raw vegetables.

In recent years, three other appliances have gained in popularity. Namely the electric casserole or crockpot, the infra-red grill, and the micro-wave oven. Electric casseroles, which usually have an earthenware pot set into an outer insulated unit with a heating element, cook very slowly at a very low temperature. They are economical to use and require no watching; they can be turned on in the morning and left to cook unattended all day.

Infra-red grills and micro-wave ovens cook rapidly. Ten minutes for a large joint is plenty in a micro-wave oven, but since the meat does not brown it must be put under the grill to give it the rich cooked look we expect.

Electric trays keep food warm at the table although, despite some food ads, food cannot be kept warm for hours on end without reducing its quality. An electric coffee pot should make up to 12 cups, if you plan to use it mainly for guests. Most pots can be filled in advance and the electricity switched on shortly before the coffee is required; when finished it automatically switches to warm.

Crockery, etc. . . .

Plates, serving dishes, glassware and cutlery all form a part of standard kitchen equipment. Dinnerware can be of many different materials, among which earthenware, stoneware and china are the most popular. *Earthenware*, because of the type of clay used and the way it has been fired, is far less durable than *stoneware*; thus the latter is generally the better buy. *China* is a general term used for a hard, long-wearing, more or less translucent ceramic. It ranges from thick, heavy, glazed material to fine bone china, thin enough to see shadows. Cups, especially, break frequently, so it is wise to get extras when you buy a set.

Serving dishes can be in the same pattern as the dinnerware or quite different, ranging from oven-to-tableware to other sorts of cooking vessels. To decide how many serving pieces are needed, consider how many vegetables you customarily serve. In general, two oval meat platters, three serving dishes (preferably with lids), and a sauce boat will be adequate for the main course. Additional serving pieces such as a large flat plate suitable for either a cake or flan, a low, wide graceful bowl for puddings and fruits, another sauce boat and a cream jug (at least 300 millimetres [10 fluid ounces] in size) will be useful.

Glassware, along with cups, seems to break more often than anything else. Thus try to get more than the minimum of any pattern you particularly like. Tumblers are needed for water, whisky (the traditional shape is short and squat) and tall drinks; mugs for beer and cider; medium-sized stem glasses for sherry; and large tulip-shaped glasses for wine. Choose your wine glasses carefully – larger sizes allow red wine to develop aroma and the shape holds that aroma in

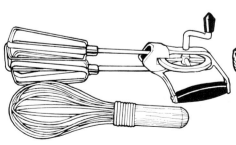

the glass for a longer period.

Choose cutlery that balances well in the hand and does not seem too light in weight. It should be easy to wash, so investigate closely whether wood and bone (plastic) handles can be soaked in the washing-up water. It will be inconvenient if they cannot. In addition to the standard cutlery, make sure you have enough serving pieces, especially serving spoons. Sauce ladles are also useful, as are a serving fork, and a cake or tart server.

Storage

Storage space in the modern kitchen must serve a variety of functions: in addition to packaged food in jars, tins, bags and boxes, it accommodates cooking equipment, dinnerware, cutlery and washing-up aids. Your storage units are likely to consist of deep below-counter cupboards, narrow wall-hung ones, a walk-in or look-in floor to near-ceiling type, and drawers. Some households have a wall area on which things are hung, or open shelving. If you are thinking of these remember that exposed objects get coated rather quickly with a film of cooking grease and dust. And that while sliding doors on cupboards are more economical in terms of space, they do get dirtier, especially along the sliding grooves.

Some of your storage areas will be warmer than others. For instance, a cupboard adjacent to, or above, the stove will be warmer than one farther away. Ideally, foods should be stored in well-ventilated-to-the-outside cupboards on a north facing wall, since they keep better in a cool place. Few of us, however, are likely to have such ideal conditions, so try to arrange storage in a way that places regular necessities close to where they are likely to be used, yet where they will not get overheated.

Cooking equipment
Cooking equipment should be placed near the stove if possible, with larger items on the below-counter shelves or a pot stand and smaller items in drawers or in open containers at the rear of the counter. Drawers for utensils are much easier to keep tidy when they have vertical

A selection of kitchen equipment used for baking, including scales, a rolling pin and a pastry blender.

dividers, since they enable you to separate knives from spoons, etc. If possible, table cutlery should be kept apart from cooking utensils. If no cupboard exists by the stove, the area below the sink is a convenient alternative.

Dinnerware and glassware fit more easily on narrow shelves above counter level or in a separate tall unit. In either case their location should be convenient to both the washing-up area and the table. If your shelves are too far apart, make or buy stacking units so that you don't have to pile different sizes of dishes on top of one another. Cups can hang on hooks attached to the underside of the shelf above.

One other non-food category needs drawer or cupboard space, namely wrapping materials. These include rolls of polythene bags, aluminium foil, grease-proof paper, cling film, and the like. Unfortunately, no two boxes seem to be the same length or width, and each has to be taken out for use. They should be located near the food preparation area.

Food storage can be divided into three categories: non-perishables; long-keeping perishables (lasting several weeks or more); and short-term perishables (lasting only a few days). Each type can be stored in a different way.

Non-perishables (which do go bad if left unused for a long time) include cans, bottles, jars and dry goods like flour, sugar and salt. These often go in an above-counter cupboard. They should be kept cool if possible and absolutely dry. Once open, dry goods keep better in airtight containers which have been clearly labelled.

Long-keeping perishables include open jars, various condiments, dripping and certain vegetables – onions, garlic, potatoes, apples – if they can be stored in a cool dry place. These should be kept in a cold larder if you have one.

Short-term perishables include milk, meat, poultry, bread, green vegetables and opened canned goods. All need to be kept at below 10°C (50°F), that is, in a cold larder or refrigerator, preferably the latter. In fact, you should think of the refrigerator as a sort of modern cold larder and use it in the same way.

A refrigerator must never be packed so full that air cannot circulate. Convection currents draw heat from the food and keep the temperature low. To keep this low temperature, it is not advisable to open

the refrigerator door more than necessary, and *never* put hot food in a refrigerator – it may cool more quickly but it will also warm up the other food already stored there.

Correct containers
Foods tend to dry out during storage in a refrigerator, so they should always be wrapped or covered. This also prevents smells and flavours of different foods cross-mingling. Do not pack goods in airtight containers, since anaerobic bacteria (those which survive without oxygen) may become active. The frozen-food compartment of your refrigerator allows for longer term storage of perishables. The star-marking system on newer machines tells you how long frozen goods can be kept on top condition (* 1 week; ** 1 month; *** 3 months or more). Only older machines with a *** rating and newer ones with a light star on a dark background are suitable for freezing fresh produce.

Our mothers and grandmothers used to shop daily, buying in small amounts. But this method does not fit our modern lifestyle very well and we tend to buy ahead. And buying at intervals means that new habits should be formed. Put just-acquired items (both frozen and non-frozen) at the back of a shelf or at the bottom of a stack of similar items. (Also date them with a felt-tip pen.) In this way the oldest will always get used first.

Avoid buying dented tins, since they have a greater tendency to spoil, and never use a tin that is bulging at the lid, because the risk of food poisoning is high. (The bulge can indicate an accumulation of gas, often caused by active bacteria.)

Make it a practice to empty airtight containers that hold flour, sugar and other items and to wash them thoroughly before filling with new supplies. This procedure prevents the new contents from being contaminated in any way by the old.

Organizing your food storage space
Try to group similar items together, with those used most frequently in the front and nearest eye level. Thus unopened items should go to the back or onto higher shelves.

The following arrangement is one of many possibilities. Arrange things in groups – soups, dry and canned vegetables; fish and meat; fruits; jam; unopened flour; sugars – so that you can see all similar items at a glance. Do not pack things so closely together that some hide others. At least twice a year take everything out, clean the cupboard, and assess your supplies. Use whatever seems to be getting old. Group together items you use in cooking. Flour, sugar, herbs and spices, stock cubes, salt and pepper should all be easily reached from the cooking and preparation areas. Since herbs and spices come in small packets you may find it useful to improvise a small two-shelf unit on the side of the cupboard or on the door; this will allow you to see them more easily.

Baking aids (castor sugar, icing sugar, cocoa, dried yeast, vanilla essence, food colouring, baking powder) form another natural grouping. Sauces should be stored together (Worcestershire, ketchup, prepared mustard).

Finally locate jams, marmalade, table salt and pepper where they are convenient to the table, since that is where they are used most often.

Maintenance

Whether we like it or not everything in the kitchen needs care, and care calls for some equipment. For washing up a basin, dish drainer, brush, sponges and gentle nylon scouring pads are necessary. For the floor, broom, dustpan and brush, and if the floor area is large enough, a long-handled sponge mop and bucket.

Washing up calls for a certain amount of organization, and if you are lucky or have planned well, you will have enough space to place the unwashed dishes on one side and the washed on the other. Glassware and cutlery washed in very hot water sparkle more and have fewer watermarks, so do these first, followed by dishes and saucepans. Both instant coffee and tea leave residues that discolour cups; this can be reduced by rinsing out the cups immediately after use. Soapy water and a hard scrub with a sponge will remove the deposits.

All pots and pans benefit from a soaking before washing. So get into the habit of putting warm water and some washing-up liquid into saucepans immediately after dishing up.

The exception is pans with fat. If you are saving the fat for dripping, pour it off while still liquid; if it is to be thrown away, let it solidify before cleaning it out

with paper towels. Either way wipe the pan out well before washing it in hot soapy water. Grease poured down a drain can spell disaster in the form of a blocked up sink! A pan that sizzles as you put water in it is being damaged by the rapid change in temperature.

Washing-up liquid has a variety of uses away from the sink. A little put on a damp sponge is excellent for cutting grease on the walls and other kitchen surfaces and for removing finger marks from paint anywhere in the house.

Cleaning the stove and refrigerator

Everyone dreads cleaning the stove and refrigerator, yet it has to be done. The instruction books that come with both appliances tell you what to do for your particular model. In general, after use wipe the hob and oven with a damp soapy sponge. Never use abrasives, such as scouring powder, which can scratch the surface. A particularly difficult spot can be softened by leaving a wet sponge over it for several minutes, after which it usually wipes off easily. Remember to clean the drip pans regularly, not just after spills.

Oven cleaners often contain caustic soda which can cause terrible burns if it gets on your skin. Since caustic soda has several different names, you can't always tell when the product you buy contains it. Therefore be especially careful if the instructions tell you to wear gloves! If an oven is particularly dirty, more than one application of oven cleaner will be needed. Roasting meat at a high temperature causes more spatter and grease than roasting at a low temperature.

Defrosting the refrigerator and freezer

To keep the refrigerator and freezer operating at maximum efficiency, they should be defrosted when the ice builds up to a thickness of $\frac{1}{2}$ centimetre ($\frac{1}{4}$ inch). Try to defrost on a cool day or when the kitchen is cool.

Switch off the power unless your temperature dial has a defrost position. Remove all food from the refrigerator to a table or other convenient surface. Pack frozen foods tightly into one or more cartons with the slow-thawing items (roasts, poultry) around the perimeter and quicker thawing ones in the middle. Pile the boxes on top of one another and cover the top one with about $2\frac{1}{2}$

centimetres (1 inch) thickness of newspaper, which is an excellent insulator (in hot weather, a layer can also be placed under the bottom box). Place a large pan in the freezer to catch as much water as possible (the chiller tray serves the same function in smaller refrigerators), leave the door open (unless there is a defrost setting), and go away for 15 to 30 minutes, returning once to empty the drip pan. After 30 minutes the frost should either have melted entirely or look grey and rotten. In a chest-type freezer, you must get the ice out before it becomes water, since water is difficult to siphon or sponge out. Theoretically you should leave the 'rotten' ice alone, but human nature being what it is, we all tend to help things along. Tease the ice off with your fingers or the spatula provided by some manufacturers. Never use sharp knives or other similar implements since these can puncture the lining. Have patience while the last bits melt off the piping, which should not be touched. While waiting for the last of the ice to melt, wash down the inside with a solution of 1 tablespoon of bicarbonate of soda dissolved in a gallon of water. Rinse and dry thoroughly. Turn the refrigerator or freezer back on. Wait 15 minutes before replacing the contents, so it has begun to get cold.

Refrigerator shelves sometimes need special attention. The solid shelf above the salad box frequently has plastic strips front and back. Spills have a way of getting under these, and it is necessary to pull or slide the strips off gently to do a thorough cleaning. Other shelves may also have decorative strips which should be removed in the same way.

Self-defrosting refrigerators and freezers have a drainage hole at the bottom which carries water to the evaporator tray. Sometimes this hole becomes clogged, and the debris must be delicately extracted with a toothpick, skewer or knitting needle. Water leaking out from under the salad box is a sign the refrigerator needs attention. A build-up of ice at the bottom of the freezer signals the problem there. If you decide to switch off the refrigerator when going on holiday be sure to leave the door open (pull a shelf out so the door cannot close accidentally). A refrigerator or freezer left switched off and with the door closed develops a terrible musty odour that is hard to get rid of, as well as mildew.

Guide to Larder Storage

Food	Storage Time (Reduced in hot weather)	Special Points
Dairy Produce		
Milk	1-2 days	Keep in original bottle with top. Store away from light, and never mix old and new milks together. Milk can be kept longer in summer by using a porous earthenware milk cover or by placing in a bucket of cold water covering the bottle with a cloth, the ends of which are dipped in the water.
U.H.T. milk	As stated on carton	Keeps well, but flavour is better when stored in the refrigerator.
Cream	1-2 days	Keep away from light in covered carton or jug.
Ice-cream	Consume as purchased	
Cheese, hard	1 week	Remove tight wrappings, Wrap in foil or polythene, or put in a non-airtight container. Mould may develop, but this is easily removed and will not harm cheese.
Cheese, soft	2-3 days	Store as for hard cheese.
Butter	2 weeks, but in very hot weather 1-2 days	Leave in wrapper or transfer to covered butter dish, or porous earthenware container that has been soaked in water.
Fats and Oils		
Margarine, hard	3 weeks	Keep in original wrapper.
soft	Up to 3 weeks	Keep in original container. In very hot weather it may become very runny and unmanageable.
Fat, lard and cooking	Up to 2 months	In wrapper as purchased or in covered dish.
Oils	Almost indefinitely	Keep in a dark place.
Eggs, whole	7-10 days	Stored pointed end down in carton or egg rack, or basket.
whites	3 days	Keep in covered container.
yolks	1-2 days	Keep in small basin, and pour a little cold water on top to prevent hardening.
hard-boiled	2 days	Leave in shells.
Bread	3-4 days	Leave in original wrapper or put in a loosely-tied polythene bag. Keep in a ventilated bread bin. Crisp rolls and bread only keep 1-2 days, but can be used for breadcrumbs or cooking, after that.
Meat and Poultry		
Raw meat, joints and chops	1-2 days	Rinse off any blood, and pat dry. Cover loosely with foil, polythene or gauze meat cover.
Raw poultry, fresh or chilled	1-2 days	Remove tight wrappings. Remove and cook giblets. Wipe clean and cover loosely with foil or polythene.
Cooked meat or poultry	1-2 days	Cool quickly. Store in covered dish or wrap in foil.
Purchased cooked meat	1 day	Wrap in foil, or store in non-airtight container.
Mince and offal	1 day	Put in a dish, or on a plate and cover loosely.
Bacon	4 days	Wrap in greaseproof paper or cling film, and place in a covered container.
Cooked made-up dishes	1-2 days	Cover dish with lid or foil.
Fish		
Fish, fresh	½-1 day	Do not put near eggs, milk, etc. as flavour can be transferred. Put on a plate, and cover loosely.
shellfish	½ day	Eat as purchased.
cooked fish	1 day	Store in a covered dish.
smoked fish	1-2 days	If possible, wrap in muslin and hang in larder. Or cover with a gauze food cover.
Vegetables and Fruit		
Vegetables, root	3-7 days	Must be absolutely dry, or they will rot. Store in a vegetable rack in a cool, dry, airy position. Can be kept for a longer time in sand or soil in a box in a shed or out of doors.
green	1-2 days	Wrap lightly in newspaper, or polythene bag in which holes have been punched. Keep in a dark, cool, airy place.
Salad	1-2 days	Keep in a closed polythene bag or lidded salad container.
Fruit, soft	1-3 days	Clean and keep in a covered container.
hard	3-4 days	Wipe. If under-ripe, leave in a bowl at room temperature. Check for over-ripe items as these can go mouldy and transfer mould to other fruits. Cut fruit should be covered with cling film to prevent drying-out.

Guide to Refrigerator Storage

Food	Storage Time	Special Points
Dairy Produce		
Milk	3-4 days	Keep in bottle or transfer to a milk jug, and cover.
U.H.T. milk	As stated on packet.	Once opened, store as fresh milk.
Cream	3-4 days	
Ice-cream	Store according to the star marking on the freezing compartment.	Keep in original wrapper, or transfer it to a lidded plastic container.
Cheese, hard	2-3 weeks	Wrap in foil, polythene, or store in non-airtight container. Always remove cheese ½ hour before serving for maximum flavour.
Cheese, soft	Up to 1 week	Keep in a covered container.
Butter	4-6 weeks	Keep in original wrapper.
Fats and Oils		
Margarine (hard and soft)	6 weeks	As butter
Lard and cooking fat	Up to 4 months	As butter
Oils	Do not store in the refrigerator as they may solidify.	
Eggs – whole	2-3 weeks	Always keep some eggs out at room temperature for cooking purposes.
whites	4-5 days	Put in covered container.
yolks	2-3 days	Store in covered container with water.
hard-boiled	5-7 days	
Bread	Up to 1 week	Keep in a polythene bag; storing in refrigerator reduces mould growth, but can hasten the staling process.
Meat and Poultry		
Raw meat – joints and chops	3-5 days	Wipe off any blood. Pat dry. Wrap loosely in foil or cling film.
Raw poultry – fresh or chilled	2-3 days	Remove tight wrapping, store giblets separately for 1-2 days. Wrap in foil or cling film.
Cooked meat or poultry	3-5 days	Wrap in foil, or store in covered container.
Purchased cooked meat	2-3 days	Wrap in foil or polythene, or put in covered container.
Mince and offal	1-2 days	Wash and pat dry. Cover loosely or put in non-airtight container.
Bacon	7-10 days	Wrap loosely in greaseproof paper, and put in a covered container.
Cooked made-up dishes	2-3 days	Cover with lid or foil.
Fish		
Fish, fresh	1-2 days	Wrap loosely but thoroughly to prevent smell escaping.
shellfish	1 day	ditto.
cooked fish	1-2 days	ditto.
smoked fish	Not necessary to keep in refrigerator.	ditto.
Vegetables and Fruit		
Vegetables, root	Do not store in refrigerator.	
green	2-3 days	Put in polythene bags and store in bottom of refrigerator.
Salad	3 days	Keep in sealed polythene bag, lidded container or salad crisper.
Fruit, soft	2-3 days	Clean and prepare. Keep in lidded container or polythene bags.
hard	3-7 days	Wrap with cling film or polythene, if necessary.

Shelf positions for refrigerated foods

Position	Temperature	Food
Freezer compartment	These have star markings as follows:	
	* −6°C (21°F) – 1 week	Ice and frozen food, ice-cream, 1 day
	** −12°C (10°F) – 1 month	Ice and frozen food, ice-cream, 1 week
	*** −18°C (0°F) – 3 months	Ice and frozen food, ice-cream, 1 month
Tray below freezing compartment	Very cold	Fish
Shelf below freezing compartment	Very cold	Meat, fish, cold desserts and jellies
Middle shelf	Cold	Cooked meat, made-up dishes
Bottom shelf	Least cold	Vegetables, salads, fruit
Rack inside door	Least cold	Milk, eggs, cheese, fats (*not* oil), fruit juices, etc.

Chapter Two

Buying wisely

One person's bargain can be someone else's great mistake. An enormous jar of honey that would last a family of six for two weeks could mean months of honey with everything for a single person.

Wise buying is an individual affair. It depends on the number of people in a household, on the amount of time at your disposal and on your financial resources. The time saved by shopping locally can sometimes be of greater value than the monetary savings obtained at a more distant supermarket. The choice of where to shop is controlled by geographic factors. In a large town numerous options will be available, but a small village may offer only one general store, a mobile van once or twice a week and an intermittent and inconvenient bus service to the nearest town.

However, all of us share a considerable number of problems and when we decide what to buy – which cut of meat or which plums – we do a constant mental juggling act, balancing quality and quantity against price. Generally the better the quality, the higher the price, and we reach our decisions by weighing these factors against one another.

Types of shops

Most people shop at a variety of shops rather than always at one type. We may get staples (flour, sugar, cooking oil, soap powders) at a supermarket or by bulk buying, meat from an independent butcher, some fresh vegetables, cheese and bread from a corner shop. We may also use market stalls for a range of in-season produce and order speciality items by mail.

Small is expensive. An independent local general store with room for limited stock cannot possibly buy on the same competitive terms as a large supermarket

with rapid turnover. It therefore has few savings to pass on to the customer. In order to compete, the corner shopkeeper is often compelled to work anti-social hours and remain open long after other shops have closed for the night. Other attractions include friendly, personal service, which contrasts with the anonymity of the supermarket, and a sense of personal responsibility towards the 'regular' customer. Some local shops, particularly in rural areas, also offer credit. Sometimes small shops (especially those in rural areas) have small-scale suppliers (perhaps local farmers) of fresh vegetables or poultry and are able to sell these items at surprisingly advantageous prices.

One way in which a small independently owned grocery can continue to trade successfully without sacrificing independence is by joining a voluntary chain group. Voluntary chain members are able to buy from their wholesaler at advantageous terms and pass some of these savings on to their customers. They also have the advantage of being able to sell the group's own-label goods at prices which will compete directly with similar own-label goods offered in supermarkets.

It is easy to spot the good points about supermarkets. The size of their operation accounts for their competitive prices, and rapid turnover ensures a constant supply of fresh perishable foods. Many supermarkets operate their own date stamping system on perishable items. (At present, government legislation does not demand that perishable goods should be date stamped, but most supermarkets have voluntarily introduced an easily understood code. And negotiations are now in progress within the E.E.C. which may make this a European, industry-wide legal requirement soon.)

Other advantages of supermarkets includes the fact that you can do all your food shopping under one roof. Although fruit and vegetables are sometimes more

expensive than they would be elsewhere, speed and convenience may outweigh monetary savings. In a supermarket you can shop at leisure and choose from a wide range of goods which carry clearly marked prices. Frequently goods can be paid for by cheque, backed with a banker's card, no small advantage, especially towards the end of the month!

Supermarkets do, however, have disadvantages, too, and one at least can be so great as to completely counteract any

potential savings: the temptation to buy things that you do not need because the goods are attractively packaged, and all you have to do is stretch out your arm and add them to your basket or trolley. Supermarkets are designed to encourage customers to spend money. Special offers are placed in an eye-catching position near the entrance, basic foods are found in the centre of the shop so that rows and rows of tempting goods have to be passed en route, and small luxury goods such as sweets and magazines are positioned close to the check-out tills where the customer will have to wait if there is a queue. The only effective way to withstand all these temptations to impulse buy is to make a list before you leave home, remember to take it with you and stick grimly to it! A sure recipe for overspending is deciding what to have for supper when you are actually in the supermarket. Keeping a rough total of what you are spending as you put goods into your basket can also

act as a horrifying deterrent to your more expensive impulses.

Convenience foods, that is prepared foods in packets or cans, can prove expensive if bought frequently. There is obviously a place for the virtually instant meal in dehydrated, canned or frozen form, as emergency food, but apart from this they have little to recommend them on grounds of cost or flavour.

Another way in which the supermarket encourages you to buy more than you actually need is through pre-packing. Pre-packed items such as cheese, bacon and meat often contain larger quantities than you need, something that particularly discriminates against people living alone since most pre-packed goods are sold in quantities suitable for at least two people.

If you are lucky enough to live near a regular street market or near a market town, you should have access to a supply of cheap fresh fruit and vegetables. Be

on the look out for in-season produce and be flexible.

Shopping at market stalls has to be done carefully. Make preliminary price comparisons between stalls before buying. Sometimes the reason why apples are twice the price at one stall as they are at another is obvious, but, as you get to know the market, you will notice that not only are prices higher at some stalls than at others, but that goods at one end of the market are dearer than at the other.

If you find a stall where prices are generally low and quality high, it is worth using it regularly. When you get to know a stallholder, he is less likely to slip in the odd rotten onion or over-ripe plum than if you were a customer whom he did not expect to see again.

It is a good idea to buy bulky, unbruisable items like potatoes and onions first and the most perishable items like soft fruit last. In this way you will not have to re-arrange your bag continually.

Buying in bulk

Bulk buying may sound like a good idea, but you need to estimate how long it will take to use up the bulk purchase. Buying seven pounds of icing sugar just before Christmas would be a good buy if you are planning to ice lots of cakes, but would be silly if you seldom make icing of any sort. On the other hand, if you use three tins of baked beans a week, a carton will last you about two months. And you will have reduced the weight of your weekly shopping bag by several pounds. Often bulk buying is not worth considering unless you have a large family or can combine with friends or relatives to share the goods.

Before going to a bulk buying centre, make up a detailed shopping list that includes the prices of the items where you normally shop. For sometimes the bulk price is the same as, or higher than, the local price.

Many of these centres cater to freezer owners who want to stock up their freezer with larger packs than are available in supermarkets. Be cautious about buying unlabelled or unknown brands of frozen food. It is impossible to assess the quality simply by looking at it so, however, cheap, 24 hamburgers that taste like sawdust will be a saving that you will regret having made. Bulk meat packs consisting of half lambs or pigs are also available at these centres, but they may include cuts that you would normally not consider or want to purchase. Although more expensive, bulk packets containing a single cut such as chops may be more useful.

Many butchers also provide meat in bulk for the home freezer. Although their meat may be slightly more expensive than that at a frozen food centre, the quality of the meat may be preferable.

Like tinned or bottled food bought in bulk, frozen food has to be stored. You will not only need enough room in the freezer to store your purchases but you should also have enough spare to maintain a balance among different types of food. A freezer containing a pig and an immense packet of peas has not been magnificently planned!

If, however, you manage to avoid the pitfalls of bulk buying, you will have the considerable advantage of saving money during a period of rapid inflation. You will also have cut down on time spent shopping, and provided yourself with

extensive supplies that will be particularly useful if you work, or if you find yourself cooking for twice as many as you had anticipated.

They're after your money

In a competitive field such as food retailing, traders employ numerous methods to attract customers. One such device is the giving of trading stamps. Double or triple stamps are offered at certain times to encourage the customer to shop when business might otherwise be slack, or to make extra shopping hours financially worthwhile for the shop.

Trading stamps appeal to the collecting urge in most people and to the idea of getting something for nothing when the stamps are exchanged for a gift. If the

goods are of the same price and quality and the shop is as clean, efficient and convenient as its nearest rival without stamps, something can be said for shopping at the one giving stamps.

Other inducements used to lure us into shops and, once in, to spend, are special offers. A loss leader is the name given to goods, usually basic foods, which are offered at reduced prices. These goods are prominently displayed inside the shop and advertised on window posters.

Once inside the customer will almost certainly buy other goods, and the increased business will more than cover the shop's slight loss on the product that drew the customer into the shop.

Date stamped food is sometimes offered for sale at reduced prices, especially near to its latest sell date. This date

24

does allow for a few days storage at home before consumption so such items are safe to buy provided they are eaten fairly quickly.

Reducing your spending

1. Plan your menus before you leave home. And stick to them.
2. Always make a list and remember to take it with you.
3. Ask yourself, do I really need it? Impulse buys are expensive. They can also be fattening, if you make a habit of buying biscuits and snacks to eat between meals.
4. Keep in touch with the price of basic goods such as butter, sugar, washing powder and the like. If you know what the current price is, you can determine whether cut-price offers are really worth having.
5. Many Citizens' Advice Bureaux and Consumer Advice Centres compile weekly lists of shopping prices. Many local radio stations and newspapers also run this type of up-to-the-minute service.
6. If you travel around from shop to shop in search of bargains, remember that you are often spending money as well as time. By the time you have deducted bus fares or petrol from your savings you may not have much left!

Extra shopping hints

1. Always compare prices and quality.
2. Check date stamps on perishable goods.
3. Save your carrier bags and take a sufficient supply with you when you go shopping.
4. Whenever possible, shop at off-peak times. It will save time and temper.
5. If you are shopping in a market, go first thing in the morning. The fruit and vegetables will be at their best and so will you.

Cleanliness in shops

The standard of hygiene in shops should be taken into consideration when shopping for food. The young and the old are particularly susceptible to food poisoning, so anyone whose family includes babies or grandparents should take special care to shop in places that maintain a high standard of cleanliness.

Bacteria that cause food poisoning can be carried in a number of different ways. Salmonella, one such bacteria, breed rapidly in undercooked meat and poultry. Cooked chicken joints that are pink in the middle, are, therefore, to be avoided. Because so much raw meat contains salmonella, raw and cooked meat should never be kept in the same refrigerated compartment, nor should they be cut with the same knife or on the same board.

Botulism, found in canned goods with bulging lids, can in extreme cases be fatal and staphylococci, another bacteria, can be transmitted to food by assistants with colds or with septic cuts on their fingers which are not adequately covered by a waterproof dressing.

Your rights as a consumer

Within recent years, rapid inflation has given rise to a fantastic growth in consumer awareness. A new word, consumerism, has entered the language, and a government department, the Department of Prices and Consumer Protection, has been set up to deal with consumer affairs.

Bodies and organizations designed to inform and protect the consumer have proliferated. These range from large official organizations such as the Office of Fair Trading and the National Consumer Council, both responsible to the Secretary of State for Prices and Consumer Protection, to small groups run on a part-time voluntary basis. The basis of consumer protection is the law. The main acts relating to foodstuffs are Weights and Measures, Food and Drugs, Labelling of Food Regulations and Prices. Collectively, these acts set food quality standards and their areas of operation range from making it an offence to give short measure to stipulating detailed regulations covering the labelling of processed and packaged foods.

Making a complaint

Achieving a satisfactory outcome to a complaint about food is simpler than if you are complaining about a pair of shoes or a malfunctioning washing-machine. Legislation covering the selling of food is comprehensive and there can be little disagreement about the fitness of a particular item of food. You can't argue with a rotten egg.

The first problem is in overcoming your apathy once the initial fury at finding the food inedible passes. Lethargy, plus the dislike of making a fuss, deters many people from making justifiable complaints. However, in the case of a serious complaint, such as finding broken glass in a carton of yogurt, it is in everybody's interest that you do tell the shop of your discovery. Any serious incident, which endangers public health, should also be reported to your local Environmental Health Officer or Trading Standards Officer.

Trading standards

Assuming that your complaint is a minor one, you should return the offending article to the shop from which you bought it as soon as possible. Take the receipt, if you had one, any packing materials and, if practicable, the article itself. Obviously you can't return a bad egg, but you could take the egg box with you. Ask politely but firmly to see the manager. Explain your complaint clearly – when you bought the goods, and what the problem is. You gain nothing by being rude and abusive. If you lose your temper you will antagonize the manager, and possibly forget the most important point you were going to make.

If for some reason you cannot return to the shop from which you bought the unsatisfactory goods, you should write to the manager. Keep a copy of all correspondence and, if you have access to a photocopying machine, you might enclose a copy of your receipt. Do not send the original. If you are unable to obtain any satisfaction from the shop, contact your local Consumer Advice Centre or Citizens' Advice Bureau with the details. A firm letter with official letterhead can often work wonders. If your complaint is more serious and unlikely to be an isolated incident but relates to the general cleanliness of a shop, or to foreign bodies found in food, you should report the matter to your Trading Standards Officer or Environmental Health Officer. Restaurants and shops selling food are frequently prosecuted under the Food and Drugs Act for running dirty premises. And many of these cases have been brought to the attention of the authorities in the first instance by members of the public.

25

Chapter Three

Preserving is the art of keeping food beyond its natural span, and is almost as old as cooking itself. The traditional methods were salting (usually meat or fish) or drying (meat, fish, vegetables or fruit), both rarely done at home now, and bottling, pickle- or chutney-making, or jam-making – these last concerned wholly with vegetables and fruit. In addition, the advent of the home freezer has added another, even easier, method of preserving nearly all food.

Home freezing

An efficient food freezer should be capable of freezing a specified weight of food from 25°C (77°F) to −18°C (0°F) while at the same time maintaining the temperature of any frozen food already stored in the freezer at about −18°C (0°F). Most freezers are now marked with the food freezer symbol (see page 29) and this distinguishes them from conservators or frozen food storage compartments in refrigerators which have star markings (see page 29) indicating that they are intended only for the storage of already-frozen food.

Freezers are available in a wide range of sizes, ranging from about 55 litres (2 cubic feet) to 800 litres (28 cubic feet). Each 28 litres (about 1 cubic foot) of space will hold about 9 kilograms (20 pounds) of frozen food. At least 55 litres (2 cubic feet) is the minimum requirement for each person in the family, though you should bear in mind the usual number of people to be catered for: families that do a lot of home entertaining will probably require a much larger freezer.

Foods for freezing

With a few exceptions (listed below) almost all fresh and cooked food can be preserved by freezing, and following a few simple rules will ensure success.

1. Choose only really fresh food of prime quality – this especially applies to fish and seafood.
2. Cooked foods should be freshly prepared and allowed to cool before packing and freezing.
3. Food for freezing must be sealed in a container or wrapped to exclude air to avoid dehydration, loss of colour, texture and flavour, and cross-flavouring during storage.
4. Pack foods in probable mealtime proportions, interleaving chops, beefburgers, fish fillets, etc., with polythene, aluminium foil or freezer paper for easy separation.
5. Follow the freezer manufacturer's instructions when loading fresh food and *avoid placing fresh food in direct contact with food already frozen.* It is good practice to depress the fast freeze switch, if one is fitted, a few hours before loading the freezer with fresh food. Return the switch to its normal position after about 24 hours. The thermostat setting for normal storage should keep frozen food at a temperature not warmer than −18°C (0°F).
6. The usual rules of hygiene in the preparation of food must be followed. In particular make sure that all packaging, kitchen tools and utensils, cutting boards and hands are thoroughly washed between handling fresh and cooked foods.
7. A few foods are not recommended for freezing. These include hard-boiled eggs, mayonnaise, baked egg custard pies and tarts, royal icings and frostings, single cream, soft meringues, boiled potatoes (except if new), stuffed poultry, bananas and vegetables intended for use in salads. Foods which contain a high proportion of gelatine also do not freeze well.

Packaging food for freezing

The low temperature air in a food freezer is very dry, and any food not properly sealed will lose its natural moisture and may develop freezer burn. Inadequately packaged food is not unsafe but will be unpleasant to eat after storage.

Packaging materials must be free from taint and odours, and be moisture and vapour proof to prevent loss of natural moisture and juices in the food. They should also be resistant to cracking and breaking at freezer temperatures and a suitable shape to ensure fast freezing.

Various packaging materials fill these requirements. Polythene bags are available in many sizes for fruits, vegetables, fish, meat, poultry, loaves of bread and baked foods. Polythene sheeting, freezer paper and heavy duty aluminium foil are especially useful for wrapping irregularly shaped food and interleaving individual portions of meat, fish, poultry, hamburgers, and yeast or pastry dough.

Polythene tubs and cartons with tightly fitting lids hold soft fruit, sauces, stews, casseroles and all liquids. Aluminium and waxed paper dishes, trays and basins using aluminium foil or polythene sheet to cover, serve the same purpose. Plastic covered wire and freezer tape are used for sealing. Each package should be labelled and marked with the contents and the date of freezing. Different colours for labels are helpful for later identification – such as green for vegetables, red for meat, blue for fish.

Meat

With all kinds of meat, prepare for freezing by trimming off all excess fat and removing bones as far as practicable to save space and packaging material. Bones which have been removed can be used for stock, which can then be frozen after skimming off all fat. The airtight wrapping of meat is especially important to prevent dehydration. Protect the outer packaging by first covering any sharp projecting bones with greaseproof paper

or clean muslin. Exclude as much air as possible before sealing in aluminium foil or polythene sheet. Larger joints of meat should be cut into mealtime or family size portions before freezing. Joints of 1 kilogram (2 pounds) and larger will probably require at least 48 hours to freeze through to the centre.

Freezing cooked meat

Home or commercially frozen meat can be used for a recipe, then refrozen after being well cooked. Providing fat has been skimmed, the storage life of cooked stews and casseroles prepared in this way is up to two months. It is especially important for hygiene and cross-contamination to avoid handling fresh and cooked meat and poultry at the same time when preparing for freezing.

Fish

Fresh fish deteriorates quickly after being caught even if well chilled, so fish purchased from an inland fishmonger is unlikely to be fresh enough for home freezing. All fresh fish suitable for freezing should be washed, cleaned, gutted and head, tail and fins removed and then washed again. Prepare the fish as for cooking, either whole, filleted or in steaks (see pages 83 to 87). To increase storage life, whole round and flat fish, after freezing and temporary packing, can be glazed by dipping in an ice cold solution of salt and water, 50 grams (2 ounces) salt to 600 millilitres (1 pint) of water.

Game birds

Game birds after being hung for a time according to the taste and flavour preferred, should be prepared for home freezing in the same way as poultry (see chart, page 38). After preparation, pack in polythene bags or aluminium foil and seal.

Vegetables

As a general guide, all vegetables which are normally cooked before eating will freeze and store satisfactorily. Some, like tomatoes and onions, lose their original crispness and texture after freezing, but are useful for stews, casseroles and sauces. After washing and trimming, most vegetables must be blanched in boiling water for a short time before packaging and freezing. This retards the action of enzymes and prevents 'off' flavours. The few exceptions are given in the chart on page 37. Blanching is most easily done by putting small quantities of vegetables in a wire basket and immersing this in a pan of boiling water, normally at a ratio of not more than 450 grams (1 pound) of vegetables to 3½ litres (6 pints) of water. Blanching time begins when the water returns to the boil, and ends by plunging the vegetables into ice cold water. Most vegetables can be packed into polythene bags or rigid cartons, and many can be frozen individually to produce a free flow pack (see under fruit below).

Fruit

Fruit can be frozen whole, in halves or in slices, in a dry pack, in dry sugar, in a sugar syrup or as a fruit purée. The sugar or sugar syrup helps to preserve colour and flavour. Light-coloured fruits like apples, pears and peaches will darken after peeling and slicing. This discolouration can be almost eliminated by working quickly and placing the fruit in a solution of ascorbic acid and water, using 1 teaspoon ascorbic acid to 600 millilitres (1 pint) of water. Do not use iron or copper pans for this solution.

Freezing separately: After cleaning the fruit, with as little water as possible, dry it and spread it out in a single layer in a polythene bag laid on a flat aluminium baking sheet. Freeze the fruit in this position. Small fruit will freeze in a few hours and can then be shaken gently down into the bag. Fill the bag using fruit from other sheets. Although time-consuming, this method is best for small fruit like raspberries, strawberries and blackberries, producing a free flow pack. (The method applies to other kinds of food as well as diced vegetables and peas, for example.)

Dry pack: This is suitable for fruits with a relatively tough skin. Gooseberries and currants, for example, need only to be washed and dried before freezing in closed bags.

Dry sugar pack: After cleaning and drying, sprinkle the fruit with sugar using 125 grams (4 ounces) of fruit, shaking or stirring the fruit gently to ensure an even coating.

Two popular types of freezer: on the left, an upright fridge-freezer and on the right, a chest-type.

Sugar syrup: Prepare sugar syrup and allow it to cool before adding to fruit. Add sugar to boiling water and simmer only long enough for all the sugar to be dissolved. Sugar syrup can be used in one of three strengths:

1. Light sugar syrup: 225 grams (8 ounces) sugar to 600 millilitres (1 pint) water.
2. Medium sugar syrup: 350 grams (12 ounces) to 500 millilitres (17 fluid ounces) water.
3. Heavy sugar syrup: 450 grams (1 pound) sugar to 500 millilitres (17 fluid ounces) water.

If recommended add 1 teaspoon ascorbic acid to the solution when cold.

Purées and juices: Fruit which has been discarded because of over-ripeness, blemishes or bruises can be frozen in purée form after the blemishes or bruised parts have been removed. Pass the fruit through a nylon sieve or food mill and add sugar at the ratio of about 125 grams (4 ounces) of sugar to 450 grams (1 pound) fruit or according to taste. Apples and tomatoes should be cooked before sieving.

Storage life: With a few exceptions, most fruit will freeze and store satisfactorily at −18°C (0°F) for up to nine months when packed in dry sugar or in sugar syrup. The storage life is normally reduced to about six months for dry packs.

Cake, breads and pastries

All cakes, except those with icing, breads, pastries, scones and biscuits freeze well. Generally cakes, breads, scones and biscuits have a better texture if they are baked before freezing, whereas dough is crisper if it is frozen before baking. If the dough is to be used for pies with a cooked filling – steak and kidney, chicken or game – then this should be cooked before covering with dough.

Uncooked bread dough can be frozen, but a better rise is ensured if the amount of yeast is increased by half. Pack the unrisen dough in a greased polythene bag, leave 2½-5 centimetres (1-2 inches) of space above the dough, and seal the bag. (To prepare for baking, remove the fastener and allow the dough to thaw out and rise in the refrigerator overnight, or for 2-5 hours at room temperature). Divide large cakes into serving pieces before wrapping and freezing. It is easier to wrap soft and sponge cakes and those with a buttercream filling and decoration after they have hardened in the freezer. Cakes that are to be filled when thawed should be packed with a piece of foil between each layer to prevent them from sticking together. Fresh white breadcrumbs will keep well in the freezer packed in polythene bags.

Bought, sliced bread should be overwrapped in foil or a polythene bag. Slices required for toast can be taken straight from the freezer and toasted while still frozen.

Dairy foods

Butter and cheese should be overwrapped in polythene or aluminium foil before freezing. Grated cheese, packed in usable quantities in a polythene bag, can be taken straight from the freezer for use in sauces and other savoury dishes. Whole milk should not be frozen, but pasteurized and homogenized milk can be frozen and stored for a short time. Freeze in wax cartons, leaving a head space.

Eggs should not be frozen in their shells as they expand and crack. The yolks and whites should be lightly beaten together with salt or sugar added – ½ teaspoon of sugar to every 6 eggs. Label the cartons with the number of eggs and whether with sugar or salt. Approximately 3 tablespoons of the thawed egg mixture is the equivalent of 1 egg.

Like whole milk, single cream does not freeze well. Double cream, with not less than 40 per cent butterfat, will however and if it separates when thawing, stirring will correct it.

Cooking home frozen foods

Small portions of fish, meat, poultry and all vegetables can be cooked straight from the freezer without thawing. Be sure however that they are cooked right through to the centre before serving. Vegetables which have been blanched should be cooked in the minimum quantity of boiling, salted water and normally need less cooking time than fresh vegetables.

It is important that large joints of meat, whole fish and all whole birds should be thawed completely before cooking. This is especially important with chickens, ducks, geese and turkeys, bearing in mind that a frozen bird of above 10 kilograms (22 pounds) will require about three days in a cool, clean place to thaw to the centre.

Home preserving

The long-term storage of fresh produce usually requires some kind of treatment to retard or prevent spoilage. Larders and refrigerators have already been discussed in terms of purchased foods, but both of these provide only short-term solutions for the problem. To keep most food for longer than a week requires more sophisticated methods.

The traditional ways of preserving are by bottling, jam-making and pickling, to name only the broadest categories. The objective is to make seasonal foods available all the year round.

Home freezer, with symbol.

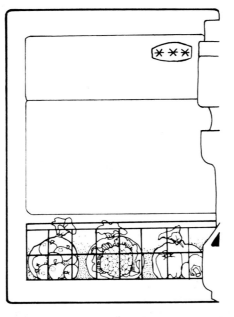

Refrigerator with freezing section.

Bottling

Bottling, one of the methods of preserving food by heat, will only be successful if the processing is efficiently, carefully and correctly carried out and the bottles are completely sealed for storage.

Home bottling of vegetables is not recommended unless a pressure cooker with a very accurate pressure control is available. Vegetables are low in acid and may contain bacteria resistant to heat. They may also develop a toxin during storage, which can cause fatal food poisoning.

On the other hand, food that contains a high percentage of acid – like fruit and tomatoes – is ideal for bottling, since the acid inhibits the growth of bacteria and prevents the formation of toxin.

Fruits vary, of course, in the amount of acid they contain, and those with a lower content need a longer processing. See the chart (page 40) for precise details.

Equipment

Two types of bottles are specially made for preserving; one with a spring-like clip and the other with a screw band. These are available in various sizes from hardware, kitchen equipment and department stores. Jam jars also can be used in most methods but *not* in a pressure cooker. Whichever type of bottle is used, it must not be chipped or cracked and should be scrupulously clean. If glass lids are used these should not be chipped.

If you are using bottles with separate rubber rings, make sure they are the correct size. Always use new rings: they stretch and will not form a satisfactory seal if they are used a second time. Before using rubber rings, soak them in warm water for 10 minutes, then quickly dip them into boiling water immediately before using.

A large container for processing the bottles is another essential. If the processing is done on top of the stove then the container must have a false bottom – a wooden or wire rack is ideal – so that the bottles do not come into direct contact with the container. If they do they will crack. The container also must be deep enough to hold sufficient water to cover the bottles completely. Special bottling pans are available, and one of these is a good investment if you do a lot of bottling each year. If you use the oven method (see opposite page), a large asbestos mat is necessary to stand the bottles on.

Other useful items of equipment are a thermometer, a long-handled spoon, a pair of tongs and heatproof jug.

Preparation of fruit

Fruit used for bottling must be fresh, firm and clean. Wash the fruit in cold water and leave to drain in a colander.

Equipment and preparation for fruit-bottling.

Remove the peel and pith from citrus fruits, cut the segments away from the tissues and remove any pips. Pears and apples are best peeled, cored and cut into slices or quarters. Apricots, peaches and plums can be bottled whole or halved with the stones removed.

Fruit may be bottled in fresh water or syrup although syrup is preferable, since it helps to preserve the colour and flavour. The strength of the syrup depends on the sweetness of the fruit and also on how it is packed. The proportions are generally 225 grams (8 ounces) of sugar to 600 millilitres (1 pint) water.

To make the syrup, dissolve the sugar in the water over moderate heat and when the sugar is dissolved, boil for one minute. If the syrup is cloudy, strain it through muslin because clear syrup gives a better finish to the fruit. The sugar used for syrup may be granulated or loaf or, for a different flavour, clear honey or golden syrup could be used instead. The syrup is used either cold or very hot, depending on the processing method.

A brine solution is best for tomatoes. Make it with 1 tablespoon of salt to 1 litre (1¾ pints) water. If they are packed solidly no water is necessary but 1 teaspoon of salt should be added to each 450 grams (1 pound) tomatoes.

Packing the bottles

Rinse the clean bottles in cold water, drain them but do not dry them – it is much simpler to pack the fruit into wet bottles since it slips down more easily. Fill with the prepared fruit and press down with the handle of a wooden spoon. Make sure the fruit is tightly packed but be careful not to bruise it. Fill the bottles to within 1-2½ centimetres (½-1 inch) of the rim, then pour the syrup or water over the fruit a little at a time. Twist the bottle from side to side after each addition to remove any air bubbles.

Methods of processing

Processing the bottles can be done on top of the stove or in the oven. There are several methods employed for both types; one example of each is detailed below. The advantages of the first are reliability and economy of fuel, but it can only be done in a container large and deep enough to allow the bottles to be completely immersed. It is more difficult to control the temperature with the oven method and the processing time is

longer. See the chart on page 40 for times and temperatures for different fruits.

Method 1: slow water-bath

Pack the bottles with fruit and slowly pour in enough *cold* syrup (or brine) to come to the top of the bottle. Place the lid on top and secure it with a spring clip or screw-band. Place the bottles in a deep container, making sure they do not touch each other or the sides of the container. Completely cover them with cold water, cover the container with a lid. (If no lid is available, a pastry board is a good substitute). Bring the water slowly to the boil. The temperature of the water should be raised gradually from cold to 55°C (130°F) in one hour and up to the required temperature (see chart page 40) in up to another half hour. If the water is heated too quickly the fruit may rise in the bottles and more time may be needed at the maximum temperature to enable heat to penetrate the fruit in the centre of the bottle.

When the processing time is finished, remove the bottles from the container using a pair of tongs and place them on a wooden table or board. Tighten bands on the screw-topped bottles and leave for 24 hours before testing that the seal is complete (see next column).

Method 2: pressure cooker

This is a quick method of bottling fruit, because the temperature of the boiling point is raised when under pressure, so reducing the processing time and saving energy. The pressure to use should be L or 5 pounds. The basic principles are the same as other methods: the cooker must be deep enough to hold the bottles and have a trivet or rack in the bottom. There should be 900 millilitres (1½ pints) of water in the cooker before the trivet or rack and bottles are put in, and it should be at boiling point before the bottles are inserted.

The fruit is packed into warm bottles and boiling syrup poured on top leaving 2½ centimetres (1 inch) headspace. Cover the bottles and place them in the cooker making sure they do not touch each other or the sides. Cover the pan and bring up to L or 5 pounds pressure over moderate heat and process for the times given in the chart on page 40. Leave the bottles in the cooker and allow pressure to reduce at room temperature. Remove the bottles and finish as in the previous method.

Method 3: moderate oven

This method can be used for all types of fruit and also for solid pack tomatoes. Preheat the oven to 150°C (Gas Mark 2, 300°F).

Pack warm bottles with the fruit and pour in boiling syrup or brine leaving 2½ centimetres (1 inch) headspace. Place the lids on top but not the clips or screw-bands. Put the bottles 5 centimetres (2 inches) apart on a baking sheet lined with newspaper and place in the centre of the oven. After the processing time (see chart page 40), secure the lids with clips or screw-bands. Leave for 24 hours and test for seal.

Testing the seal

This is necessary to ensure that a complete vacuum has been formed during the processing and that no air remains in the bottles.

After the bottles have been left for 24 hours and are completely cool, remove the clips or screw-bands. Lift the bottles carefully by the lids. If these are tight and secure the seal is complete. The clips should be washed, dried and set aside for future use. The screw-bands are replaced after being washed, dried and greased on the inside with a little oil – be careful not to screw them back on too tightly, or they may be difficult to remove after the bottles have been stored. If the lids are loose the fruit should be reprocessed – the liquid should be poured off and reheated separately except when using Method 1 – or used within two days.

Label each bottle, with the name of the fruit, date processed and whether with water, light or heavy syrup, or brine. They should be stored in a cool, dry dark place until required.

Bottling vegetables

As already emphasized, the bottling of vegetables should only be done in a reliable pressure cooker – if you are in any doubt it is wise to check with the manufacturer of the cooker. As the processing is rather lengthy, it is sensible to bottle only the more expensive vegetables and those with a short season, such as asparagus and sweetcorn.

Vegetables should be young and very fresh, and processed as soon after gathering as possible. After preparation – sweetcorn kernels removed from the cob, and asparagus trimmed – they should be washed in cold running water.

Vegetables need to be blanched before bottling. This is done by plunging them into boiling water for two to five minutes, depending on the vegetables, then dropping them in cold water. Drain them well before packing into sterilized, warm bottles. This helps to retain their colour and causes them to shrink slightly, making it easier to pack them into the bottles. Do not pack them tightly or press them down. Fill the bottles with boiling brine made with 25 grams (1 ounce) of salt to 1 litre (2 pints) of water, leaving 1 centimetre (½ inch) headspace.

Cover the bottles in the same way as for fruit. Follow Method 2 for the processing *except* for the pressure and length of time (see chart on page 41 for this). Place the covered cooker over medium heat and reduce it to low when steam starts to escape through the vent. Bring up to M or 10 pounds pressure and maintain this for the required time. Time may vary according to the type of pressure cooker, so be sure to check in your instruction manual first.

When the bottles have been sterilized the seal should be tested (see page 31). If it is not tight the bottles may be re-sterilized, although there will be a loss of quality. Otherwise, use the contents as quickly as possible.

Chutney-making is easy and fun – and the results are well worth the effort.

Pickle and chutney making

Chutneys and pickles are condiments made with a mixture of fruits and/or vegetables, preserved by the addition of vinegar, salt and spices. They require similar equipment but differ in the length of cooking time required and the consistency of the end product. Chutney is usually made from a combination of ingredients while pickles often have only one basic ingredient.

Equipment

Pans should be large enough to contain all the ingredients – a preserving pan is ideal. Brass, copper or iron pans should *not* be used as they react with the vinegar and give a metallic flavour to the finished product.

A long-handled wooden spoon is required which should be reserved for chutney- and pickle-making only.

Heatproof jars of any type can be used to contain the chutney or pickles. These should be clean, dry and warmed before pouring in the mixture.

A large ladle or heatproof jug is useful, especially when making a large quantity, to make it easier to fill the jars.

For chutney-making, the covers are most important. Paper or jam covers should not be used as these allow the vinegar to evaporate and after a month or so the mixture will shrink and become very dry. Special vinegar-proof paper is

available, usually in rolls, and this is secured to the jars by tying with a piece of string. Special preserving or bottling jars are suitable, either with screw-on or clip-on lids. Jars with tight-fitting corks may also be used, providing the corks are new. They should be boiled before using, then covered with a piece of greaseproof paper and tied into the tops of the jars with string. Make sure that any metal cover is well lacquered and not scratched. To be on the safe side it is advisable to place a disc of vinegar-proof paper on top of chutney before screwing on metal lids.

Both chutneys and pickles should be labelled with the name and date then stored in a cool, dry, dark place. Most will keep for one to two years.

Chutney making

Vinegar is one of the most important ingredients in successful chutney-making, so it should be of good quality and have an acetic acid content of at least 5 per cent. Bottled vinegar is better than that sold from barrels. Any well-known brand of malt vinegar is suitable, or use wine vinegar for a special flavour.

As vinegar has a slightly hardening effect on some produce, particularly onions, carrots and other firm vegetables, it is advisable to cook them in water for a few minutes, then drain them, before adding to the other ingredients.

Sugar used may be granulated or brown; the latter is often considered

especially suitable for dark-coloured chutneys.

Ground spices are preferable to whole ones in chutney-making as they give a better flavour. If whole spices are used, double the amount given in the recipe, bruise them and tie them in a muslin bag before adding to the pan. The bag is then removed before the chutney is poured into the jars.

Pickle-making

Pickles may be made from a wide variety of fruit and vegetables. As with all methods of food preservation, the produce must be of good quality, fresh, firm and clean. Large vegetables – cauliflowers, cucumbers, cabbage and marrows – are best if they are separated or cut into pieces. Small vegetables such as onions (the small pickling variety), mushrooms and tomatoes can be left whole and only require to be peeled, halved or quartered and the pips removed. Vegetables to be pickled should first be soaked in brine or dry salt for anything up to two days. Fruits that are usually pickled whole, such as damsons, plums and cherries, should be pickled before the preliminary cooking otherwise they will shrivel and dry up. Generally fruits that are most suitable for pickling are larger ones like apples, pears and peaches – berry fruits go mushy and are not pleasant to eat.

As well as fruit and vegetables, boiled eggs may be pickled and also some nuts, particularly walnuts.

Block, coarse or sea salt gives better results than refined table salt; the latter may give a cloudy effect to the finished product.

Vinegar must be good quality, and have an acetic acid content of at least 5 per cent. Brown malt vinegar is suitable for all pickles but if a light colour is required, particularly for light-coloured fruit and vegetables, then white malt, wine or cider vinegar may be used.

Spices are added to vinegar to give it a good flavour and they also help as a preservative. Whole spices should be used for spiced vinegar as the ground ones will make the vinegar cloudy. The spices used may be varied depending on the type of pickle and personal taste. A basic spiced vinegar for pickling vegetables could be as follows: 5 centimetre (2 inch) piece cinnamon; 1 teaspoon cloves; 2 teaspoons allspice; 1 teaspoon black peppercorns; 1 teaspoon mustard

seed; 2-3 bay leaves, 1 litre (2 pints) vinegar. Place the spices and vinegar in a saucepan, cover and bring just to the boil (do not allow the liquid to bubble). Remove the pan from the heat and set aside for 2½-3 hours. Strain the vinegar and if it is not going to be used immediately pour it into clean, dry bottles.

Spiced vinegar is used either hot or cold. Usually cold vinegar is best for the vegetables that should be kept crisp – onions, cauliflower and cabbage – while hot vinegar gives a better result to the softer fruit pickles.

Mango Chutney
Makes about 1¾ kg (4 lb)

1⅓ kg (3 lb) green mangoes, peeled, halved and stoned
75 g (3 oz) salt
2 l (3½ pints) water
450 g (1 lb) sugar
600 ml (1 pint) vinegar
75 g (3 oz) fresh root ginger, peeled and finely chopped
6 garlic cloves, crushed
2 teaspoons hot chilli powder
5 cm (2 in) piece cinnamon stick
125 g (4 oz) raisins
125 g (4 oz) dried dates, chopped

Cut the mangoes into small pieces and place in a mixing bowl, sprinkle the salt over the top and pour in the water. Cover and set aside for 24 hours.

The finished product – spicy, piquant Beetroot Pickle.

Drain the mango pieces and set aside. Place the sugar and vinegar in a preserving pan and bring to the boil. When the sugar is dissolved add the remaining ingredients and mangoes and bring the mixture back to the boil.

Reduce the heat and simmer the chutney, stirring frequently, until it is thick; then discard the cinnamon stick.

Bottle, seal and label.

Beetroot Pickle
Makes about 1¾ litres (3 pints)

6 medium-sized beetroots, preferably uncooked
Cold water
350 ml (12 floz) wine vinegar
1½ tablespoons dry mustard
½ teaspoon salt
275 g (9 oz) sugar
2 onions, sliced
2 teaspoons dill seeds

Boil the beetroots until they are tender. Drain and set aside, reserving 300 millilitres (10 fluid ounces) of the liquid. When the beetroots are cool, slice off the tops and bottoms. Then, using your fingers, slip off the skins. Slice the beetroots and set aside.

In a medium-sized saucepan bring the vinegar and reserved cooking liquid to the

the boil over moderate heat. Add the mustard, salt and sugar. Stir to mix, and bring to the boil again. Remove the saucepan from the heat and set aside.

Arrange the beetroot slices and onions in layers in clean, screw-top jars. Add the dill seeds. Cover with the hot vinegar mixture. Tightly screw on the tops of the jars. Cool and place in the refrigerator. Allow the beetroot to stand for a few days before using. Serve very cold.

Note: Small, whole beetroots could be pickled in the same way.

Jams and marmalades

Jams and marmalades are probably the most popular and widely used forms of fruit preservation. They are the best way of using up surplus fruit and despite the excellence of some commercially produced jams nothing is better than really good home-made ones.

General information

Although different methods are used for jams and marmalades, the basic principles are the same. The fruit must be fresh, firm and under-ripe; over-ripe fruit will not make successful jam since it does not set. Fruit sets when boiled with sugar because it contains a natural pectin. The acid in fruit helps to extract the pectin thus ensuring a good set and a bright, clear colour, which helps to prevent sugar from crystallizing when the jam is stored.

Equipment

A suitable preserving pan is the most essential requirement since jam is usually made in substantial quantities. The pan should only be half full when the sugar is added to the fruits, so that when the jam boils up quickly, during cooking, it will not rise over the side. Aluminium, stainless steel or unchipped enamel are the best. Jam made in a metal pan must not be left to stand in it longer than necessary. If the second stage (when the sugar is added) has to be delayed for some reason the fruit should be transferred to a plastic bowl and returned to the pan when the process is ready to be completed. A little glycerine or butter rubbed over the bottom of the pan will help to prevent sticking and lessen the amount of scum.

Jam jars can be any type of jar, providing they are unchipped, clean and dry. They should be warmed slightly in the oven to prevent them from cracking when the jam is poured into them.

Jam covers can be bought in most stationers; they consist of waxed discs which are put on top of the jam when it is hot (they should exactly fit the surface and not overlap the edge of the jar); and parchment or cellophane circles which are placed on top of the jar, when the jam is cold, and secured with an elastic band. Commercial jam jars often have screw tops which provide an airtight seal. If the metal cover is lined with a thin piece of card, this should be removed and the cover washed and dried. Place a wax disc on the surface of the jam before the lid is screwed on. Plastic push-on lids are available to fit standard-sized jars, and although they cost more, they can be used over and over again. If metal or plastic lids are used, they must be put on while the jam is hot – if the jam is warm or actually cold, mould may form after a short period.

A heatproof cup is useful for pouring the jam into the jars, together with a long-handled wooden spoon for stirring and a slotted one for removing scum.

A sugar thermometer is a useful item if large quantities of jam are made, since it is the most accurate way to test that setting point has been reached.

Labels are essential to identify the type of jam and date on which it was made. They are often included with packets of jam covers or may be bought separately.

Fruits to use

Most fruits can be used for jam making but, as mentioned previously, they must be fresh, dry and slightly under-ripe. After preparation, the first stage for jam and marmalade is to soften the fruit. The fruit should be cooked slowly with a little water so that the skins soften and the pectin is released. The amount of water and cooking time depend on the ripeness of the fruit and also the quantity – the more fruit, the less water. Soft fruits such as blackberries, raspberries and strawberries do not require any water and the softening time will be much shorter. Fruits which are most easily made into jam are those which are high in pectin, although those low in pectin can be successfully made with the addition of high pectin fruits or substitutes.

High pectin fruits include citrus fruits, cooking apples, cranberries, damsons, gooseberries, plums and quinces. Medium pectin fruits include apricots, blackberries, greengages and raspberries. Low pectin fruits include cherries, figs, grapes, pears, pineapples, rhubarb and strawberries.

To make successful jam from low pectin and acid fruit, extra pectin should be added and this can be done in one of the following ways.

1. Mix the low or medium pectin fruit with a high pectin one, for example apple and blackberry or rhubarb and plum.
2. Add commercially-made pectin, which is generally available in liquid or sometimes powdered form.
3. Add lemon juice or citric acid.

Commercial pectin must be well softened before it and sugar are added to the fruit. The amount of pectin needed varies according to the fruit used, but a general guide is 150 millilitres (5 fluid ounces) pectin stock to 2 kilograms (4 pounds) fruit. Alternatively 50-125 millilitres (2-4 fluid ounces) of commercial liquid pectin or 2 teaspoons dried pectin can be added to each 450 grams (1 pound) of fruit. If using lemon juice, 2 tablespoons to 2 kilograms (4 pounds) of fruit is generally sufficient.

Sugar

Granulated, preserving or cube sugar can be used for jam and marmalade making. The advantages of using preserving sugar, although slightly more expensive, are that less scum is formed and the jam generally has a clearer appearance. Brown sugar gives a dark colour, so it is best used for chunky marmalade or black cherry jam

The amount of sugar required to give a good set depends on the pectin quantity of the fruit and should represent 60 per cent of the final weight of jam. Therefore, if a recipe uses $2\frac{3}{4}$ kilograms (6 pounds) of sugar, the final yield should be about $4\frac{1}{2}$ kilograms (10 pounds) jam. The following is an approximate guide to the quantity of sugar needed for the different types of fruit, depending on their pectin content:

High pectin fruits – 575-675 grams ($1\frac{1}{4}$-$1\frac{1}{2}$ pounds) sugar to 450 grams (1 pound) fruit.

Medium pectin fruits – 450 grams (1 pound) sugar to 450 grams (1 pound) fruit.

Low pectin fruits – 350 grams (12 ounces) sugar to 450 grams (1 pound) fruit.

If too much sugar is used, the jam may

In jam-making, test for set with a sugar thermometer or by the saucer method.

When setting point is reached, carefully fill the jars with the hot jam.

crystallize with storing; and if too little is used, it may ferment. However, when a less sweet jam is preferred, less sugar can be used – although it will not keep for so long, and the yield will be smaller. The jam will however have a much more fruity flavour.

Tests for setting

A test that setting point has been reached should be made after the jam or marmalade has been cooked for the suggested time in the recipe you are following. Care should be taken not to boil beyond the setting point, otherwise the colour, texture and flavour will be spoiled. Thus the pan should always be removed from the heat during testing. Testing the setting point can be done as follows:

1. The simplest way is to put a teaspoon of the hot mixture on a saucer and leave it to cool. (This can be done in a few seconds in a freezer.) When cool, the surface should be set and the jam should wrinkle when pushed with a finger. If it is still runny, return the pan to the stove and continue boiling and testing until set.

2. A sugar thermometer is the most accurate way of testing the set. Place the thermometer in a jug of hot water before and after testing. Stir the jam, then immerse the thermometer in it – do not allow the bulb to touch the bottom of the pan which could cause it to break. If the temperature is between 104 °C (220 °F) and 106 °C (222 °F) the jam is at setting point.

Finishing off

When the jam or marmalade is ready, remove any scum from the surface with

a slotted spoon. If the jam contains whole fruit, such as strawberries, or peel as in marmalade, leave it to cool until a thin skin forms on top (this prevents the fruit from rising to the top). Stir the jam gently and pour it into the warm jars. Place a waxed disc on the surface and press it down gently to exclude any air. Wipe the rims of the jars with a damp cloth if they are sticky, then cover when either hot or cold depending on the covering used. Label and store the jars in a cool, dark place.

Jam making

Prepare and cook the fruit, with or without water, over low heat until it has softened and broken down. Add the sugar and pectin, if necessary, cook slowly, stirring frequently until the sugar dissolves. Raise the heat and boil the jam rapidly without stirring. Take care that the jam does not rise to the top of the pan – if it does, give it a gentle stir to cool it down a fraction. If the initial cooking of the fruit has been sufficient, the jam should reach setting point within 5-25 minutes. Then pour the jam into the jars leaving 1 centimetre (½ inch) headspace, cover and label.

Strawberry Jam

2¼ kg (5 lb) strawberries, hulled and washed
125 ml (4 fl oz) lemon juice
2 kg (4½ lb) sugar

Put the strawberries in a preserving pan and add the lemon juice. Simmer, stirring frequently, until the berries are soft.

Add the sugar and stir until it has

dissolved. Bring to the boil and boil rapidly for 15-20 minutes. Test for setting. When set, leave the jam for 10 minutes before pouring into the bottles. Cover, seal and label.

Marmalade

Marmalade is traditionally made with citrus fruits, such as oranges, lemons, limes, grapefruits or tangerines, each imparting its own tangy flavour, but citrus fruit can also be mixed with other fruits to make a pleasant combination, or flavoured with ginger or other spices if wished.

The main difference between marmalade and jam making is that citrus fruit skin requires long slow cooking in a larger amount of water to soften it before adding the sugar. However, the cooking time can be shortened considerably by using a pressure cooker.

The fruit to be used in marmalade-making must be fresh and just ripe. It should be washed and if necessary scrubbed with a clean brush. Remember that the pectin content is in the pulp, white pith and pips, *not* in the peel, so these must be added to the fruit while cooking.

In some recipes lemon juice or citric acid is added. This is because the acid content of the fruit may be lowered, owing to the high proportion of water and sugar used in making marmalade. Extra acid is unnecessary when marmalade is made with two or more fruits, or for lemon and lime marmalades.

To make the marmalade, scrub and scald the chosen fruit in boiling water (this makes it easier to remove the peel). Remove the peel as thinly as possible and cut into thick or thin shreds. Place the peel, acid (if used) and half the quantity of water in a preserving pan. Bring to the boil, then simmer for 1½-2 hours or until the peel is soft.

Meanwhile, cut the fruit and pith into pieces and simmer in another pan for 1½ hours. Strain the mixture through a colander placed over a bowl. Discard the pips, coarse tissue and pith and add the pulp to the peel. If a thicker marmalade is required the pulp should be pressed through a fine nylon sieve. Add the sugar and cook over low heat stirring frequently until it dissolves. Bring to the boil and cook rapidly until setting point is reached (see column one). Remove any scum from the top, allow the marmalade to cool slightly and finish off as above.

Freezing Chart

Food	Preparation	Storage life up to
Bread and cakes Bread, rolls, croissants, Danish pastries	Bake and cool before wrapping in polythene bags, seal and freeze. If sliced, individual slices can be toasted without thawing. Freeze bread crumbs in convenient sized polythene bags.	1 month
Cakes, scones, biscuits	Bake and cool before wrapping in polythene bags or sheet. Preferably fill and decorate cakes during thawing. In recipes use egg yolks rather than whole eggs, high quality margarine instead of butter. Interleave layers of sandwich cakes with freezer paper or polythene sheet.	6 months
Unbaked yeast dough	Yeast does not remain stable very long when frozen. Pack the unrisen dough in greased polythene bags. Leave headspace and seal. Rising time may need to be increased: compensate by adding more yeast in doughs to be frozen.	2 months
Unbaked pastries and pies	Pastry is better frozen unbaked. Prepare in conveniently sized thin slabs. Wrap in foil or polythene sheet, roll out after thawing. Pies with a pastry base and/or covering should be prepared as for cooking. Cook and cool savoury fillings before covering with pastry. Fruit does not require cooking. Foil dishes are ideal for packing: over-wrap with foil before freezing.	6 months
Dairy Foods Whole eggs	Lightly beat yolks and whites together either with 1 tablespoon sugar or 1 teaspoon salt to every 6 eggs. Pack in waxed carton or tub leaving headspace. Seal well. Alternatively freeze in ice cube tray and store frozen blocks in polythene bag. Seal well.	6 months
Egg yolks	Store better than whole egg. Gently mix yolks. Add a little sugar or salt. Freeze and pack as for whole eggs.	9 months
Egg whites	Pass through sieve, mix gently, add a little sugar or salt. Freeze and pack as for whole eggs.	9 months
Milk	Freeze only homogenized milk in waxed carton leaving head space.	3 months
Cream	Freeze only double cream (not less than 40 per cent butter fat) and whipping cream. Preferably add sugar – one tablespoon to each 600ml (1 pint) cream. Pack in waxed cartons leaving head space.	3 months
Ice-cream	Store ice-cream in original container. Home-made in wax cartons, leaving headspace.	3 months
Butter	Overwrap commercial packaging or tubs with polythene sheet or aluminium foil. Seal well.	salted up to 3 months; unsalted up to 6 months
Cheese	Hard cheese may become crumbly after freezing. Cream and cottage cheeses mixed with whipped cream make good sandwich fillings. Grated cheese freezes and stores well for use in recipes or for garnishing. Pack in tubs or cartons and grated cheese in polythene bags.	soft cheese up to 3 months; grated hard cheese up to 6 months
Fish White fish – cod, haddock, plaice, sole, whiting etc	Small fish can be frozen whole after preparation. Glaze if preferred and pack in polythene bags or aluminium foil. Larger fish should be filleted or cut into steaks. Interleave individual fillets and steaks with aluminium foil, polythene sheet or freezer paper. Pack in flat wax or foil containers. Wrap in polythene or foil.	6 months
Oily fish – halibut, herring, mackerel, mullet, salmon, turbot, trout, etc	Prepare and freeze as for white fish. Storage life for oily fish is shorter than white fish.	3 months
Shellfish – crab, lobster	Only freeze shellfish if it is less than 24 hours since it was taken from the water. Cook crab and lobster, remove meat from shells and claws and pack in tubs, cartons or aluminium foil containers leaving head space.	3 months
Oysters, scallops	Best frozen uncooked, remove from shells, retain natural juices. Wash fish in salt and water then pack in polythene tubs, cartons or aluminium foil containers with natural juices. Leave head space before sealing.	3 months
Prawns and shrimps	Best frozen uncooked after washing in salt and water. Remove the heads and tails and pack in tubs, cartons or aluminium foil containers. The shells and veins should be removed during thawing.	3 months
Beef and lamb Large cuts	Remove bones and excess fat. Pad any projecting bones and seal as snugly as possible in aluminium foil or polythene bags. Seal well. Make stock from bones, freeze in ice-cube trays and pack in polythene bags.	9 months
Small cuts	Remove excess fat, wrap in aluminium foil or in polythene bag. Interleave chops, steaks etc with aluminium foil, freezer paper or polythene sheet, draw out as much air as possible before sealing well in aluminium foil or polythene bags.	6 months

Freezing Chart

Food	Preparation		Storage life up to
Pork and Veal Large cuts Small cuts	Prepare and pack as above.		4 months 3 months
Offal	Prepare and pack as for small cuts. Maintain strict hygiene standards.		2 months
Minced meat and sausages	Prepare and pack as for small cuts. Freeze only freshly minced meat and bought sausages. Avoid salt in sausages as this reduces storage life.		1 month
Poultry and game	Remove head, tail and feathers. Clean and truss as for cooking, pad any projecting bones. Do not stuff poultry before freezing. Pack in polythene bags, excluding as much air as possible, and seal well. Make stock from giblets, skim all excess fat after cooling and freeze in tubs or cartons leaving head space.		Chickens up to 9 months Ducks, geese, turkeys and game up to 6 months.
Poultry joints and quarters	Freeze and wrap individually in polythene bags or aluminium foil. Several portions can be frozen in one package providing pieces of poultry are interleaved with aluminium foil or polythene sheet.		Chicken up to 9 months. Duck, goose, turkey portions up to 6 months.

Vegetables	Preparation	Blanching time in minutes	Storage life up to
Artichokes (globe)	Trim off coarse outer leaves, stalks, tops and stems. Add lemon juice to blanching water.	7	12 months
Asparagus	Wash, scrape stalks, trim to approx equal lengths. Divide up into thick, medium and thin stalks. Pack in rigid containers.	thin – 2 thick – 4	12 months
Aubergines	Wash well and cut into about 1cm ($\frac{1}{2}$in) slices with stainless steel knife. Pack in rigid containers.	4	12 months
Beans (broad)	Pick young tender beans. Shell and discard any blemished beans.	3	12 months
Beans (French and runner)	Wash and trim ends, leave whole or slice thickly or cut into pieces about 2$\frac{1}{2}$cm (1in) long	whole – 4 sliced – 3	12 months
Beetroot	Select young and small beets. Cook whole beets until tender, rub off skins and pack in rigid containers. Large beets should be sliced or diced after cooking.	none	6 months
Broccoli	Wash, and trim stalks cutting away any woody stalks. Divide up into thick, medium and thin stems. Pack in rigid containers, sprig to stalk. Separate layers with polythene film or freezer paper.	thick – 5 thin – 3	12 months
Brussels sprouts	Trim and remove discoloured leaves. Cross-cut the stalks and wash in salted water. Can be frozen individually. Pack in rigid containers or polythene bags.	small – 3 large – 5	12 months
Cabbage	Trim outer coarse leaves. Wash in salted water. Cut or tear into shreds. Drain well and dry. Pack in rigid containers or polythene bags.	2	6 months
Carrots	Remove tops and tails. Scrape and wash. Leave small new carrots whole, but slice or dice larger carrots. Small whole carrots can be frozen individually.	whole – 5 sliced – 3	8 months
Cauliflower	Select firm white heads. Remove most of outer coarse leaves. Separate into equal sized sprigs. Wash in salted water, drain and pack in rigid containers. Add lemon juice to blanching water to retain colour.	3	8 months
Celeriac	Wash, trim, scrape and slice, dry and pack into rigid containers or polythene bags.	6	9 months
Celery	Best suited after freezing for use as ingredient in recipes. Remove outer coarse stalks and strings. Cut into 5 to 7$\frac{1}{2}$cm (2-3in) lengths. Freeze hearts whole. Pack in containers or polythene bags.	hearts – 8 stalks – 4	12 months
Corn on the cob	Remove outer husks, trim ends and wash. Freeze separately and pack in polythene bags.	5 to 8 depending on size	12 months
Corn kernels	Remove outer husks, and scrape kernels off the cob. Wash, drain and pack in rigid containers or polythene bags. Can be added to other vegetables before freezing, eg peas.	5	12 months

Vegetables	Preparation	Blanching time in minutes	Storage life up to
Courgettes	Wash and cut into 2½cm (1in) slices. Drain and pack into rigid containers interleaving layers with freezer paper or aluminium foil.	3	12 months
Leeks	Remove coarse outer leaves and trim root end. Wash well, leave whole or slice and pack into rigid containers or polythene bags. They freeze well in white sauce. Seal well to prevent cross-flavour in storage.	whole – 4 sliced – 2	6 months
Mushrooms	Wash and peel field mushrooms. Trim stalks. Leave whole or slice. Add lemon juice to blanching water – or sauté in margarine – dry well and pack in rigid containers without blanching.	whole – 4 sliced – 2	12 months
Onions	Use only for cooking after freezing. Peel, slice into rings. Pack in small rigid containers and seal well to prevent cross-flavour in storage. They freeze well in white sauce.	2	3 months
Parsnips	Choose young and small parsnips, scrape and wash. Cut into quarters or slices. Drain and pack into rigid containers or polythene bags.	3	12 months
Peas	Choose young sweet peas, pod and discard any blemished peas. Blanch in small quantities. Drain well and pack in containers or polythene bags.	1½	12 months
Peppers (red and green)	Wash, halve and remove seeds and stalk. Can then be sliced if preferred. Remove only tops and seeds if later to be stuffed. Freeze individually, whole or sliced. Drain and pack in polythene bags.	2	12 months
Spinach	Choose young tender leaves. Wash well in running water, drain and press out as much water as possible. Pack in rigid containers or polythene bags in portions or family mealtime quantities.	2	12 months
Turnips and swedes	Remove thick peel and cut into 2½cm (1in) cubes. Pack in rigid containers or polythene bags.	3	12 months
Herbs – mint, parsley, sage, thyme etc.	Wash, drain and dry. Chop finely and freeze in ice cube tray. Wrap cubes in aluminium foil or polythene bags. After freezing and storage, colour and flavour may be reduced.	1	3-6 months

Fruit	Preparation	Storage life up to
Apples	Peel, core and slice. Use ascorbic acid to prevent browning. Blanch (see vegetables) for two or three minutes for dry pack. Alternatively pack in dry sugar or medium sugar syrup with ascorbic acid. Pack in bags or tubs. Leave headspace in syrup pack.	9 months
Apple purée	Peel, core and slice, cook until tender and sieve. Add sugar and pack in tubs leaving headspace.	6 months
Apricots	Peel, remove stones and freeze in halves or slices in medium sugar syrup with ascorbic acid. Pack in tubs leaving headspace.	9 months
Avocados	Peel, remove stone and convert flesh to purée, adding 1 teaspoon of lemon juice to each 600ml (1 pint) of purée. Season with salt and pepper and pack in tubs leaving headspace.	2 months
Bilberries and blackberries	Pick firm berries, remove stalks, wash and dry. Freeze as dry pack, individually, or as dry sugar pack or in heavy syrup. Pack in tubs leaving headspace.	9 months
Blackcurrants	Strip firm currants off stem, wash and dry. Freeze as dry pack individually for jam making, or in dry sugar pack or in heavy sugar syrup. Pack in tubs leaving headspace.	9 months
Cherries	Pick fully ripe, firm fruit, wash and dry. Remove stones and freeze as dry pack for jam making or in light sugar syrup. Pack in tubs leaving headspace.	9 months
Citrus fruits: lemons, oranges, grapefruit	Peel and remove pith and pips. Separate into segments and pack in tubs with medium sugar syrup leaving headspace. Alternatively wash, dry and freeze whole, especially Seville oranges for marmalade making.	9 months
Cranberries	Remove stalks, wash and dry. Freeze whole in dry sugar for sauce or sieve for purée, then pack in tubs leaving headspace.	6-9 months
Damsons	Wash, halve and remove stones. Pack dry for jam making, in dry sugar pack for cooking and dessert varieties in heavy sugar syrup. Pack in tubs leaving headspace.	9 months

Freezing Chart

Fruit	Preparation	Storage life up to
Grapes	Seedless varieties of grapes can be frozen whole; otherwise halve, remove seeds and pack in a light sugar syrup leaving headspace.	9 months
Loganberries	Select firm berries, remove stalks, wash and dry and pack dry, individually or in dry sugar; pack in tubs leaving headspace.	9 months
Melon	Peel and halve the fruit to remove the seeds. Cut into slices, cubes or balls and immerse immediately into light sugar syrup. Alternatively sprinkle prepared melon pieces with lemon juice and pack in dry sugar. Leave headspace in cartons or tubs.	9 months
Peaches	Peel, remove stones and cut into slices. Immediately immerse in medium sugar syrup with ascorbic acid. If dry sugar pack is preferred, dip slices into ascorbic acid solution before sprinkling with sugar.	9 months
Pears	Peel, core and cut into quarters or slices. Immediately sprinkle with lemon juice to avoid discolouration. Then cook for about five minutes in light sugar syrup. Drain the fruit, cool and pack in tubs in medium sugar syrup with ascorbic acid leaving headspace. Freeze and store best as a purée.	6-9 months
Pineapple	Peel and core, then cut into slices, rings or cubes. Pack into light sugar syrup using any juice from the fruit. Leave headspace in tubs and cartons.	3 months
Plums	Wash, halve and remove stones. Pack dry or in dry sugar pack for jam making. For dessert use pack in heavy sugar syrup with ascorbic acid, leaving headspace in tubs.	9 months
Raspberries	Select firm berries and wash only if necessary. Freeze individually or in dry sugar pack.	9 months
Redcurrants	Strip currants off stems, wash and dry. Freeze individually or dry pack for jam making. Alternatively pack in tubs leaving headspace with heavy sugar syrup for desserts.	9 months
Rhubarb	Select only young and tender stalks. Cut into 2½cm (1in) pieces and lightly cook. Drain and cool and pack in dry sugar for pie fillings and jam making, or in heavy sugar syrup for dessert use, leaving headspace in tubs.	9 months
Strawberries	Remove hulls and wash only if necessary. Freeze individually or in dry sugar pack.	9 months
Tomatoes	Best frozen as a purée, otherwise wash, dry and freeze individually whole if to be used for cooking.	6-9 months

Bottling Chart

Fruit	Preparation	Temp	Method 1 *Time maintained minutes	Method 2 Time maintained at L (5lb) pressure in minutes	Method 3 Time 450g-1.75kg (1-4lb) minutes	2.25kg-4.5kg (5-10lb) minutes
Apples (in syrup)	Peel, core and quarter or slice. Keep under salted water (1 teaspoon salt to 1 litre [2 pints] water). Drain and rinse before bottling.	74°C (165°F)	10	1	30-40	45-60
Apples (solid pack)	Prepare as above. Blanch in boiling water for 2 to 3 minutes or steam over boiling water until just tender. Pack warm.	83°C (180°F)	15	3-4	50-60	65-80
Apricots	Remove stalks. Pack whole or cut in half and remove stones.	83°C (180°F)	15	1	40-50	55-70
Blackberries	Remove stalks and leaves.	74°C (165°F)	10	1	30-40	45-60
Cherries	Remove stalks.	83°C (180°F)	15	1	40-50	55-70
Citrus fruits (Oranges, lemons, grapefruit etc). (For marmalades)	Remove peel and white pith. Divide into segments and discard pips.	83°C (180°F)	15	1	40-50	55-70
	Wash and cut the fruit into pieces. No liquid is required for Method 2.	83°C (180°F)	15	15	50-60	65-80
Currants (Black, red, white)	Remove stems and broken fruit.	83°C (180°F)	15	1	40-50	55-70

Fruit	Preparation	Temp	Method 1	Method 2	Method 3	
Damsons	Remove stems.	83°C (180F)	15	1	40-50	55-70
Gooseberries (for cooking)	Top and tail. If using syrup, nick the ends to prevent shrivelling.	74°C (165°F)	10	1	30-40	45-60
(for use uncooked)		83°C (180°F)	15	1	40-50	55-70
Greengages	Remove stalks. This fruit is often cloudy when bottled.	83°C (180°F)	15	1	40-50	55-70
Loganberries and raspberries	Remove stalks. This fruit attracts maggots so pick carefully.	74°C (165°F)	10	1	30-40	45-60
Peaches	Peel (see Tomatoes). Pack in halves or whole.	83°C (180°F)	15	3-4	50-60	65-80
Pears	Prepare as for apples in syrup. Pack and process as quickly as possible after preparing. Cooking pears should be stewed until tender.	88°C (190°F)	30	4	60-70	75-90
Pineapples	Remove peel and centre core. Cut into rings or cubes.	83°C (180°F)	15	3	50-60	65-80
Plums	Remove stalks. Pack whole, or cut in half and remove stones. Replace a few kernels if liked.	83°C (180°F)	15	1	40-50	55-70
Rhubarb	Best bottled when young so no need to peel. Wipe and cut stalks.	74°C (165°F)	10	1	30-40	45-60
Strawberries	Remove hulls. This fruit loses colour and may rise when bottled. A few drops of red food colouring may be added if liked.	74°C (165°F)	10	1	30-40	45-60
Tomatoes (whole)	Remove calyx. Pack with or without skins. The skins can easily be peeled off if the tomatoes are put into boiling water for 5 to 15 seconds and then dipped in cold water.	88°C (190°F)	30	5	60-70	75-90
Tomatoes (solid pack)	Peel, cut in halves or quarters. Pack tightly in the jars, sprinkling salt on each layer – 2 teaspoons to every 1kg (2lb) of tomatoes. A teaspoon of sugar added to each jar will improve the flavour. Press the tomatoes well down in the jars but do not add any liquid.	88°C (190°F)	40	7	70-80	85-100

*Increase process time for large jars when using Method 1
2kg (3-4lb) size by 5 minutes all packs except Tomatoes Solid Pack 10 minutes
3kg (5-6lb) size by 10 minutes all packs except Tomatoes Solid Pack 10 minutes
4kg (7-8lb) size by 15 minutes all packs except Tomatoes Solid Pack 30 minutes

Vegetables	Preparation	Blanching Times (minutes)	Time maintained at M (10lb) pressure
Asparagus	Peel or scrape the stalks and trim to equal lengths. Tie in bundles (about 6 in each). Pack into bottles with stalks uppermost.	2–3	35
Beans, broad	Remove and discard pods. (Note: broad beans may turn brown during sterilization.)	3	40
Beans, French	Trim ends and remove string if necessary. Wash and pack whole.	3	35
Beans, runner	Wash, string and slice.	3	35
Peas	Remove and discard pods. Ideally select peas of even size for each bottle.	2	45
Sweetcorn	Remove and discard the husks and silk thread. Cut the corn kernels from the cob, making sure the kernels are not damaged.	3	50

Note: It is advisable to use bottles of 600ml to 1 litre (1-2 pints) capacity to ensure the sterilizing process is complete. The above times are based on these sizes. If larger bottles are used an extra 5-10 minutes should be added. Bottles larger than 4 litres (8 pints) capacity must not be used for bottling vegetables.

Chapter Four

The common ingredients of cooking – sugar, flour, milk, cheese, to name only a few – are so taken for granted that few people think seriously about how and why they work. Once you understand the ingredients, however, you will find them far easier to work with. You will be able to read and interpret recipes more easily and will notice how ingredients behave as you work with them.

Long-life foods

Sugar

Sugar is a crystalline substance used to sweeten foods and beverages and as a preservative – for example, in the preparation of jam. It is obtained from various plants but made commercially from sugar cane and sugar beet.

Sugar cane, the major source of sugar, is a bamboo-like grass which grows in tropical and sub-tropical climates. Sugar beet grows in mid-latitude climates. There is no noticeable difference, either in flavour or appearance between cane and beet sugar.

The first stage of the refining process is the formation of *massecuite*, which is a mixture of crude crystals and syrup. The crystals are separated from the syrup by a spinning process and the isolated syrup is then used for the preparation of golden syrup, treacle and molasses.

Golden syrup is a pale-coloured syrup which is less sweet than sugar. It contains more water and glucose and a higher proportion of calories. It can be substituted for light corn syrup in North American recipes. Both golden syrup and black treacle contain invert sugar which prevents crystallization.

Molasses is a dark, sweet syrup, which comes in two forms, sulphured and unsulphured. Sulphured molasses is the by-product of cane sugar making, which requires sulphur fumes. Unsulphured molasses is made from mature, sun-ripened canes and, if available, is preferable to the sulphured type.

The partly refined sugar crystals, which are brown, may be finely ground to form **soft brown sugar,** or coarsely ground for **demerara.**

White sugar is produced after further processes of refining. Granulated sugar is the coarsest and cheapest of the white sugars and is the most commonly used sugar in cooking. It is perfectly acceptable for sweetening liquids, preserving, rubbed-in cakes and biscuits, and boiled sweets.

Castor sugar is obtained either by separating the finer from the coarser grains of granulated sugar by grinding down granulated sugar. Castor sugar is less gritty than granulated and is therefore most often used in making cakes, pastries and biscuits.

Cube or **loaf sugar** is made by compressing white sugar into lumps. This type of sugar is used to sweeten beverages or remove the zest from citrus fruits.

Icing sugar is very finely milled white sugar which is mixed with a maximum of 1.5 per cent calcium phosphate to prevent lumps from forming.

Coffee sugar or **crystals** may be white, brown or multi-coloured and were originally developed for the benefit of coffee connoisseurs because they dissolve more slowly than other sugars.

Preserving sugar is composed of smaller granules than coffee sugar but larger than those of granulated sugar. This sugar produces brighter and more translucent jams and jellies, whose appearance justifies their extra cost.

Sugar, whether it is brown or white, is an almost pure carbohydrate. Black treacle and molasses contain calcium and iron, but in such small quantities as to be almost negligible. Sugar provides energy which is quickly assimilated into the body, but recent research has also disclosed the fact that a regular and large consumption of sugar contributes to dental decay.

Sugar substitutes such as saccharine have been developed for the diabetic and weight conscious. These are suitable for sweetening liquids but are less satisfactory in cooking. If they must be used it is best to use recipes specially designed for them. Most are low in calories but not calorie free. Recent research has now cast some doubt on the general safety of using saccharine, especially in large quantities, and they are now no longer available in the United States.

In baking, sugar not only sweetens but improves texture. It gives cake a soft consistency when dissolved in a little liquid (including eggs). The resultant syrupy liquid also slightly softens the gluten in the flour. Creaming sugar and fat encloses air, making for a lighter mixture that rises more.

Sugar boiling

Cooked sugar is the basis for most sweet-making, some icings and the preservation and cooking of fruit. It is important when cooking with sugar to completely dissolve it before the mixture is brought to the boil. A heavy-based saucepan should be used if possible, so

A selection of sugars, including preserving, granulated, brown sugars, cube and icing.

Sugar Boiling Chart

Temperature	Description	Use
102°-104°C (215°-220°F)	Short thread	Thin syrups
107°-110°C (225°-230°F)	Long thread	Thick syrups
115°C (240°F)	Soft ball	Fondants and soft fudges
118°-121°C (245°-250°F)	Hard ball	Hard fudges
155°C (310°F)	Crack	Soft toffees
163°C (325°F)	Hard crack	Hard toffees and spun sugar
193°-199°C (380°-390°F)	Caramel	Coating fruit, gâteaux and cakes, also as a colouring agent for savoury sauces.

that an even temperature may be maintained. For skilled sweet-making a sugar thermometer is required, but simple sweets can be made without one, in which case the condition of the sugar solution when cooled rapidly is used as a guide to temperature.

To test a sugar solution, drop about ½ teaspoon into a cup half-filled with cold water. A *short thread* means that the cooled sugar will feel sticky to the fingers and will form a short thread when the thumb and forefinger are pulled apart. A *long thread* means the syrup is slightly tackier and a longer thread can be formed when the thumb and forefinger are pulled apart. A *soft ball* means that the cooled sugar forms into a small lump which is very malleable. A *hard ball* means a firm, but still malleable lump is formed. A *crack* means that the cooled sugar sets into a brittle thread which will bend and break as soon as it enters the water. A *hard crack*, that the brittle thread formed snaps without bending. A *caramel* means the colour of the sugar solution changes to light golden, then to deep brown and the cooled sugar is very brittle and breaks easily. (See the chart above for sugar thermometer equivalents and uses).

While the sugar solution is boiling, it should not be stirred because this causes sugar crystals to form, which in excess causes grainy-textured sweets. When a fine texture is required, as in fondant, a little acid such as lemon juice or tartaric acid is added.

Honey

Honey is natural liquid sugar made by bees. The bee converts the sucrose in the nectar of flowers into glucose and fructose by means of an enzyme it carries in its body.

Honey is an easily assimilated source of energy and the oldest known method of sweetening food. It was used extensively in cooking and preserving before cane sugar became available. The flavour depends on the herbs and flowers from which the bees take the nectar; rosemary and heather are among the most prized, and the honey of Mount Hymettus in Greece is particularly famous.

Honey can be substituted for sugar in many recipes, but more honey than sugar will be required and a reduction should be made in the liquid used. Only clear honey should be used in cookery.

Honey has hygroscopic properties – which means that it absorbs moisture. For this reason, bread and pastries made with honey remain moist for a long time and thus keep well.

Flour

Flour is a finely ground cereal. Commercially, the cereal is always wheat except when otherwise qualified, and again if not qualified it means white wheat flour. Other flours are obtained from grains, fruits and vegetables such as oats, barley, buckwheat, corn, rye, beans, bananas, cassava, peanuts and potatoes and are always labelled accordingly.

Finely ground wheat flour consists basically of the starch and gluten of the grain, the bran having been milled out. When all the bran is included in the flour it is called wholemeal or wholewheat and if only 10 per cent of the bran is removed it is called wheatmeal.

The way you use flour depends on how much gluten and starch it contains. Gluten is the nitrogenous part of flour which absorbs water, and the higher the proportion of gluten the more water the flour will absorb, which means that the mixture will rise more and the yield will be greater. Flours with a high gluten content are known as 'strong' flours and are particularly suitable for making breads and other yeast doughs. The less gluten there is in flour, the higher the proportion of starch. Starch absorbs fat and so flours with low gluten content are the types most commonly used for making cakes and biscuits. Self-raising and plain flour are both of this 'soft' type.

Plain flour: Plain flour is used to make biscuits, scones, cakes, pastry and batters, and for thickening sauces.

Self-raising flour: Self-raising flour is said to have too much raising agent for rich cakes and too little for scones, and because its gluten content is low it is not suitable for pastries and yeast doughs. But it is convenient and the results are on the whole satisfactory. Self-raising flour may be used to make most cakes and biscuits. If you use it to make scones, add 2 teaspoons of baking powder to 450 grams (1 pound) of flour.

Strong flour: Strong flour is used in yeast dough and for flaky and puff pastry. It is usually available in larger supermarkets and in health food stores. Wholewheat, wholemeal and wheatmeal flours make splendid bread. So does rye flour, but oatmeal, cornmeal, rice flour and barley meal must all be mixed with wheatmeal as they have little gluten.

In recipes where flour is called for, this means plain flour, otherwise the type of flour (self-raising, etc.) is specified.

Flours differ from nation to nation, incidentally, so if you are using a foreign recipe, you may have to adjust amounts.

Raising agents

Baked mixtures are induced to rise by air, steam and carbon dioxide gas. Raising agents are the means by which air and gas are introduced into a flour mixture.

Air is incorporated by sifting flour and by beating sugar, fats and eggs well. (See creaming and whisking cakes, page 133.) Steam is given off by the liquid in the mixture during cooking. This is why preheating the oven is important. Carbon dioxide gas is produced by chemical change; when heated gases expand, the mixture is stretched. Carbon dioxide gas is produced by yeast, bicarbonate of soda and baking powder.

Yeast is a minute, single-celled fungus which is used both as a raising agent and as an agent of fermentation. Its properties are utilized in the baking of bread and brewing of alcohol.

Yeast is activated into growth by the addition of carbohydrates – in the form of sugar – liquid and warmth, in the correct proportions. An excess of sugar, cold, fat or salt will retard growth, while too much will kill the plant altogether. This happens during the baking of bread but by that time the yeast has done its work. As the yeast grows a ferment is produced which breaks down the carbohydrates and converts them into carbon dioxide which causes the dough to rise.

Fresh yeast is moist and crumbly in appearance and is preferred by some people to dried. Fresh yeast is obtainable from specialist food stores and bakeries where bread is made on the premises, and may be kept, well wrapped, in the refrigerator for two to three days, or in the freezer for several months. Dried yeast is a concentrated form of fresh yeast which is available from most food stores in tins and packets. Providing the container is airtight, dried yeast will keep for up to six months. If substituting dried yeast in a recipe which specifies fresh, use only half the quantity and follow the directions on the tin or packet on how to prepare it.

The alkaline **bicarbonate of soda,** used alone or combined with an acid, releases a gas when heated with a liquid. Used alone it gives up only half its carbon dioxide, leaving a disagreeable taste and smell. When mixed with an acid, all the gas is released. Thus recipes calling for soda usually contain vinegar, sour milk, jam, marmalade, molasses, honey or spices. Without an acid ingredient, soda is usually combined with cream of tartar or tartaric acid, both of which begin to give off gas as soon as they are mixed with a liquid. Any mixture containing this combination should be baked as soon after preparation as possible.

Baking powder is a commercially made soda-acid raising agent. Most brands are now comparable in the amount of gas they will produce.

Thickening agents

Thickening agents have the ability to absorb liquid and to increase viscosity. The major thickeners are flour, corn-flour, arrowroot and egg yolks (see page 58). In addition, semolina, tapioca, potato and other starches thicken well under some circumstances. Reduction, or boiling down, will concentrate a gravy or sauce, and small pieces of butter stirred into a sauce just before serving have a slight thickening power.

Beurre manié (made with equal weights of butter and flour kneaded together – see page 114), whisked by

small bits into a hot liquid, will thicken it. Simmer for 1-2 minutes to cook the flour; if you boil the sauce, however, the beurre manié loses its thickening power.

Cornflour is made from the ground kernel of maize. It has twice as much thickening power as flour and makes a translucent sauce. It has a raw taste if not cooked enough, and cornflour sauce should therefore be simmered or cooked over hot water for 5-10 minutes. Do not overheat these sauces because that thins them. Overcooking over high heat also causes loss of thickening power.

Cornflour thickens acid fruit fillings better than flour because it loses its thickening power less quickly in the presence of acid. A little cornflour added to an egg custard mixture dispels the worry about scrambling through over-heating, for eggs added to a cornflour mixture can be boiled.

Cornflour should be mixed with a little cold water or other liquid and stirred to a smooth paste before it is added to a hot liquid. If it is being used with sugar, sift the two together so the cornflour is evenly distributed. This prevents lumps when the liquid is added.

Arrowroot is a pure starch obtained from the sun-dried roots of several different tropical plants. The roots are ground to a fine white powder that is nutritious, easily digested and need not be cooked. It makes clear, delicately textured sauces. Use only half as much arrowroot as flour to thicken sauces, soups and puddings; when substituting it for cornflour use an equal amount.

Arrowroot should be blended with a cold liquid and then added to the hot liquid. Simmer it gently because, like cornflour, it cannot stand high heat or boiling. After 3-5 minutes, the sauce should become clear and slightly thickened. Serve the sauce soon after making, because its thickening powers do not last long.

A tablespoon of arrowroot is sufficient to thicken 300 millilitres (10 fluid ounces) of liquid.

Gelatine

Gelatine is a colourless solid made from boiling bones, cartilage and tendons. Sometimes it is extracted from fish (isinglass) and seaweed (agar-agar and carrageen moss). The seaweed types are used by vegetarians. In its pure form it is used in cooking to set desserts, sweets, salads

and savoury dishes. Commercially it is used in canned meat products, soups, confectionery and ice-cream.

Gelatine is tasteless and odourless and its main characteristic is that when dissolved into a solution with a liquid it will 'gel' or set on cooling, and melt or liquefy on warming. Thus gelatine dishes must be refrigerated or kept in a cold larder until ready to use. They cannot be frozen, however, unless the fat content is high, as with some ice-creams.

In warm weather and without a refrigerator, use one-third more gelatine. Too much gelatine, however, results in an unpleasantly rubbery substance – it should wobble when shaken gently.

Gelatine is available for cooking in powdered or sheet form. Both forms are usually soaked in a little cold water or other liquid until soft and then dissolved over low heat. To set 600 millilitres (1 pint) of liquid use 20 grams ($\frac{3}{4}$ ounce) of sheet gelatine or 15 grams ($\frac{1}{2}$ ounce) of gelatine. If a sheet of leaf gelatine is used, it must be soaked for 2-3 hours then dissolved in a little water over low heat.

Generally speaking, and unless a recipe particularly specifies it, do not dissolve gelatine directly in milk or add it to hot milk, as this will cause the milk to curdle. Dissolve the gelatine first in water and, when it is cool and begins to set, add it slowly to cool but not cold milk.

If fruits, nuts or candied peel are added they must be folded in when the jelly is on the point of setting, or else they will sink to the bottom of the mould and appear as a solid layer on top when unmoulded.

Most fruit is suitable for making jellies, but those with attractive colouring and a strong flavour, such as blackcurrants, oranges, lemons and pineapple, are particularly successful. Pineapple contains an enzyme which breaks down the gelatine and destroys its setting properties, so when using fresh pineapple it is necessary to boil the juice for 2-3 minutes to kill the enzyme.

Bavarian creams and some mousses are based on flavoured egg custard made with gelatine. Stiffly beaten egg whites and whipped cream are folded into the custard when it has cooled and begun to set. If it has become too set, it should be put over warm water for a few minutes.

Simple aspic is made with gelatine and stock. To coat a mould, fish or other savoury food successfully, the object to be

coated must be chilled and the aspic just beginning to set. Working quickly, cover the object with a thin layer of aspic. Let it set. Add any decorations, then cover with another layer of aspic. For special occasions, replace 25-50 millilitres (1-2 fluid ounces) of the liquid with wine or liqueur. Dry white wine, vermouth and sherry go well with savouries; sweeter wines, cognac and fruit-flavoured liqueurs suit sweet jellies.

Fats and oils

Fats and oils used in cooking come from both animal and vegetable sources. They are compounds of fatty acids and glycerol and consist of carbon, hydrogen and oxygen. Fats at normal temperatures are solids, whereas oils at similar temperatures are liquid. The main animal fats are butter, lard, suet and dripping.

Butter is a natural food, free of all preservatives, made from cream (solidified milk fats). There are two main kinds of butter. The first, sweet cream butter, is made from fresh cream in New Zealand, Australia, Eire, the British Isles and the United States. The second, lactic butter, comes mainly from continental Europe and is made from ripened cream, that is, cream to which special bacterial cultures have been added to enhance the butter flavour and develop a mild acidity.

Sweet cream butter is mild and delicately flavoured. Its texture is firm, waxy and smooth. This makes it an ideal ingredient for pastry and biscuits, where the dough has to be rolled. Lactic butter has a full flavour and a fine texture. It creams easily and so is an excellent ingredient for all kinds of cakes, especially for spicy ones such as ginger and Dundee. Lactic butter is also used for making fudge, caramels and toffees. Both types of butter have a small amount of salt added for flavour.

Lard is the white fat of a pig, melted down to produce cooking fat. The best lard is made from the fat inside the ribs, around the abdomen, and about the kidney. Most commercially made lard, however, uses fat taken from all parts of the animal. Stored in a cool, dry place, lard will keep for several months. Pure lard is excellent for deep-frying because it can be heated to a high temperature before it burns. When used in biscuits and pastry it creates a flaky texture, but it is not suitable for most types of cakes.

For salmon in aspic, first carefully skin the salmon.

Using a spatula, spread mayonnaise evenly over the surface of the fish.

Spoon aspic on the point of setting over the fish to cover completely.

Decorate with cucumber skin, radishes and olives as used here.

Spoon over another layer of aspic, then chill until set.

Arrange on a serving dish and garnish with leftover chilled chopped aspic.

Suet is the fat which is found around the kidneys and loins of sheep and bullocks. Commercially prepared shredded suet, which has been minced and mixed with a little flour and preservative to keep the shreds separate, is readily available. Fresh suet can be bought from butchers' shops. Prepare it by discarding the membranes and fibres and chopping or mincing it finely. Suet is used in making suetcrust pastry, dumplings, mincemeat and steamed or baked puddings.

Dripping is the fat which flows from meat when it is roasting. Clarified dripping can be used for frying and roasting. Beef dripping is regarded as best for this. Pork or chicken drippings are sometimes used in pastry making. Lamb and mutton drippings should be discarded because they give a tallowy taste.

To clarify dripping, melt it in a saucepan over moderate heat. Strain it into a mixing bowl through a sieve lined with muslin. Pour boiling water (three times the volume of the fat) over the dripping and leave it to cool. The clean fat rises to the surface when it is quite cold and solid, and can be skimmed off the top. All sediment in the bottom of the fat should be scraped off with a knife or dabbed off with paper towels.

Vegetable fats are solids made by chemically processing oils from a variety of plants. **Vegetable oils** are made from the same raw materials, but are processed in a different way. Some of the major oils are corn, coconut, groundnut, olive, safflower, sesame, soya and sunflower. Except for olive oil, which has a distinct flavour, these oils are refined after processing so they are not particularly distinguishable from one another in odour or flavour.

Some oils, however, are higher than others in polyunsaturated fats. Among the most beneficial in this way are corn and sunflower oils. Most margarines and cooking oils are blends, and unless the label says 'high in polyunsaturated fats' or the product is unblended, you have no way of knowing how much saturated fat they contain.

Medical authorities believe that too much saturated fat causes a build-up of cholesterol in the bloodstream and of fatty deposits on the walls of the arteries, which can cause strokes and contribute to heart attacks. Polyunsaturated fats do not create deposits and help to break down those caused by saturated fats. Since the typical western diet is high in hidden saturated fats (in meat, eggs, cheese and chocolate), using polyunsaturated fats daily helps maintain a balance.

Margarine is a commercially manufactured substitute for butter. It is now made with vegetable oils, though animal fats could also be used. It is deliberately constituted to have the same proportion of fat and water as butter, and is coloured and flavoured to resemble it. For most purposes it can be used interchangeably with butter.

Margarine is not recommended for frying or for greasing cake tins, since when it is melted a sediment is deposited which causes food to stick to the pan. It gives a light texture to pastry, cakes and biscuits.

Soft or table margarines are increasing in popularity. They are made from a special blend of oils which remain soft at low temperatures. Like regular margarines they can easily be substituted for butter in any recipe.

White vegetable fats are sold under a variety of brand names. They are essentially flavourless and are designed to be used as a vegetable-oil substitute for lard. They contain no water and can therefore be used for frying.

Cooking

Connoisseurs state that nothing can surpass butter for all cooking purposes except deep-frying; health authorities feel butter (and all other saturated fats) should not be part of the normal diet; the rest of us have our budgets to consider and margarines are, on the whole, certainly cheaper. Thus, most people use both, employing margarine in strongly flavoured foods, perhaps combining it with butter in more delicate cakes, and using butter alone for sauces and as a spread.

Fats for frying The best fats for deep-frying contain no water or solids. The best for this purpose are lard (which has a distinct flavour), white cooking fat and vegetable oils except groundnut which has a low smoking point. These three types can all be heated to above the temperature required for frying. Dripping is extremely variable, depending on how well it has been clarified, and it is better for shallow-frying. Butter and margarine both contain water and solids, which make them unsuitable for deep-frying. They also burn at low temperatures.

Butter, but not margarine, is suitable for sautéing, as is cooking oil.

When butter begins to melt in a pan, the liquids in it begin to evaporate causing the butter to foam. When the foam subsides, the butter is still not very hot, but it is time to add the food to be sautéed. Butter mixed with an equal amount of cooking oil can be heated to a higher temperature before burning. Add the oil first, let it heat a few seconds and then place the butter in the oil. This combination foams in the same way as butter alone. Therefore, as the foam begins to subside, add the eggs, meat, fish or vegetables to the pan.

Butter can be heated to a higher temperature if the water, salt and solids are removed. This is known as *clarifying*. To clarify, melt the butter in a saucepan over moderate heat and cook gently without browning until all bubbling has stopped. This shows that the water has evaporated. Let the pan sit off the heat for 2-3 minutes while the milk solids and salt settle to the bottom. Strain the butter through muslin into a bowl, leaving a milky residue behind. Clarified butter is used for making black butters (really a medium brown in colour) for brains, fish and other dishes. It is known as *ghee* in India and is widely used for cooking in that country.

Deep-frying fat should be strained after use to remove food particles and to ensure nothing remains to cause 'off' flavours. Add a little fresh fat each time you fry to prolong the life of your fat. When the fat becomes thick and dark it should be discarded because the smoking point will have dropped below normal frying temperature and the flavour will be unpleasant.

Fats for baking Butter, margarine, lard, white cooking fat and oil can all be used in pastry making. The last three, which are water-free, make the shortest crust, that is, the most crumbly, but they are all lacking in flavour so butter or margarine, the least short of all the fats, are sometimes added.

The differences in shortening power are explained by what happens when fat is rubbed into flour. The fat encloses flour particles giving them a waterproof coating. Thus only the loose flour particles absorb the water added after the rubbing-in. The pure fats do a better job of enclosing than those with moisture.

During baking the fat melts and the

flour cooks as separate particles bound together by fat. The air caught inside the fat along with the flour expands, assisting in making the layers inside good pastry.

Fats are incorporated into cakes by two methods, creaming and melting. The creaming method requires a fat that creams easily, that is, can be beaten to a smooth fluffy mass which has absorbed a lot of air. The fat should also have either good flavour or no flavour. Butter has excellent flavour, but creams only moderately well. Margarine, especially the soft type, has fairly good flavour and creams easily. White cooking fats are easy to cream, but other ingredients must supply the flavour. Lard's rather distinctive flavour makes it unsuitable for most cakes and biscuits.

Fats for creaming should be at about 21°C (70°F). A fat taken from a cold place should not be warmed by heating, however, because the outside is likely to melt before the inside has warmed. If you cannot wait, use the following method for creaming with a wooden spoon. Warm the bowl, cut the fat into small pieces and mash each with a spoon Continue hitting and beating until the fat has softened and become a creamy mass, then add the sugar and beat until light and fluffy. With electric beaters, the fat should be cut into pieces and whipped until the butter begins to fall away from the beaters. Then add the sugar.

Melted fats are added to dry ingredients in some recipes. Plain cakes require a good-flavour fat, but highly spiced cakes can be made with any fat including dripping, but excluding suet.

Vinegar

Vinegars can be made from a variety of raw materials. Natural vinegar results from bacteria working on an alcoholic liquid to produce acetic acid. It can also be distilled chemically like distilled white vinegar.

Malt vinegar is based on beer, others are made commercially from cider and red or white wine. Other bases can be used though those are found only in specialty shops or home-made. Herb and spiced vinegars use a common vinegar as a base and are flavoured by adding fresh herbs – marjoram, thyme, or a mixture – or spices such as ginger, clove, allspice, alone or in combination.

Try various brands of the same type of vinegar, say malt; for you will find some harsh, others sharp, mild or mellow. A good flavour makes all the difference in food preparation, especially in salad dressings (French, mayonnaise) and other sauces. Vinegars for pickling should contain 5 per cent acetic acid to have adequate preserving powers.

Vinegar is also essential in the preparation of dishes such as soused herring, and is also used in cakes with bicarbonate of soda, for the two blended together act as a raising agent.

Remember that all vinegars are corrosive and should be kept away from copper, zinc, aluminium and iron. Use them in glass, ceramic, enamel and stainless steel containers.

Chocolate and cocoa

Chocolate and cocoa both come from the beans of the *cacao* tree, a shrub native to Central and South America, but now grown throughout the tropics. The difference between chocolate and cocoa is that chocolate contains cocoa butter, or another fat as a substitute, whereas cocoa has had 75-90 per cent of the cocoa butter removed.

Cocoa butter is a pure fat, shiny yellow-white in colour and with a faintly sweet chocolate flavour. It is used as a sun tan

Herb vinegar (such as marjoram, as below) makes a pleasant change from commercial varieties and is easy to make.

oil and in many pharmaceutical preparations as well as in confections and as a butter substitute in some diets. It is high in saturated fats. Under normal storage conditions, it will keep for years without going rancid.

There are three main types of chocolate. For bars or filled sweets eaten as a confection, a particularly refined chocolate with a higher proportion of cocoa butter is required. Although eating chocolate bars can be used in cooking, they are less successful than cooking chocolate. Eating chocolate can be plain (that is, dark and semi-sweet) or milk (lighter in colour and sweeter). Cooking chocolate, sold in slabs or chips, is a semi-sweet, usually dark, chocolate that is designed for use in home baking. Con-

50

fectioners' chocolate, known as *couverture*, is a high quality chocolate ideal for cake decorating or for coating cakes. It gives a smooth, shiny finish.

Chocolate scorches easily and therefore it should never be melted over direct heat. The best methods are to place the chocolate in a double saucepan or in a heatproof bowl set over hot but not boiling water. (The steam rising from boiling water can enter the chocolate and make it cloudy.)

When the chocolate has just melted, remove the bowl from the heat, stir it to melt any solids, and cool it to tepid but still liquid before adding it to cakes, puddings or biscuits. Sometimes a liquid – coffee, brandy, rum – is added to the bowl before the chocolate is melted.

Cocoa comes in two forms; an unsweetened powder used in cooking and a sweetened powder which is diluted with water or milk to form a drink. The cocoa specified in recipes is always the unsweetened type.

Cocoa often becomes lumpy when combined with liquids. To avoid this, either sift it with other dry ingredients or add a very little water to the cocoa and stir to form a thick, smooth paste. To make a plain cake or biscuit chocolate flavoured, replace 2-4 tablespoons of flour with cocoa.

Rice

Rice is one of the most important food grains in the world, and is the staple food

of millions of people.

Because it keeps well, cooks more quickly and has a better appearance, most rice is milled before it is marketed. Milling removes the bran skin which lies under the husk, therefore some of the protein, minerals and vitamins are lost. Brown rice which has only the husk removed is more nutritious than other varieties and is often used in vegetarian dishes. There are about 7000 varieties of rice and almost as many colours – rice can be red, brown, blue, purple, black or ivory. Long, short and round grain rice are the three most commonly used varieties in western cooking.

Rice can be bought in several forms, among them are parboiled, pre-cooked (which only requires reconstituting in hot water) and boil-in-bags. Rice is also ground and used for puddings, or very finely ground to make rice flour for use in cakes and biscuits.

Rice which is to be served as an accompaniment for a curry or used to make a pilaff or biryani should be a long-grain variety such as Patna or basmati, the latter being the better. Risottos are best made with absorbent Italian rice such as avorio or crystalo. Round-grain rice is most suitable for rice puddings.

Rice absorbs liquids in varying amounts. Each variety, and sometimes different crops of the same variety, have unequal powers of absorption. The amount of liquid given in any recipe therefore, can only be approximate. When cooking rice, check halfway

A selection of different types of rice: from left to right, brown rice, avorio (Italian-type rice, Basmati (long-grain), wild rice, round-grain (for puddings), rice flour and natural rice.

through the cooking time and add more liquid if necessary.

Rice, when cooked, increases two and a half to three times in bulk, so 1 cup of uncooked rice will yield between 2½-3 cups of cooked rice. Servings vary with individual appetite and type of meal. For rice-based meals such as Chinese and Indian, allow 25-40 grams (1-1½ ounces) of uncooked rice per person. If it is to be used as a potato substitute in a western style meal, 15-20 grams (½-¾ ounce) should be enough.

Boiled rice

Plain boiled rice should be made with a long grain variety. Many techniques can be used in cooking rice, and sometimes one works better than another for a particular brand or package. One method of cooking is to have the rice absorb all the liquid by the time it is done. This retains all the nutrients, but requires planning ahead and may not work well for some brands.

Wash 275 grams (10 ounces) of long grain rice thoroughly in cold running water. When the water runs clear, leave the rice to soak for 30 minutes, then drain. Put the rice in a saucepan and pour over 600 millilitres (1 pint) of water and add 1 teaspoon of salt. Place the pan over high heat and bring the water to the boil. Cover the pan, reduce the heat to low and simmer for 15-20 minutes or until the rice is tender and all the liquid has been absorbed. Remove from the heat and serve hot.

A second method is to boil the rice in a large quantity of water, drain and put in a colander to steam. Nutrients are said to be lost when the cooking water is drained off, but the end product is dry and fluffy. Rinse 275 grams (10 ounces) of long grain rice and add it slowly to 1¾ litres (3 pints) of rapidly boiling water. Let the rice boil rapidly, uncovered, for exactly 10 minutes, stirring once with the back of a fork to loosen any grains stuck to the bottom. Bite a rice grain in half; it should have no hard core nor should it be limp. Cook 30 seconds more and test again if too hard. Drain the rice into a colander and rinse under running water. Now shake the colander well to remove as much water as possible. Refill the saucepan with an inch or two of water, place the colander, covered, on top and return to the stove to steam for 10 minutes or longer. (Don't let the saucepan boil dry.) Alternatively, place the colander on an ovenproof plate and stand in a low oven 120°C (Gas Mark ½, 250°F) for 8 minutes to dry out. Do not leave it in the oven any longer than this or it will become too dry.

Boiled rice can be reheated most easily by steaming it in a colander placed over boiling water.

Italian rice

Italian rice is cooked in a completely different way from long grain. It is a thick, short grain, highly absorbent rice and requires slow cooking. The liquid is added a little at a time, the first amount being absorbed before more is added. Cooking times vary between about 20 and 30 minutes. The end result is creamier and more moist than long grain.

Basic rice pudding

Rice pudding is made with short or round grain rice. This absorbs liquid to form a soft, smooth mass. Preheat the oven to cool 150°C (Gas Mark 2, 300°F). Grease a 1¼ litre (2 pint) baking dish with butter. Place 40 grams (1½ ounces) of round grain rice, 2 tablespoons sugar, 900 millilitres (1½ pints) milk and 1 teaspoon vanilla essence or a dash of grated nutmeg in the dish. Place the dish in the oven and bake the pudding for 3 hours. For a richer pudding, beat in 2 egg yolks 30 minutes before the end of the cooking time. For a more attractive appearance, remove the dish from the oven, sprinkle the top of the pudding with 1 tablespoon of sugar and place the dish under a hot grill for 1 minute to glaze.

Pasta

Pasta is a name that is almost synonymous with Italian cuisine, and is a farinaceous product made from flour, water and sometimes eggs. The flour used is hard or durum with a high gluten content, which gives the dough its slightly brittle consistency.

Pasta is usually made commercially, although some types – most particularly egg noodles, ravioli and gnocchi – are still made at home. Spinach is sometimes added to the basic pasta dough – thus fettuccine verdi and lasagne verdi.

Some Italian specialty shops sell freshly made pasta which is soft and pliable because it has not been fully dried. This should be cooked on the same day it is purchased. It is finer in flavour and texture than ordinary commercial pasta.

All pasta should be cooked in a large saucepan with at least three times as much water as pasta – 2½ litres (4 pints) of water for each 225 grams (8 ounces) of pasta. Bring the salted water to a rolling boil and add the pasta slowly so that the water never stops boiling. Long types of pasta should be pushed in gently and as they soften, more can be pushed in. Keep the water at a rolling boil throughout the cooking. Stir gently once with a fork to separate any clumps that have stuck together. If the pasta does show indica-tions of sticking, add a few drops of olive oil to the pan.

Never overcook pasta. It is ready to serve when 'al dente', which in Italian means the pasta still offers some resistance to the teeth. Cooking time varies greatly with the size and age of the pasta. Home-made varieties may be ready in 5 minutes, whereas thick or long stored pasta can take as long as 15 minutes. Always test just before the minimum cooking time is up. Drain well in a large colander and serve immediately. It does not reheat well. Unsauced leftovers should be dropped briefly into boiling water to heat through. Those with sauce should be reheated over low heat, stirring gently and often.

Pasta is always served with a sauce of some kind – even though it may be as simple as melted butter and grated cheese. In Italy, pasta is served as the course before the main, usually meat, course of the meal, although in other parts of Europe and the United States, pasta is more often served as a main course. The lighter, smaller pasta, such as vermicelli, is often used in soups, and heavier pasta, such as macaroni, can be made into substantial sweet or savoury puddings.

Short-life foods
Milk

Milk, which is produced by all mammals, is the most complete form of food. However, each species has unique require-ments, and the milk differs in the amount of fat, protein and minerals in it. Thus, cow's milk, although good, is not ideal for humans. While most milk in the west comes from cows, goats and sheep are also suppliers, though today their milk is mainly used in cheese-making.

Cow's milk in all its forms (butter, cheese, yogurt) is used extensively as a food and in cooking. Soups, sauces, custards and puddings all require milk. As befits a food with so many uses, milk is processed in a variety of ways. Bottled or cartoned fluid milk is most commonly used in the home. This milk is perishable and should be kept at 5°C (40°F). It also needs to be protected from sunlight, which destroys the B vitamins.

Fluid milk is available in numerous forms. Untreated or raw milk has had no processing before bottling. It is now hard to obtain, since only a few farmers are

allowed to produce it for sale. Almost all of the milk sold is now **pasteurized** to destroy disease-carrying bacteria. The milk is heated to 72°C (161°F) for 15 seconds, then rapidly cooled to 10°C (50°F), placed in sterile bottles and sealed. The cream separates out from the milk and rises to the top of the bottle.

Homogenized milk has been pasteurized and then, before bottling, been forced under high pressure through a tiny valve to break up the clusters of milk fat globules to a uniform size. This distributes the globules evenly throughout the milk and no cream rises to the top of the bottle. In cooking, fresh homogenized milk gives a different texture – sauces are stiffer and fat separation is greater; gravy, cooked cereal and custards all tend to curdle.

Skimmed milk has the same protein and mineral value as whole milk, but the fat content has been reduced to less than 1 per cent, thus reducing its caloric value by half. This type of milk is recommended for people on low fat diets, and those who need to watch their cholesterol levels.

Filled milk has also had its cream removed. But in this case it has been replaced by another form of fat, usually vegetable oil.

Milk is also processed to improve its keeping qualities. **Ultra heat treatment (U.H.T.)** and **sterilized** milk are both whole milks that need no refrigeration until they have been opened. The ultra heat treatment process is similar to pasteurization except the milk is heated to 132°C (270°F) for 1 second. It is then packed into cartons under sterile conditions and will keep without refrigeration for several months. Its flavour is similar to that of pasteurized homogenized milk.

Sterilized milk has been homogenized before being poured into bottles which are closed with a hermetic seal. The bottles are then heated to 110°C (230°F). Because of the high heat the milk appears thicker and creamier than pasteurized milk and often has a slightly 'cooked' flavour. It will keep almost indefinitely, unopened, without refrigeration.

Tinned milk with a reduced water content is sold as **evaporated** and sweetened **condensed** milk. Evaporated milk is unsweetened full-cream or skimmed canned milk. The milk is reduced by evaporation (hence the name) to about one-third of its original volume. It is then sterilized and canned while still hot. Evaporated milk, when reconstituted to its original volume with water, has the same nutritional value as fresh pasteurized milk.

Evaporated milk is often used in cooking, as a substitute for cream in desserts, for example. Some varieties can be whipped and will thicken slightly. It will keep for a long time in the store cupboard.

Condensed milk has also been reduced by evaporation until the water content has been reduced by as much as 60 per cent. This means that 400 millilitres (15 fluid ounces) is the equivalent of 750 millilitres ($1\frac{1}{4}$ pints) of ordinary milk. Condensed milk contains a large amount of sugar – as much as 125 grams (4 ounces) in a 400 millilitre (14 fluid ounce) can. This high proportion of sugar linked with the low proportion of water helps to prevent the condensed milk from deteriorating once the can has been opened. Because condensed milk tends to settle, the can should be turned over every two weeks. Condensed milk can be used in place of fresh milk for fudge, puddings and ice-cream.

Milk can also be kept a relatively long time when dried. **Dried** milk is prepared from whole, partly skimmed or skimmed milk. The skim milk powder keeps better than the full cream type after opening, since the removal of the fat prevents the milk from becoming rancid. They should be stored in a lightproof container in a cool place.

Dry milk is frequently used to enrich foods such as bread, cooked cereals and puddings. Dieters sometimes replace cream in soups with skimmed milk enriched with 3 to 4 tablespoons of dried for each 300 millilitres (10 fluid ounces). It can also be reconstituted with water for drinking and cooking. For drinking, always make the milk up several hours in advance and have it well chilled before serving. Its somewhat unpleasant odour and flavour will then have disappeared. The powder will blend smoothly if you first mix it with only a small amount of liquid to form a lump-free paste. Stir as you add the rest of the water. In cooking, dried milk should be sifted with the other dry ingredients. Reconstituted dried milk scorches more easily than whole milk and extra care must be taken when making sauces. Use a double saucepan or low heat and never use more than 3 tablespoons of powder to 300 millilitres (10 fluid ounces) of water.

Milk is also fermented to form cheese (see below), yogurt, buttermilk and sour milk.

Yogurt: Yogurt is a semi-solid dairy

53

product produced by fermenting milk with a culture of bacteria. During fermentation the lactose (milk sugar) is converted to lactic acid causing the milk to clot.

Yogurt has the same food value as milk, though the sugar level is sometimes lower. It is a good source of protein and calcium, but despite the obvious dietary benefits of yogurt and the fact it is easily digestible, there is no evidence to support claims that it aids longevity or has any therapeutic value which cannot be obtained from an equivalent amount of milk or cheese. Because yogurt continues to mature even in cold storage, most commercial yogurts are marked with a date stamp and have a shelf life of about two weeks. This does not mean that the yogurt is unfit for consumption after the date stamp has expired, but it will become considerably more acidic.

Diet conscious people sometimes substitute yogurt for sour cream in sauces, soups and salad dressings. Once it is added to cooked dishes they should not be heated to above a simmer or the yogurt will curdle.

Buttermilk: Buttermilk is the liquid left after churning butter. It is about 90 per cent water, 5 per cent sugar, 3 per cent casein, mineral salts and lactic, which gives it a sour taste. It is now also made from pasteurized skim milk to which a bacterial culture is added to develop flavour and a thicker consistency. It is good for both drinking and baking.

Buttermilk is used with bicarbonate of soda as a raising agent, in the proportion of 300 millilitres (10 fluid ounces) of buttermilk to ½ teaspoon of soda. Although buttermilk is available commercially in cartons, you can make a substitute for cooking using ordinary milk. Place 1 tablespoon of lemon juice or vinegar in a measuring jug and add 300 millilitres (10 fluid ounces) of fresh, evaporated or reconstituted dried milk at room temperature. Stir, then let the milk stand for 10 minutes to clabber, that is, thicken to approximately the consistency of yogurt.

Sour milk: Sour milk can only be made from unpasteurized whole or skimmed milk that has been allowed to ferment (sour) naturally. It is, therefore, virtually unobtainable today. Pasteurized and scalded milk will spoil rather than sour if left at room temperature or in the refrigerator for too long In recipes that call for sour milk either use buttermilk, or

sour fresh milk by using 1 tablespoon of lemon juice or vinegar to 300 millilitres (10 fluid ounces) of fresh milk and letting it clabber. Like buttermilk, sour milk combines with bicarbonate of soda to act as a raising agent. The presence of lactic acid in both produces a tender crumb in baking, while in sauces it gives an attractive, slightly acid flavour. Sour milk and buttermilk should never be allowed to boil.

The term 'scalding' is frequently used in conjunction with milk. It means to heat the milk to the point at which bubbles appear at the edge of the pan (80°C, 180°F). Before pasteurization this was done to kill harmful bacteria, but now scalding is used exclusively to hasten or improve a food process. Scalding is most frequently called for in bread and baked custard making.

Cream

Cream is the part of milk which contains all the fat. If fresh milk is left undisturbed, the cream will rise to the top and can be easily skimmed off.

Cream is available fresh, canned, bottled, frozen and processed. Fresh cream is classified according to its thickness and the proportion of butterfat it contains. **Single cream** is fairly thin and contains not less than 18 per cent butterfat. **Double cream** is thick, can be whipped until it holds a shape and contains a minimum of 45 per cent butterfat. **Whipping cream** is neither as rich nor as thick as double cream but can be whipped thick enough to hold a shape. Two parts of double cream combined with one part of single cream will whip up like whipping cream (or use three parts of double cream and one of rich milk).

Clotted cream – a British specialty – comes from Devon or Cornwall in England where the milk has a particularly high fat content. Clotted cream is made by leaving fresh milk to stand for 12 hours or more. It is then gently heated in a large shallow pan and the cream is skimmed off in layers, the last layer forming a crust.

To whip cream, use a wire whisk, a rotary beater, an electric beater or lacking any of these, a plain fork. Put the chilled cream in a cool mixing bowl and whip slowly. When the cream begins to thicken, whip it faster until it is as thick as you

require. Do not over-whip or the cream will turn to butter. The volume of whipped cream may be increased by folding a stiffly beaten egg white into 600 millilitres (1 pint) of cream. This produces a lighter cream which, though it is suitable for most decorative pruposes, does not pipe well.

Milk can be substituted for cream in recipes that call for a lot of cheese, such as cheese and onion flan or quiche lorraine.

Soured cream is single cream which has been fermented by adding a bacterial culture. It has a tangy flavour and a smooth, semi-solid texture. Like the fermented milks (see above) it should not be heated above simmering point or it will curdle.

Soured cream can be made at home by vigorously shaking together 300 millilitres (10 fluid ounces) of single cream and 2 tablespoons of commerical buttermilk. Stir in another 300 millilitres (10 fluid ounces) of single cream and let the mixture stand for 24 hours at a temperature between 21-27°C (70-80°F). It is now ready to use, though another 24 hours in the refrigerator makes a smoother product. A thicker soured cream can be made by replacing some of the single cream with double cream.

Cheese

What cheese is

Cheese was originally a method of solidifying and preserving milk, but it has become a favourite food for its own sake. It is versatile and nourishing, containing a high proportion of protein and fat. Since a pound of cheese is made from a gallon of milk, its nutrients come in a concentrated form.

The milk used in cheese-making in Europe and America usually comes from cows, goats or ewes. The processes used in the cheese-making and the climate and animal diet that produced the milk vary so greatly that many cheeses cannot be reproduced outside their original districts. Others are more easily made, however, and are produced commercially in large quantities.

Cheese is made by curdling milk, which can be full cream, partly skimmed or skimmed and pasteurized, or raw. This curdling can be achieved by the natural souring of unpasteurized milk, by the addition of rennet or of a bacterial starter culture, or by a combination of these methods. All help to form the cheese curd. This is cut into pieces, heated, stirred, salted and put to drain. After draining the curds are put into moulds of a variety of shapes and sizes.

Soft cheeses are cured without pressure being applied. They retain between 45 and 85 per cent of their moisture, are highly perishable and need to be kept under refrigeration. They can be un-ripened (cottage), mould-ripened (Brie) or bacteria-ripened (Limburger). All are

A selection of cheeses guaranteed to make a fitting end to any meal.

mild in flavour. Of the soft cheeses, only cottage, curd and ricotta are generally used in cooking. And they must be heated very gently.

Semi-hard cheeses have been cured under some pressure to press out a greater amount of moisture, retaining only 40 to 45 per cent. If they are aged for more than 60 days they need not be made from pasteurized milk, which gives them a superior flavour. They can be mould-ripened (Stilton) or bacteria-ripened (Bel Paese). Most are poor for cooking.

Hard cheeses retain 30 per cent or less moisture and are excellent for cooking.

All are bacteria-ripened; some for a few months, others for more than a year (Cheshire).

Processed cheeses are pasteurized mixtures of young cheeses, aged cheeses, emulsifiers and milk or water. They have good keeping qualities but little real flavour or texture. They should not be confused with the real thing!

Types of cheese for cooking
Although cheese is used regularly in cooking, it does not take kindly to excessive heat or overcooking. Thus it is important to choose the right type of

cheese and to cook it properly. First, try to employ the cheeses that heat well. These are mainly hard types: Cheddar, Edam, Gruyère, Emmenthal, Cheshire, Parmesan, Lancashire, Leicester, Derby, Mozzarella. Second, have the other ingredients hot before adding cheese, except when cold ingredients are mixed together before baking, as for cheese flans. Third, heat the cheese for the minimum time needed in a moderately hot oven or under the grill. Fourth, never keep a cheese dish hot; serve it within a few minutes of being done.

If cheese is heated for too long or at too high a temperature, the fat and protein separate, causing the protein to become tough and stringy. If cheese is melted over low heat as in a cheese sauce, the fat is less likely to separate out. For *gratin* dishes, mix the grated cheese with half its volume of dried breadcrumbs. The breadcrumbs will absorb the fat and a crisp, brown surface will be achieved more easily.

Dessert cheeses

Hostesses at dinner parties often produce a cheese board either before or after the dessert. Generally a selection of two to four cheeses of different texture and flavour is presented, accompanied by butter, biscuits or crusty bread, and sometimes dessert fruits such as apples, cherries, grapes and pears.

All types of cheese should be served at room temperature. If soft runny types of cheese are provided, be sure to remove them from the refrigerator and unwrap them on to the board three to six hours in advance. This will allow them to ripen and spread out before serving.

Storing cheese

Once cut, cheese deteriorates fairly rapidly and it is advisable to buy only enough for a few days or a week at most. Store it in a cool place, such as a cold larder. It should be covered loosely, but not so as to make it airtight.

If it is airtight it may become mouldy, while if it is entirely exposed to the air it will become hard and dry. Cheese can be stored in the refrigerator for about one week but should be wrapped in waxed paper or aluminium foil, otherwise it will dry too rapidly.

Cheese can be hardened and dried by hanging it in a muslin bag where the air can circulate around it. Dried, grated cheese can be stored in a screw-top jar for several weeks. If you have a home freezer, freshly grated cheese, packed in polythene bags, is a useful standby to have to add to sauces and savoury dishes.

Eggs

Eggs have always been symbols of birth, re-birth, fertility, fortune and even witchcraft. The Easter egg, for instance, inherited from a pagan past, is a symbol of spring and rebirth.

Nowadays, however, it is chiefly regarded as a basic and versatile food, which can be prepared by itself or used in cooking. It is high in protein and fat as well as in calcium, iron and some vitamins. The fat, however, is saturated and eggs, particularly the yolks, should be avoided by those on low fat diets.

Hen's eggs are most commonly used in cooking, but duck and goose eggs are also suitable.

Hen's eggs have either brown or white shells, but colour is of no significance since the food value of all eggs is the same. The flavour of eggs, however, is somewhat dependent on the hen's diet, and you may find that eggs from one source, say free-range hens, more tasty than those from another. It is pointless, though, to use the more expensive eggs in combination cooked dishes because the subtle flavour difference will be unnoticed.

Eggs eaten on their own should be as fresh as possible, but for most cooking they need to be at least three days old. If you hard-boil eggs less than that they will be difficult to peel and turn slightly greenish; when you beat them they will not retain air well and will fail to reach proper volume.

You can tell if an egg is fresh by placing it in cold water. Lay it horizontally in the bowl and if it stays that way it is fresh, but if it stands vertically it is too stale to eat. In practice, however, few eggs are likely to be bad unless they have been in the house for too long, and this is only likely to happen if you mix new and old eggs together. Make it a practice to put cartons of new eggs behind or under the older ones.

Eggs keep best under refrigeration at a temperature below 7°C (45°F) and preferably below 5°C (40°F). At these temperatures they will keep for as long as two months. Since they pick up odours, keep them away from strong-smelling foods. Store eggs round end up (notice this is the way they are packed in egg cartons) because this keeps the yolk suspended in the right place, surrounded by the white. This positioning retards spoilage since the less perishable white part envelopes and protects the yolk. An egg left lying on its side will lose this protection as the yolk comes into contact with the shell. No matter how dirty, never wash an egg before storing it, just wipe it off with a damp cloth. Washing will remove the protective film over the shell which keeps air out.

Grading: Before eggs are boxed they are graded first for freshness and quality by candling. This means each egg is held in front of a light and inspected. A newly laid egg has a transparent, unclouded white, a small air space at the rounded end, and a pinkish yolk with no dark spots. Those that don't meet these criteria are labelled 'seconds' and are graded no further.

Quality eggs are graded by size into *large*, *standard* and *medium*. It is important to use the right sized egg in recipes. For example, two standard eggs have the same volume as three medium eggs. Most recipes that only specify 'egg' mean the standard egg.

Breaking eggs: Not everyone has mastered the art of breaking eggs. If you hit them too hard or on the wrong surface they shatter leaving a mess of egg and shell in some inconvenient place. Your aim is to crack the shell midway between the round and pointed ends, so that when the egg comes apart you will have two equal-sized 'egg cups'.

1. Tap the egg sharply but not hard on an edge or rim. In most kitchens the edge of the counter is the best place because it forms a sharp right-angle corner. The edge of a cup or bowl is less satisfactory because it tends to be round and wide or too thin. Additionally both move too easily on impact. The tap should crack the egg but not shatter the shell; no liquid should run out. Nonetheless do the cracking adjacent to the bowl into which you are putting the egg.

2. Hold the cracked egg over a bowl. Put your two thumbs up to the crack so they touch. Gently force the shell apart, allowing the contents to fall into the bowl.

3. If you are separating the white and yolk, have three bowls handy: one for the white, one for the yolk and one to break

the egg into. Never try to save time by separating the white directly into the egg-white bowl. It is far too easy to have a yolk break and get into the whites, which is disaster.

Separating eggs: Crack the egg open as described in steps 1 and 2. Open it only wide enough to let the white but not the yolk spill out, which in practice means to hold the egg almost vertical as you pull it apart. To get all the white out, slowly and gently transfer the yolk from one half of the shell to the other, letting the white slide into the cup below. Should the whole egg yolk fall into the cup, scoop it out with the egg shell.

If the yolk looks as if it will break, STOP. Empty the white from the cup into the larger bowl and then try to get the rest of the white out. A little white with the yolks won't hurt.

If the yolk does break and get into the white in the cup it can sometimes be removed by scooping it off with a corner of paper towel. If things are too bad, put the egg in a jar, beat it lightly, film it with water and save it for another use within four days.

Although eggs should be stored at low temperature, both the yolks and whites work better in cooking if they are at 21-24°C (70-75°F). But eggs at room temperature are difficult to separate because the yolks break easily. Therefore separate the eggs as soon as you take them from the refrigerator and let them warm up after.

Egg yolks

Egg yolks generally behave like whole eggs. When beaten with sugar they will turn almost white and form a ribbon. In sauces, custards and other uses, they cannot be cooked at a temperature above 78°C (170°F) without scrambling; on the other hand, if they are cooked with other ingredients at just below this temperature they will thicken to a mayonnaise consistency. Cooked at the same low temperature, they are able to thicken sauces.

Egg yolks can be stored in a lidded jar in the refrigerator for up to three days, covered with a little water to prevent a hard skin from forming. They can also be frozen if they are stabilized to prevent them from becoming pasty on thawing. Gently fork the raw yolks, then add $\frac{1}{4}$ teaspoon of salt or a teaspoon of sugar or clear honey to each 50 grams (2 ounces) of yolk, depending on the future use.

Freeze in small quantities, making sure you label what stabilizer you have added and the number of yolks in a package.

Egg whites

Egg whites have the unique characteristic of being able to increase seven times in volume when whisked. To achieve this result some care must be taken. First, the egg whites and utensils must be completely free of fat and contain no speck of yolk. Second, for best results the utensils should be chosen with some care. Last, a specific method of beating should be followed.

If you are beating by hand, an unlined copper bowl and a large thin-wired whisk half the diameter of the bowl give the best result. A pinch of salt is added to the egg whites which creates a slightly acid condition which stabilizes the beaten whites. But copper is expensive and hand beating somewhat hard, so you may prefer the alternative in excellence, a stainless steel bowl and electric beaters. In this case, measure the diameter of your beaters and get a deep bowl about twice that width in diameter. In this case, cream of tartar is added to stabilize the whites.

A pottery, glass or china bowl, however, works well enough if it is shaped to suit the whisking utensil. Use a scant $\frac{1}{4}$ teaspoon of cream of tartar for each 4 egg whites. Aluminium bowls turn whites grayish and plastic bowls cannot be kept absolutely fat-free, so neither of these is recommended.

Cream of tartar should not be added in one type of recipe, namely the small group of puddings that are supposed to separate into a sponge top with a sauce below. With cream of tartar they fail to separate.

Whatever type of bowl you use, wash it with detergent and hot water along with the beaters. As extra insurance they can also be rubbed with a piece of lemon. If you are making meringues, have the oven heated before you begin whisking. The egg whites should go into the oven the moment they are ready.

Begin beating slowly until the whites begin to froth. Add the salt or cream of tartar and quicken the speed of beating gradually until you are beating vigorously. Try to keep the entire mass in motion continuously. When the mixture forms soft rounded peaks slowly, by the spoonful, add any sugar the recipe calls for.

Continue beating until the whites stand in stiff pointed peaks when you lift up the whisk. The traditional method of being able to turn the bowl over without the whites falling out means the eggs are a trifle overbeaten and too dry. Although the whites then have maximum volume the cells break down somewhat when cooked.

To incorporate beaten egg whites into other ingredients, tip the whites on top, and, using a large metal spoon, lightly cut and fold them together. Be careful not to over-mix.

Leftover egg whites can be stored for three or four days in a screw-top jar in the refrigerator. They can also be frozen without any further preparation. Either freeze each egg white separately in individual ice-block trays or keep adding whites to a single jar, keeping note of how many you have in it. Either way they are good for meringues, yolkless soufflés and angel cake. Be sure that thawed whites have returned to a warm room temperature before you try to whisk them.

Meringues: Meringues are basically a confection or cake-topping made from egg whites and sugar. Depending on the type of meringue you wish to make, there are several basic methods of preparation.

To make meringue shells, beat 3 egg whites together in a large bowl with a whisk, beater or electric mixer until they form stiff peaks. Beat in 2 tablespoons of castor sugar and continue beating for 1 minute or until the peaks are stiff and glossy. Fold in 150 grams (5 ounces) more castor sugar with a metal spoon. Spoon the mixture into a forcing bag with a plain nozzle and pipe the mixture, spaced apart, on to a baking sheet lined with non-stick silicone paper. Bake in the oven preheated to very cool 130°C (Gas Mark $\frac{1}{2}$, 250°F) for 1½ hours, or until the meringues are crisp on the outside and pale beige in colour. If they brown too quickly, open the door of the oven. Remove from the oven and turn the meringues over with a palette knife. Gently press the undersides to form a small pocket and return to the oven. Bake for a further 30 minutes. Cool completely before filling with cream, fruit purée, etc.

Meringue topping is discussed more fully under cakes on page 139.

Eggs in cooking

The four major uses of eggs in cooking are emulsifying, thickening and binding,

To make a meringue case, draw a 23cm (9in) circle on non-stick silicone paper.

Spread a third of stiff meringue mixture over the circle, about ½cm (¼in) thick.

Pipe the remaining mixture round the sides to make a case.

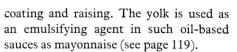

When the case is cooked, and cooled, transfer it to a serving plate.

coating and raising. The yolk is used as an emulsifying agent in such oil-based sauces as mayonnaise (see page 119).

Beaten eggs are used to thicken and bind sauces and custards. Croquettes, fritters and fish or meat cakes are coated in beaten egg before frying to prevent them from disintegrating.

Eggs are used as a raising agent in such foods as whisked sponge cakes. The whites may be beaten separately to 'lighten' a dish such as a soufflé.

In cooking, the two most significant properties of eggs are their ability to hold air when beaten and their extremely low cooking temperature. Their air-holding ability has been discussed in connection with other ingredients, and here only the art of beating is discussed.

Eggs can be beaten with a fork, a wire whisk, a rotary beater or an electric beater. Whole eggs and yolks should be beaten vigorously, unless the recipe says otherwise, until they are light in colour and texture. If sugar is added they become almost white and so thick they will run off the beater in a long stream or

ribbon rather than falling off in globules. This can take 5 minutes or more with an electric mixer. Sponge cakes are made in this manner. (Beating egg whites is discussed on page 58 under that heading.)

Beaten whole eggs begin to cook when their temperature is as low as 70°C (150°F); yolks alone cook at 75°C (160°F). When milk is added the setting temperature rises slightly. If eggs are heated to a higher temperature they begin to scramble. If you catch this happening quickly, put the base of the saucepan in cold water and stir hard; a spoonful of cream sometimes also helps.

When eggs are added to hot ingredients, you must first add about a quarter of the hot mixture by spoonfuls to the eggs in order to warm them gently. Once the eggs are warmed they can be poured on to the rest of the hot mixture. Unless this contains cornflour the eggs should not be heated above 78°C (170°F).

When egg mixtures such as custards are overcooked or overbaked they become watery, develop small holes and are rather tough. These signs indicate that the egg part of the mixture has shrunk, squeezing out the liquid's moisture.

The basic methods of cooking eggs are boiling (hard or soft), scrambling, frying, poaching and baking. They are also made into omelets and soufflés or eaten raw – as in steak tartare or egg flip.

Boiled eggs: Boiled eggs should not, in fact, be boiled but simmered gently to prevent them from cracking. There are two chief ways of soft-boiling an egg.
1. Lower the egg into a pan of boiling water. Boil for 1 minute. Turn off the heat, cover the pan and leave for 5 minutes.
2. Place the egg in a pan of boiling water and simmer for 3-4 minutes according to the size of the egg and its temperature. At the end of this time the egg white will be lightly set and the yolk runny.

For hard-boiled eggs, put the eggs in a pan of boiling water and bring the water back to the boil. Simmer over moderate heat for 10 minutes. With a slotted spoon, remove the eggs from the pan and place them at once under cold running water to prevent the yolks from discolouring.

Scrambled eggs: In a small bowl, beat 2 eggs together with seasoning to taste and, if liked, 2 tablespoons of milk, cream or water, until the mixture is

A fluffy omelet.

frothy. Melt 1 tablespoon of butter in a saucepan and pour the egg mixture into the pan. Cook for 3-4 minutes, stirring constantly with a wooden spoon, until it thickens.

Fried eggs: Heat 1 tablespoon of oil, butter or bacon fat in a frying-pan. When the oil or fat is sizzling, break an egg carefully into the pan. Reduce the heat to low and cook gently, basting frequently with the hot fat, until the white is set and the yolk firm. Remove from the pan with a spatula or fish slice.

Poached eggs: Poached eggs may either be cooked in boiling water, or steamed in a poaching pan. For the first method, half fill a saucepan with water. Add ½ teaspoon of salt and 1 teaspoon of vinegar. Place the pan over moderate heat and bring the water to the boil. Break an egg into a cup. When the water is boiling, carefully tip the egg into the centre of the bubbling water. Reduce the heat to moderately low and simmer gently for 3 minutes. Remove with a slotted spoon.

To use an egg-poaching pan, half fill the bottom of the pan with water. Place ¼ teaspoon of butter in the centre of each cup, unless you are using a non-stick pan. Place the pan, with the cups in place, over the heat. When the water boils break the eggs into the cups. Cover and simmer for 3-5 minutes or until the eggs are lightly set. Loosen with a knife and slide them on to a plate.

Baked eggs: Baked eggs are usually prepared in individual cocotte dishes, although several may be baked together in a small ovenproof dish. Place the dish or dishes on a baking sheet. Put ½ teaspoon of butter in each dish and place the baking sheet in the oven preheated to fairly hot 200°C (Gas Mark 6 400°F) for 2 minutes. Break an egg into each dish, season to taste and return the dishes to the oven. Bake for 4-5 minutes, or until the eggs are lightly set.

Omelet: To make perfect omelets every time you will require a special omelet pan – to be used for nothing else. However, few of us can aspire to this happy state of affairs, especially if we are just beginning to equip a kitchen. Any medium-sized, heavy-based frying pan can be substituted; use an 18 centimetre (7 inch) size for a 4-egg omelet and a 23 centimetre (9 inch) size for a 6-egg one. You should not attempt to make a larger-size omelet than this.

Omelets must never be overcooked,

the perfect one will still have a soft, creamy semi-liquid centre. To make an omelet for three people, break 6 eggs into a bowl. Season to taste and add 2 tablespoons of cold water. Beat well to mix with either a fork or wire whisk. Heat the pan over moderate heat for 30 seconds, or until it is quite hot. Add ½ tablespoon of butter and, when the foam subsides, pour in the beaten eggs. Stir the eggs, then leave them for a few seconds until the bottom sets. Reduce the heat to low. Using a palette knife or spatula, lift the edge of the omelet and at the same time tilt the pan away from you so that the liquid egg escapes from the top and runs into the pan. Put the pan down flat again over the heat and leave until the omelet begins to set. Tilt the pan away from you again and, with the help of the palette knife, flip one-half of the omelet over to make a semi-circle. Slide the omelet on to a plate.

Soufflé: To make a cheese soufflé for four, first generously grease a medium-sized soufflé dish with butter. Sprinkle about 4 tablespoons of grated cheese (preferably a hard cheese, such as Cheddar) around the inside of the dish.

In a large saucepan, melt 50 grams (2 ounces) of butter. Stir in 4 tablespoons of flour with a wooden spoon to make a smooth paste and cook, stirring constantly, for 1 minute. Remove the pan from the heat and gradually stir in 300 millilitres (10 fluid ounces) of milk. Return to the heat and cook, stirring constantly, for 1 minute, or until the sauce is thick and smooth. Add spices and seasonings to taste and remove from the heat. Beat in 5 egg yolks, one by one and set aside to allow the mixture to cool slightly. Meanwhile, beat 6 egg whites until they form stiff peaks.

Stir about 125 grams (4 ounces) of the grated cheese used to line the dish into the egg yolk mixture until it has blended. Quickly fold in the egg whites and pour the mixture into the prepared soufflé dish. Cook in the oven preheated to 200°C (Gas Mark 6, 400°F) for 25-30 minutes, or until the soufflé is well risen and golden brown.

Breadcrumbs

Three types of breadcrumbs are used in cooking: fresh breadcrumbs, dried breadcrumbs and browned breadcrumbs.

Fresh white breadcrumbs: Fresh white breadcrumbs are used for panades, for stuffings and bread sauce and for some desserts and cakes. Prepare them from bread which is at least one day old. Remove the crusts and reserve for browned breadcrumbs. Blend, grate or rub the rest through a wire strainer.

Dried white breadcrumbs: Place the fresh white breadcrumbs on a baking sheet and bake in a very slow oven, so that the crumbs do not brown. Dried white breadcrumbs are used for coating foods for frying (see frying instructions on page 74).

Browned breadcrumbs: Place the bread crusts on a baking sheet and bake in a very slow oven until dry. Crush finely with a pestle and mortar, with a rolling pin or in a blender. Browned breadcrumbs can be used for coating for frying, but they are more often used for covering the surface of ham before baking or for *gratins*. They are also served hot, on their own, with game.

Storage

White breadcrumbs soon become mouldy but they will keep for up to two days stored in a screw-top jar. To store longer, freeze in a polythene bag. Dried white

breadcrumbs will keep for several weeks in a screw-top jar. They too can be frozen. Browned breadcrumbs keep indefinitely in a screw-top jar in a cool, dry place.

Seasonings, Herbs and Spices

Seasoning is both an art and a term that covers the whole range of things we add to our food to enhance its flavour. Seasoning can be delicate and subtle to bring out natural flavour, or emphatic, though it should never overpower the basic food's flavour. Failure to season results in dull, uninteresting food.

The art of seasoning is something you have to learn by trial and error. You have to try seasonings alone and in combination; tables showing what goes together are a help (see page 66). In general add seasonings towards the end of cooking in small quantities and let them cook for a short time to bring out maximum flavour.

In many recipes the last instruction is 'correct the seasoning' or 'season to taste'. This means you should taste in all parts of the mouth, not just on the tongue, and add more seasoning if needed. In practice this means more salt and perhaps pepper. Often when a dish tastes flat or uninteresting it is undersalted. Add salt in small amounts, stir and taste. Remember that as the salt dissolves it will become somewhat stronger.

The foremost seasoning is without a doubt salt, followed by pepper, the onion family, herbs and spices.

Salt and pepper

You may have assumed that all salt is the same, but since it is obtained in several ways and undergoes preparation, it is available in several forms. Salt is obtained from sea water and brine wells by evaporation and purification.

Rock salt is mined, then purified, crushed and graded.

Sea salt, as its name implies, comes from sea water. Usually the individual grains are quite large. This is the salt to use in grinders. It is often sprinkled on meats and other foods just before serving, and because it dissolves relatively slowly, is also sprinkled on breads and pretzels that come with a salted surface. Malden salt is a special form of sea salt which comes in flat, multi-sided shapes. It is

unsuited for salt grinders and should be served in little salt bowls and crushed between the fingers before use. Kosher salt is a coarse sea salt.

Ordinary salt, usually evaporated from brine pumped from deep wells, comes in several forms. **Cooking salt** is pure salt with no additives; **table salt** usually contains a small quantity of magnesium carbonate and calcium phosphate to help it stay dry and shake easily. Some authorities say cooking salt can be sprinkled on meat before grilling or roasting, but if table salt is used it toughens the meat; others simply say do not salt before cooking because it toughens the meat.

Pepper, in all of its various forms is discussed later, on page 64.

The onion family

The onion or *allium* family is important in seasoning. In addition to the onion, other members include chives, garlic, shallots, leeks and spring onions. Some of these are used only as seasoning others are also a vegetable in their own right.

Onions used as seasoning in cooked dishes are usually sliced or minced (see page 91 for technique). They are then sautéed in a little hot fat or butter. For a mild flavour cook them until they are translucent; for a strong flavour brown them slowly. But remember that high heat and long frying create strong odours and an unpleasant taste; scorching causes bitterness.

Garlic is still regarded with suspicion. in many households, but correctly used it imparts a lovely flavour to meats and other dishes. Garlic can be used peeled or unpeeled, the latter giving the milder flavour with no after taste. Garlic is stronger if cut lengthwise and even more so if crushed in a garlic press or with salt using a round-ended knife. When it is used whole in stews and braising, remove it before serving. Never brown garlic because it gives a bad taste. Add it after the other vegetables and cook for only a few minutes. At the greengrocer you buy a bulb, or head, of garlic. This separates into many smaller pieces when you remove the outer skin. Each of these little pieces, also encased in a skin, is called a clove. Fresh garlic will keep well in any cool place where you keep root vegetables, but often it is more conveniently stored in the refrigerator. As long as you do not pierce the skin around the cloves, it will give off no offensive odour.

Shallots have a delicate flavour some-

The onion family, including leeks, spring onions and garlic.

where between onion and garlic and are especially used in wine cookery and delicate dishes. They are not particularly easy to find in many areas, but since they keep well in a cool place, a pound, if you find them, should last at least half a year. Often the bulb part of spring onions is substituted, but the flavour is not identical.

Chives and **spring onions** are most frequently used raw in salads and as a garnish. Chives can be minced easily by cutting with scissors (a trick that can be used with other herbs as well). Since they are best very fresh and are also hard to find commercially, keep a pot plant on a sunny window sill. Both the green stem and white bulb of spring onions are used in salads. Thinly slice or mince, discarding only the coarse upper part of the green stem.

The onion family's characteristic smell can be removed from hands, knife and cutting board by rubbing on salt, lemon juice or vinegar and washing under cold water (beware of open cuts which will sting). Eat raw parsley to remove onion and garlic odours from your breath.

Herbs and spices

Herbs are mainly the leaves and seeds of herbaceous plants that grow in mid-latitude countries. Some are annuals resown each year, others are perennial. Most can be grown in your garden or window box, doing best in a sunny location with poor, even dry, soil. The flavours of herbs are best when freshly picked. When you have to use dried herbs, buy them in small amounts and store them airtight in a cool, dry, dark place, which generally means not on a pretty spice rack next to the stove. Replace herbs regularly, at least once a year, because they lose flavour and become musty. When you substitute dry herbs for fresh, use half the quantity, that is 1 teaspoon of fresh herbs equals $\frac{1}{2}$ teaspoon of dry.

The terms **fines herbes** (fine herbs) and **'bouquet garni'** appear frequently. **Fines herbes** is the French culinary term for a finely chopped fresh herb mixture, usually parsley, tarragon, chives and chervil. The term can also mean parsley alone. Fines herbes are used as a flavouring for soups, sauces, omelets and grilled meats.

A **bouquet garni** is a mixture of thyme, parsley and bay leaf. The proportions are up to you and your personal taste. It is used primarily to flavour stews and casserole dishes.

A chart relating specific herbs to food is given on pages 66–67.

Spice is the collective name given to various aromatic substances which are used to season and flavour sweet and savoury foods. Most, but not all of them, come from tropical lands. They are mostly hard and can be crushed and grated to form a powder – nutmeg, all-spice, pepper, cinnamon. Unlike herbs they are often used in sweet cookery.

Spices, like herbs, are more pungent when freshly bought – you have only to compare the smell and taste of new and old spices to recognize the great difference. Like herbs, spices should also be bought in small amounts and kept tightly covered in a cool, dry, dark place. Keep ground spices no more than a year, after this they do rapidly lose pungency. If spices are being used in a savoury dish like a curry, add them to the fat and fry over low heat for a minute without scorching. This process will enhance their aroma and flavour.

Spiced foods lose flavour when frozen for any length of time. Therefore, use them within two or three weeks of freezing. When doubling a recipe do not automatically double the spices; let taste be your guide.

Pepper is undoubtedly the most widely used spice. **Peppercorns** are the dried fruit of a climbing vine native to India. They are sold green (unripe fruit) and soft, black (sun dried) and white (ripe fruit with outer hulls removed before drying). Generally black pepper is used in cooking, since it is the most flavourful. White pepper is for white sauce and other dishes where black flecks would be undesirable.

Peppercorns bought whole and ground coarsely in a peppermill taste fresher and have more flavour than the pre-ground commercial powder sold as pepper. A single layer of peppercorns can be cracked easily in a garlic press.

Chilli powder is a blended pepper made from sweet paprika, cayenne, turmeric, cumin, coriander, oregano and cloves. Fresh red or green chillis should not be substituted for chilli powder. To substitute dried chillis for fresh, drop 6 chillis in 300 millilitres (10 fluid ounces) of water and simmer for 20 minutes or until tender. Working carefully wearing rubber gloves, split and seed the chillis. Then scrape off the soft red pith to add to your recipe; the cooking liquid can also be used. The problem with this method is that you have no way of comparing the strength of the chilli pith with that of fresh chillis, therefore be prudent and use a small quantity at first; taste and add a little more. Repeat this several times if necessary.

Other speciality flavourings

Anchovies, though neither herb nor spice, add a piquant taste that is not easily identifiable, though pleasant, to sauces, meat and gravy. But you must use it sparingly; no more than $\frac{1}{8}$ teaspoon of mashed fillet or paste to 300 millilitres (10 fluid ounces) of sauce (the paste is weaker in flavour and saltier). For a sauce soak the fillet in warm water for 5–10 minutes, then drain. For a salad or antipasto soak in cold milk or water for up to 1 hour; drain and dry before using. Anchovies keep well as long as they are completely covered with either brine or oil, depending on which they were originally packed in. Worcestershire sauce has an anchovy base.

Herb chart

Herbs	Cheese	Eggs	Meats
Basil	Pizza Rarebit Cream cheese Cheese spreads	Devilled Scrambled Egg salad spread Soufflé	Beef, lamb and veal – roasts and stews Meat pies Lamb chops
Bay leaf			Beef, lamb and veal stews and pot roasts Tongue Bacon Pâté

Chervil	Cottage cheese
	Cream cheese
	Curd cheese
		Omelet (with parsley
		  and chives)
		Scrambled
			Beef, lamb and veal
			  stews and pot roasts
			Pork chops

Chives	Cheese spreads	Omelet Scrambled	
Coriander, crushed seed		Omelet Curried Scrambled Egg salad spread	All meat curries Pork sausages Meatballs Marinated meats
Dill, seed or weed	Cottage cheese Cream cheese Canapés	Devilled Egg salad spread	Pork and lamb chops, roasts and stew Meatballs Curries
Marjoram (M) (including Oregano [O])	Pizza (O) Cheese spreads	Devilled (O) Omelet Sandwich spread (O) Scrambled (M) Soufflé (M)	Beef and lamb roasts, stews and pot roasts Pork dishes (M)
Mint	Cream cheese spreads		Lamb stews and roasts Mint sauce for lamb
Parsley	Cottage cheese Curd cheese Cream cheese Soufflé	Devilled Omelet Scrambled	Beef, lamb and veal stews Meat pies

Poultry	Seafood	Soups	Vegetables	Other
Fried chicken	Fish Shrimp Crabmeat Lobster	Minestrone Pea Potato Spinach Tomato Vegetable	Asparagus, beans, broccoli, cabbage, carrots, celery, cucumbers, aubergine, peas, tomatoes, turnip, spinach, onions, courgettes	Goes especially well with tomato in all forms. Gives a Mediterranean flavour to salads
Chicken stew and fricassée Venison Rabbit	Shellfish Fish Soused fish	Consommé Chicken Vegetable Stocks	Artichoke, cabbage, carrots, tomatoes	A leaf is used in a bouquet garni. Tomato sauces
Chicken fricassée Chicken and turkey pie Stuffing	Shellfish	Cream of potato Cream of spinach Tomato	Aubergine, celery, cucumbers, lettuce, peas, potatoes, spinach, tomatoes	Good in all salads
		As a garnish	As a garnish on new potatoes, carrots, turnips, tomatoes, peas, beans, cauliflower, mushrooms	Chopped as a garnish for salads, especially tomato, lettuce and potato
Chicken curry Stuffing		Pea Stocks	Cauliflower, onions, spinach, tomatoes	Leaves also known as Chinese parsley, and *cilantro*; can be chopped and used like parsley in Chinese-style meat and poultry dishes. Seed good with cooked fruit
Chicken and duck curries Stuffing	Shrimp Lobster Halibut Herring Curries Salmon	Cabbage, borscht dried bean, cucumber, tomato, courgette	Beetroots, beans, broccoli, brussels sprouts, cabbage, potatoes, cucumber, French beans, turnips.	Dill leaves, known as weed, can be chopped and sprinkled on salads and on rice
Fried chicken (M) Chicken fricassée (M) Roast duck and turkey (M) Stuffing (M)	Grilled fish Prawns Crabmeat (M) Stuffing	Creamed celery (M) Cream of chicken (M) Onion (M) Potato (M) Spinach (M) Bean (O) Minestrone (O) Tomato (O)	Broccoli (O) Asparagus (M) Aubergine (O) Brussels sprouts (M) Cabbage (O) Marrows Courgettes Lentils (O) Dried beans (O) Mushrooms Tomatoes (O) Celery (M) Peas (M) Potatoes (M)	Oregano gives an Italian or Mediterranean flavour to many dishes. Do not cook more than 10-15 mins for best flavour
		Cream of pea Potato Cucumber	Carrots, peas, new potatoes, spinach	Fruit salad Fruit juice Melon balls Yogurt and cucumber salad
Chicken fricassée Chicken and turkey pie Stuffing	Fish and shellfish Stuffing	Vegetable soups Court boullion Poultry and meat stocks	Cabbage, cauliflower, celery, onions, potatoes, tomatoes, turnip, aubergine	Chopped as garnish for most savoury dishes. Stems in bouquet garni

Herbs	Cheese	Eggs	Meats
Rosemary		Omelet Scrambled Soufflé	Lamb roasts and stews Kebabs Pot roasts
Sage, rubbed or ground	Cheddar cheese spread Omelet Fondue		Pork Veal Sausage Stuffing Marinades
Savory, Winter or Summer		Devilled Omelet Scrambled	Roasts of beef, lamb, pork, or veal Meat pies Mince
Tarragon		All egg dishes	Lamb dishes Veal dishes Lamb and pork Grilled steaks and chops
Thyme	Cottage cheese Cheese spread	Devilled Scrambled Baked	All roasts and stews

Spice chart

Spice	Cheese	Eggs	Meats
Allspice ground or whole			Beef, lamb and veal pot roasts plus stews
Anise	Cottage cheese Mild-flavoured cheese spreads		Beef and veal stews
Caraway seed	Cheese spreads Cottage cheese	Omelet Egg salad spread	Beef roasts and stews Pork goulash Sauerbraten
Cardamom seed			Curried meats
Cayenne pepper	Cheese wafers and straws Macaroni cheese Soufflé Welsh rarebit	Omelet Soufflé Devilled	Pork sausage Paprikash Curried meats

Poultry	Seafood	Soups	Vegetables	Other
Any chicken or turkey dish Stuffing	Fish casseroles Scallops Stuffing	Chicken Lamb broth Tomato Fish chowder Pea	Cauliflower, potatoes, turnip, carrots, aubergine, mushrooms, peas, spinach	
Chicken, duck, turkey casseroles, fried chicken Stuffing		Chicken Turkey Tomato	Beetroots, brussels sprouts, celery, onions, marrows and courgettes, tomatoes, aubergines	
Chicken and turkey dishes	Grilled fish Fish casseroles Stuffing	Chicken Cucumber Potato Tomato Vegetable Split pea	Asparagus, beans, Brussels sprouts, cucumbers, potatoes, tomatoes, carrots, marrows, courgettes	Traditionally cooked with all bean dishes. Part of fines herbes
Chicken Turkey	Fish Prawns	Chicken Mushroom Pea Tomato	Beets, artichoke, beans, carrots, marrows and courgettes, French beans, mushrooms, onions, new potatoes	Salads Wine vinegar
All chicken and turkey casseroles and pies Fried chicken Roast duck Stuffing	Tuna Scallops Crabmeat Fish Lobster Prawns	Fish chowder Chicken and mushroom Tomato Vegetable	Carrots, beans, onions, potatoes, mushrooms, marrows and courgettes, spinach, turnips	Spray part of bouquet garni

Poultry	Seafood	Soup	Vegetables	Other
Chicken and turkey fricassée and pies Braised chicken Duck stew	Poached fish	Chicken Consommé Potato Tomato Vegetable	Parsnips, turnips, spinach	Often used as an alternative to pepper in Middle Eastern cookery. Good in fruit salad, gingerbread, pumpkin pie, mince pie, steamed puddings, fruit cake
Braised chicken Roast duck Chicken and duck pilaffs				Used mostly in sweets; cakes, biscuits, apple pie, fruit salad, stewed fruit, baked apple, also sweet rolls and breads
Roast goose	Grilled fish Crab and Lobster Poached fish Stuffed fish	Borscht Potato	Potatoes, cabbage, carrots, celery, cucumbers, onions, sauerkraut	Used on breads : rye, onion, pumpernickel. Used in cakes, biscuits, apple pie
Curried poultry	Curried seafood		Carrots, pumpkin	Ground, on all melons except water melon. Danish pastry, sweet yeast breads, apple pie, stewed fruits baked apple
Grilled chicken Paprikash Curried chicken	Grilled prawns Crab and lobster	Vegetable	Cabbage, spring greens, turnip greens	Use sparingly since it can be very hot

Spice	Cheese	Eggs	Meats
Celery seed	Cheese wafers and straws Cheese spreads	Omelet Scrambled Soufflé	Pot roasts and stews
Chilli powder	Cottage cheese Spreads Fondue	Devilled Omelet Scrambled Egg salad spread	Chilli con carne Beef stew Meatballs Tamale pie
Cinnamon, ground or stick			Beef stew (stick) Sauerbraten
Clove, ground or whole			Gammon Pork Tongue
Cumin seed	Cheese canapés Spreads	Eggs Curried	Curried meat Meatballs
Fennel seed			Italian sausage Beef Lamb Pork
Ginger, fresh, ground, preserved			All meats
Mace, ground	Welsh rarebit		Veal chops
Mustard, seed or ground	All cheese dishes	Devilled Sandwich spread	Coating for lamb roast Gammon, pork
Nutmeg, whole or ground		Custard	Swedish meatballs Meat pie
Paprika	As a garnish	As a garnish	Beef and veal paprikash Garnish
Pepper (black or white), whole or ground	All cheese dishes	All egg dishes	All meat dishes
Sesame seed	Fondue Omelet Spreads	Scrambled	
Turmeric		Egg salad spread Devilled	Meat curries

Poultry	Seafood	Soups	Vegetables	Other
Chicken fricassée			Beetroots, braised lettuce, cabbage, cucumbers	
Grilled chicken Poultry casseroles Fried chicken	Prawns Fish	Black bean Pea Tomato	Aubergine, broad beans, onions, sweetcorn, tomatoes	Used as a substitute for fresh chillis in Indian and Mexican cooking
			Carrots, onions, pumpkin, rice	Used in sweets and breads: sweet rolls, tea bread, all apple desserts, chocolate desserts, rice pudding, gingerbread, stewed fruits
Braised chicken		Onion	Carrots, onions, pumpkin, mushrooms	Used in sweets and breads: sweet rolls, tea bread, fruit compote, steamed puddings, chocolate desserts, gingerbread, apple purée
Curried poultry Stuffing	Prawn Lobster			Used in cakes and biscuits
Chicken and duck pilaffs	Seafood Pilaff Baked and poached fish	Potato	Cabbage, onion, potato	Gives an Italian flavour to foods. Can be used in apple desserts, cakes, biscuits
Fried and roast chicken Baked duck Chicken and duck casseroles			Carrots, pumpkin	Gives an oriental flavour to meat and poultry dishes. Used on fruit desserts, gingerbread, biscuits, steamed puddings
Chicken fricassée		Vegetable	Beans, onions, sweetcorn, tomatoes, aubergine	Used in sweet breads, tea bread; chocolate, lemon, lime and orange desserts
				Spice cake, gingerbread, molasses biscuits
		Black bean Pea Tomato Potato	Aubergine, beans, onions, sweetcorn, tomatoes, spinach, mushrooms	Tea bread, sweet rolls, banana bread, puddings, apple dessert and pies
Chicken paprikash Garnish	As a garnish	Pea	Cauliflower, spinach, sweetcorn	Comes in several strengths. Much used in Hungarian cooking, frequently instead of pepper
All poultry dishes	All seafood dishes	All soup dishes	All vegetable dishes	Used in some spiced breads (tea bread) and cakes (gingerbread)
Fried, grilled and roast chicken Roast duck	Grilled fish Crabmeat Prawns		Sweetcorn	Used on breads and rolls and in cakes, biscuits and pies
Chicken, duck and turkey curries	Seafood Pilaffs		Rice Vegetable curries	Gives a rich yellow colour to all it touches

71

Chapter Five

Once you understand what you are doing and why, cooking becomes much easier. While the number of recipes is infinite, the preparation techniques are limited. So an experienced cook can read a recipe and mentally reduce its apparent complexities to a series of well-known techniques. Sole *Bonne Femme*, for instance, is identified as oven-poached fish with a white sauce made with the poaching liquid.

Before you get down to cooking you must figure out the timing and order of events. Again, some experienced cooks can do this in their heads, but many prefer to write everything down. Preparing a meal for either the family or guests requires the cook to ask and answer a series of questions.

What will the main course be? What will go well with it? What vegetables, fruit, are in season? What have we not had to eat recently? What is needed for balanced nutrition? For good colour contrast? How much work will it require and when will I do it? Will it fit my budget?

Decisions based on these questions will result in a menu for the week or day.

Next the cook asks: What can be prepared in advance? What needs to be done early because it will be needed in another step of the recipe (a flan case baked blind before the filling is made for instance)? What needs long cooking? What can be partly prepared in advance? What must be done at the last minute? The answers to these questions may lead to modifications in the menu to even out the work load.

Many people find it helpful to write out the menu then make a time chart listing when to do things. A time chart should show when to prepare things for cooking, when they should start and finish cooking. For a dinner party, especially, include such details as washing the salad greens, making the salad dressing, setting the table and clearing up. Above all *begin early* and don't have lots of last minute details.

Reading a recipe

At the time you are menu planning and before you go shopping *read through the recipe*. Check that all the ingredients are available. Be sure you understand the entire process described.

Before you begin work on a recipe clear off the work surface and get out all the ingredients you will need. Start with those in the refrigerator to give them the maximum time to warm up. Gather up bowls, pans, utensils and measuring equipment. Now you are ready to begin making the recipe. Clean up and wash up as you go.

How to measure

The three types of measurements used in European cookery are: scales for solids, a measuring jug for liquids and spoons for small amounts of either. Americans do everything by volume, using a standard measuring cup that holds 225 grams (8 ounces).

Scales are measured in grams, ounces or both. With a balance scale, stand the correct weights on their stand and pour the ingredient to be measured into the pan. When the weight and ingredient arms are balanced, that is, neither is higher than the other, the weight is correct. With a spring balance scale with a dial and pointer, make sure the needle points to zero before adding the ingredients. Always measure dry ingredients before moist or sticky ones. Although this may seem obvious, in practice it is extremely difficult to remember.

Butter and margarine need not be weighed if you mark them out into 25 gram (1 ounce) rectangles. A round tub of margarine can be divided into eight equal wedges weighing either 25 grams (1 ounce) or 50 grams (2 ounces) each, depending on the size of the tub. Care must be taken, however, in getting these wedges out correctly.

Measuring jugs are marked off in millilitres, fluid ounces, or both. When you fill a jug be sure to hold it at eye level, otherwise you can be off by quite a bit. Experiment first by partly filling a jug at eye level and then putting it first below and then above and noting how much the liquid seems to increase and decrease in amount.

The spoons used in cooking are carefully measured and should not be confused with spoons found in a canteen of cutlery. Thus the standard metric teaspoon holds 5 millilitres, the standard tablespoon 15 millilitres. The standard imperial tablespoon based on ounces was one-thirty-second of a pint, which makes

it slightly larger than the metric one; the difference, however, is too small to be of significance in cooking. It is useful to know, too, that 3 teaspoons equal 1 tablespoon, and 2 tablespoons hold approximately 1 fluid ounce.

When a recipe in this book calls for a teaspoon or tablespoon, it means a *level* spoon, that is, even with the rim of the bowl. Not all cookbooks, however, use a level spoon; some mean the contents of the spoon are rounded, that is, as much above the bowl as in it. A rounded spoon is equivalent to two level spoons. With luck the introduction to your book will tell you which system is being used. All American books use the level spoon system.

Types of heat

At least half the food we eat is heated in some way. Heat can be either moist or dry. Moist heat means the food is in contact with a hot liquid or steam. Dry heat means no water (or water-based liquid) comes into contact with the substance being cooked.

Moist heat cooking

Boiling: The term 'to boil' means water has reached the temperature of 100°C or 212°F and has many big bubbles breaking above the surface. By regulating the heat, water can be kept at a fast boil (lots of large bubbles breaking well above the surface) or a slow boil (fewer large bubbles).

When the heat is reduced further only tiny bubbles form and rise to the surface just breaking it. This is called *simmering*. When the surface quivers but no bubbles come to the surface is termed *poaching*. It is important to know and remember the difference between these terms. Water alone never boils over, but as soon as another substance is added to water the mixture can boil over.

Strangely, English terminology is often in conflict with the process used. Thus the term 'boiling' is often applied to foods which are in fact simmered. Boiled beef, for instance, would be a tough, tasteless disaster if cooked above a simmer. True boiling is too fierce a heat for meats, poultry, fish and some vegetables and fruits. True boiling is the method used for cooking some suet puddings and vegetables such as cabbage, that need to be cooked quickly. It is used in jam and marmalade making to evaporate the water and concentrate the fruit and sugar solution. Liquids that need to be reduced in volume, and so made more concentrated, are boiled rapidly without a lid to drive off the excess water. This is the case for syrups, purées, and savoury glazes.

Some starchy foods such as rice, macaroni and pasta are best cooked by boiling, because the rapid bubbling keeps the grains moving and prevents them from sticking together.

Simmering: Simmering occurs at a temperature just below the boiling point, when a slow stream of bubbles reaches the surface without breaking. It is much more gentle than boiling, and does not toughen meats and poultry. Salt beef, bacon joints, poultry, stocks and soups are all cooked by this method.

Unfortunately, on many newer gas and electric stoves it is hard to maintain a simmer and, without constant watching, the liquid keeps coming to the boil. If something needs to be simmered for a long time and your stove is a problem one it is best to do it in a cool oven 140°–160°C (Gas Mark 1–3, 275°–325°F). Bring to the boil on the hob, then transfer to the preheated oven. Check it after a while and reduce the heat if necessary.

On top of the stove keep the saucepan partly covered to reduce evaporation. Ideally the pan should have a tight-fitting lid, but on most stoves this guarantees a boil. Cover tightly for oven simmering.

Stewing is a type of simmering—the term is applied to the mixture of meat and vegetables cooked in liquid which forms a rich gravy. Certain fruits such as apples, apricots and rhubarb are stewed in a sugar syrup. The liquid and solid parts mingle and are served together.

Poaching: To poach means to cook in a liquid which is just below simmering point. Water, stock, milk, wine and cider can all be used as the liquid. Poaching is mainly used for foods with a delicate structure that need gentle, low temperatures, such as fruit, fish and eggs. It can be done on top of the stove in a shallow open pan or in the oven. Often a lid or poaching paper covers the food lightly to make the process self-basting. Generally, fruit, eggs, gnocchi and small pieces of fish are poached on top of the stove, and larger pieces of fish are poached in the oven. Kippers or other smoked fish can be poached in a special way called the jug method. The kippers are placed in a jug or deep bowl and covered with boiling water. They are left for 5–15 minutes (depending on the type and thickness of the fish used), then drained and served.

Steaming: Food is cooked in the steam from boiling water. It is slow but economical of fuel and produces light, easily digested foods with little loss of nutrients.

Sometimes foods, especially vegetables, are placed on a perforated surface above the water. They can be loose or set in open dishes. At other times a covered basin is set in or over the water.

For either method, a tightly fitted lid is necessary to keep the steam in. If a lid needs to be removed, this must be done quickly with a cloth to prevent the condensed steam dripping on to the food or, indeed, on to the arm or hand.

Roasting bags and aluminium foil placed over a joint or turkey both entrap steam. Thus the meat is cooked in moist heat rather than roasted, which is a dry heat method.

Pressure Cooking: This is another form of steaming that on average reduces cooking times to a quarter, greatly saving on fuel and time. Busy people find pressure cookers invaluable, since most things take less than a half hour to cook. During the cooking period, however, the cooker cannot be left unattended because the pressure must be watched closely. All types of food can be cooked in them.

Dry heat cooking

Baking: Baking is cooking in an oven by heat which is radiated from the lining of the oven, circulated by convection currents, and passed to the food by conduction through its container. A wide range of temperatures can be achieved in a domestic oven which makes this method one of the most versatile. Baked food should not be in contact with liquid, and should have a brown, crisp surface as is the case with pastry, bread and cakes.

Roasting really means cooking on a rotating spit over an open fire, so today oven roasting is, in fact, baking. The term roasting, however, continues to be applied to meats and potatoes cooked in dry heat. Meat to be roasted should be put on a wire rack raised a little above the roasting pan, to allow air to circulate all around the joint. It should never be covered. Basting with pan juices during roasting keeps the exterior moist.

Rotisserie Cooking: Rotisseries can be fitted on to some stoves or bought as a separate unit. The food is secured on the spit, which is turned electrically, and cooks under direct heat. Because of the continuous rotation it does not usually need basting.

Grilling: Grilled food is cooked by intense direct heat under or over gas, electricity or charcoal. This method is only suitable for tender foods which do not need prolonged cooking: steak, chops, fish, liver and kidneys. These should not be much over 2½ centimetres (1 inch) in thickness. Meat should be subjected to a fierce heat to 'seal' the surface, after which the heat is reduced until the meat is cooked. Poultry and fish need a moderate heat throughout. Whole round fish, such as herring or mackerel should be scored three or four times before grilling to allow the heat to penetrate quickly.

All foods should be turned once during cooking. This is best done with tongs or two spoons; never pierce the surface with a fork because this allows juices to escape. Grilling is also sometimes used to brown the top of dishes describes as *au gratin*.

Infra-red grills use rays of shorter wave length than ordinary grills. They greatly reduce cooking time, since the heat penetrates the food quickly.

Frying: Frying is considered a dry heat method of cooking because of the high temperatures involved and the absence of a water-based liquid. When the food comes into contact with hot fat, moisture evaporates rapidly from the surface, causing shrinking, and the outside is quickly sealed. There are various ways of frying: pan broiling, sautéing, shallow frying and deep-fat frying. Each uses a different amount of fat. Many consider the first two methods far better for health, though little fat is absorbed if deep-fat frying is done at the correct temperature.

Pan broiling or dry frying is suitable for beef steaks, hamburgers, lamb chops, sausages and bacon. Pork chops are usually too dry. A heavy frying pan is preheated and rubbed with a small amount of fat so that the bottom is covered with a film of fat but there is no excess. Sear the meat until blood rises to the surface, then turn it without piercing and brown the other side. Reduce the heat and continue to cook until the meat is done to taste. Pour off fat as it accumulates or the meat will be fried rather than grilled in quality. Never cover the pan. Sautéing uses high heat and a small amount of fat, usually clarified butter or equal parts of vegetable oil and butter. The heat must be kept high throughout cooking in order not to draw juices. The food must be small and uniform in size and the surface dry. The pan must not be crowded. Rather than turning the contents often, shake the pan to keep them moving.

This method is suitable for thin meats and some vegetables. Often the cooking is finished with moist heat by reducing the temperature, adding a liquid covering and simmering for a short time. In other cases, the food is ready to serve with no further cooking. A good pan gravy can be made by deglazing the pan with stock and wine. Shallow frying is used more in Britain than elsewhere. Enough fat (vegetable oil, dripping, lard) is heated in a wide, shallow frying pan to come halfway up the side of the food to be cooked. The fat must be hot before the food is placed in the pan, otherwise too much fat is absorbed and the food becomes greasy. If the fat is *too* hot the outside will cook too quickly and the inside will be undercooked. A good test before adding the food to be fried is to see if a cube of bread will brown in 1 minute. At one time a guide to the correct temperature was when a blue haze rose from the fat. This is no longer recommended, since modern cooking fats smoke at much higher temperatures than that needed for cooking.

All foods should be lowered gently, one at a time, into the pan to prevent splashing. Never fill the pan too full. Always drain fried foods on paper towels before serving.

Deep-fat frying is best done in a special deep-frying pan with wire-basket and lid, or in a strong deep saucepan with well-fixed handles to make it easy and safe to lift. A wire draining spoon is useful to have for removing single pieces of food or crumbs which may become burned and give a bitter taste to the fat or oil. Suitable fats are clarified dripping, lard and vegetable or corn oil. Sunflower oil is recommended for those on a low-cholesterol diet. The pan must not be more than half full with fat or oil because the fat bubbles up when food is immersed. Flames should not be allowed to come up the side of the pan, and it should never be left unattended during cooking. Do not allow water from a kettle or nearby saucepan to splash into the fat, because the fat will spurt out, burning whatever it hits. In case the fat catches fire, have the pan's metal lid handy to drop over the burning fat. Salt will also smother flames. Under no circumstances should you try to move the pan. And *never use water* which will only spread the fire.

The fat or oil should be heated gradually to the desired temperature so that any moisture has time to evaporate. The temperatures for deep-fat frying are harder to judge than those for shallow-frying, so a deep-fat thermometer is recommended. Frying temperatures vary from 170°–200°C (330°–390°F), and individual recipes should be consulted for specific temperatures.

Meat, Poultry and Fish

Meat, poultry and fish form an important part of most people's diet. Not only are they rich in protein, vitamins and fats, but they also taste delicious when well-prepared. They require careful cooking and repay attention to detail.

Learn to look at meat as it cooks, so that with experience you will be able to tell when it is finished, whether it is cooking too quickly or too slowly, and whether it needs basting. The appearance of fish, especially fillets, tells a lot more about doneness than time cooked.

Listen to meat and poultry cooking. Chickens being braised or roasted make gentle crackling noises. If they are too loud or too frequent, the temperature is too high. Not enough noise warns you the temperature is too low. Sound also warns you that the simmer has become too close to a boil.

Overcooking is the worst thing you can do to meat, poultry and fish. The result is dry, uninteresting and even tough and stringy. This happens most easily to fish, some poultry, and meat that lacks fat. None of these should be cooked in advance and kept waiting; rather, let the diners wait for them.

Interestingly some cuts of meat that are tender when slightly underdone become tough when well cooked, then tender again after further slow cooking. Liver is a prime example; also beef skirt as used in Chinese stir-fry cooking.

Meat

The term 'meat' encompasses beef (from ox, bullock and sometimes cow), veal (calf), lamb and mutton (sheep), pork, ham and bacon (pig). It forms a basic part of most diets and is one of the largest expenditures in any family budget. Each carcass consists of meat of various qualities. Some are tender, others tough. Tender cuts are naturally more expensive than the others, though cheaper cuts, if they are cooked with care, can become tender and have good flavour.

Meat is cooked by all the methods described on pages 73–75. Dry heat should be used only for tender cuts; moist is best for all the others. Cooking meat not only destroys bacteria but also causes changes to take place in meat that makes it more tender. Fat marbled through as well as on the outside of roasts and chops melts during cooking, which helps meat to stay moist when cooked by dry heat. Moist heat causes connective tissue to dissolve, and fibre falls apart, making the meat more tender. Acid (lemon juice, vinegar, tomato) added to the liquid hastens the process.

Preparations

Meats to be cooked by dry heat do best if they are brought to room temperature (21°C, 70°F), because they then respond better to heating. Unless a roast is very lean it needs no special preparation. The custom of adding dripping to the pan before putting the roast into it is unnecessary except in the case of lean meat and only means the oven will have to be cleaned more frequently. Basting is also unnecessary, and opening the oven door lowers the temperature drastically, especially in an electric oven. Roasting information for specific cuts of different meat is given in the chart on page 96. For grilling and frying, cut excess fat off and score the remaining fat so the edges will not curl. If the tenderness of your meat is in doubt, pound it with a rolling pin, the edge of a heavy plate, or a mallet to crush the fibres and reduce stringiness. It can also be marinated for several hours then dried well.

Have the grill or frying pan very hot before introducing the meat. Remember that overcooking toughens meat, especially borderline cuts which are often still tender when they are slightly underdone.

Cuts for braising or pot-roasting do not need any particular preparation, though sometimes they are marinated first, which helps to tenderize them. The vegetables on which the meat will rest in braising should be great enough in number to raise the meat about 2½ centimetres (1 inch); add more if necessary.

Beef

Beef can be more variable in quality than other meats. Obviously, prime, tender cuts are always more expensive because they are a minority of the carcass.

When buying beef, look for meat with a fresh red colour that has a brownish tinge. Too bright a colour means the meat has not aged sufficiently and will be tough and lacking in flavour. The meat should be marbled with a creamy-coloured fat.

The amount of meat you buy depends on your diet and appetite, but an approximate guide is 125–175 grams (4–6 ounces) of boned meat, or 175–225 grams (6–8 ounces) of meat with bone per person per serving.

The prime cuts of beef include fillet, top rump, sirloin, and ribs. These cuts are usually either roasted, grilled or pan fried. Cheaper cuts include topside (used mainly for pot roasting or braising) chuck and minced beef.

Lamb

A lamb is a young sheep. In culinary terms the word refers to either an unweaned baby lamb or to an animal less than a year old.

When buying lamb, look for meat with a light colour, fine grain and firm texture. The fat should be creamy-white and soft. Imported lamb has a whiter, firmer fat. Yellowish fat indicates an older animal and brittle white fat one that has been frozen too long. Serve approximately 175-225 grams (6-8 ounces) of boned meat per person. For meat on the bone, allow 350 grams (12 ounces) of leg, 350–450 grams (12 ounces–1 pound) of shoulder, saddle and loin and 225–350 grams (8–12 ounces) of breast or best end for each serving.

The prime cuts of lamb are the saddle, leg and shoulder. The saddle is the choicest and biggest cut, from which the best end and the loin are cut. These are always roasted. The leg, which may be cut into two, the fillet end and the shank or knuckle end, is suitable for roasting, braising and, when boned, for casseroles.

Mutton

Mutton is the flesh of a sheep over one year of age. Good mutton is bright red in colour, close grained and firm in texture. The fat is firm and white. In France, where mutton is popular, salt meadow mutton is the most highly praised. It comes from sheep reared on the coast where aromatic plants grow. In England, the Southdown crossbread is thought to produce the best mutton.

Mutton, being older than lamb, should be cooked from 5–10 minutes to the half kilo or pound longer. So if you cannot obtain mutton and have to substitute lamb in any recipe, reduce the cooking time accordingly.

Like most other meat, mutton is cut differently in Britain, the United States and Europe, but as a general guide, the cuts and methods of cooking are as follows: the leg is roasted, boiled or cut into pieces and used in stews, kebabs and curries; the shoulder is roasted and also cut up for curries and stews; the loin is roasted or casseroled, and loin chops are fried or grilled; the neck, scrag and breast are stewed.

Pork

Pork is the fresh meat from a pig, as opposed to ham and bacon which are cured before cooking.

When buying pork look for fine-textured, firm, pink-coloured, smooth flesh with no gristle. All pork should be thoroughly cooked and never served underdone, because it sometimes harbours a parasite dangerous to man which is destroyed by thorough cooking.

Serve approximately 175–225 grams (6–8 ounces) of boned meat or 225–350 grams (8–12 ounces) with bone per person.

The prime cuts of pork are the leg, which is sometimes divided into fillet and knuckle; loin, the best and most expensive joint from which loin chops are cut and which is sometimes divided into hind and fore loin; blade or blade bone, which is a joint cut from the top part of the foreleg. These cuts are usually roasted, grilled or in the case of fillet and chops, baked. The medium cuts include hand and spring; belly, spare ribs from which cutlets and neck chops are cut; and chump chops. Fillet is a fatless cut which is removed from either side of the backbone.

Bacon, Ham and Gammon

Bacon is the cured meat from a specially bred pig. The meat is immersed in brine, then (in the case of smoked bacon) hung over smouldering oak sawdust chips; unsmoked bacon, also called green or white bacon, has a white rind and a milder flavour than smoked bacon.

Ham is the name given to the meat from the thigh of the pig. It is removed from the side of the pig before salting and then cured. There are regional differences in methods of preparation—some hams are smoked before they are cured, others are not. A ham should have a thin rind and not be too fatty. When buying cooked ham, look for fresh, pink flesh and white fat.

Veal

Veal is the flesh of calves less than 10 months old. The flesh is pale pink in colour and darkens as the animal gets older. It has little fat and, because of this, the leanest cuts should be barded, that is, covered with salt pork or streaky bacon, before cooking. Good veal is soft and moist in texture. If the flesh has a blue or brown tinge, it is stale and should not be bought. Veal bones contain a large amount of gelatine, and this makes veal stock ideal for moulds and pies.

Two kinds of veal are available: from milk-fed calves and from grass-fed calves. Milk-fed calves are considered to have the more delicate flavour and finer texture, and are more expensive. Serve approximately 125–175 grams (4–6 ounces) of boned meat per person; for meat on the bone, allow 225 grams (8 ounces) of leg; and 350–450 grams (12 ounces–1 pound) of shoulder, neck, hock and knuckle.

The prime cuts of veal are the legs, fillet, loin, shoulder and saddle. Loin chops, chump chops and cutlets are cut from the loin and should be grilled or shallow-fried. Leg, fillet, loin and saddle are usually roasted. The cheaper cuts, breast, neck, hock and knuckle are suitable for roasting when boned, stuffed and rolled, and for braising, boiling and stewing. Neck is suitable for pies.

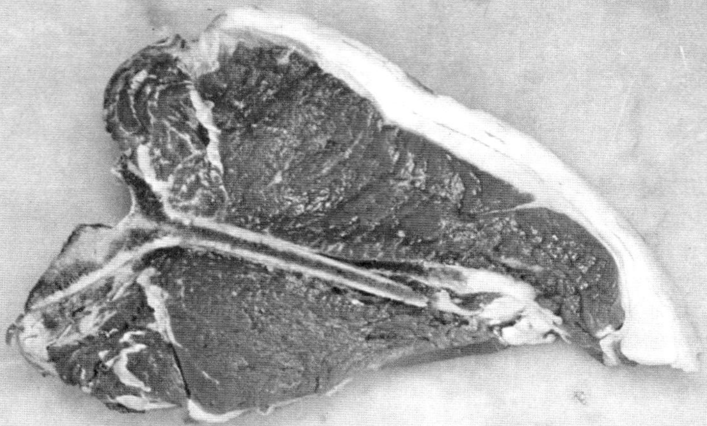

Beef – a T-bone steak

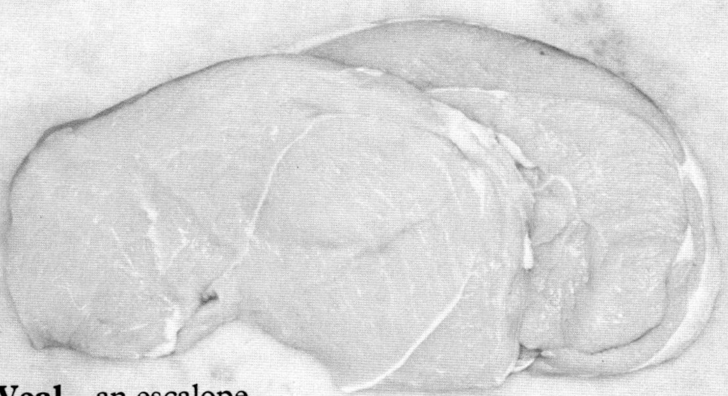

Veal – an escalope

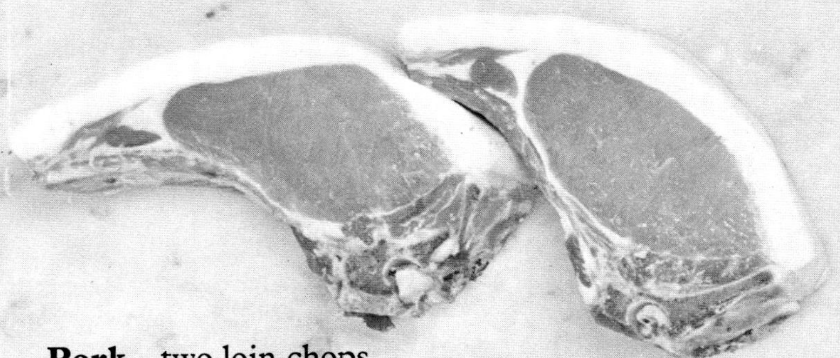

Pork – two loin chops

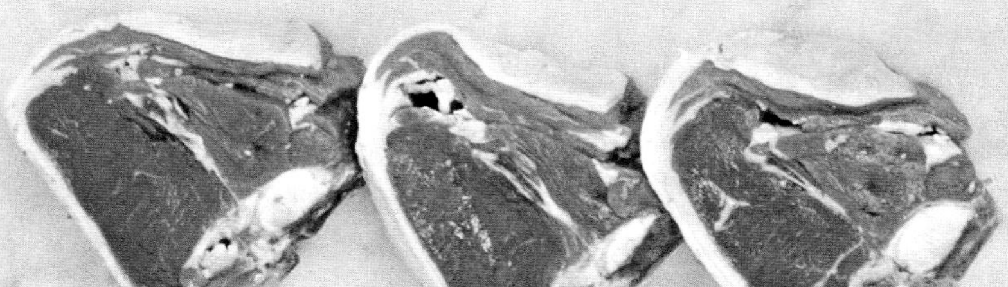

Lamb – three chump chops

Offal

Liver

The livers of calves, oxen, pigs, sheep, poultry and game are all used in cooking, but calf's liver is generally considered to be the best and is the most tender. Serve approximately 125–225 grams (4–8 ounces) per person.

Preparation: Add a little butter and oil to the frying pan and preheat. Lightly coat the liver with flour before frying.

Cooking: Frying and grilling are the best ways of cooking tender liver slices. When done, liver should be pale brown on the outside and slightly rare in the centre. If it is overcooked it will be tough.

Kidneys

Lamb and veal kidneys are the most delicate in flavour. They are suitable for grilling and frying, and need only a short cooking over medium heat. When cooked centres should remain slightly pink, since overcooking toughens them. Never boil them in a sauce; instead remove them, thicken the sauce and return them for 2–3 minutes to warm through.

Ox, pig and sheep's kidneys are tougher and have a stronger flavour. They benefit from soaking in acidulated water and from slow moist cooking.

Preparation: The white membrane around kidneys should be removed along with the fat, which is highest quality suet and should be rendered down. Allow 2–3 lambs' kidneys per person, $1\frac{1}{2}$–2 mutton, 1 small veal or pork, and $\frac{1}{2}$ or less of ox. Lay the kidneys on a wooden board and, with a pair of scissors or a sharp knife, nick the skin. Peel off the skin with your fingers, taking care not to break the flesh beneath. Remove as much of the fatty core as possible.

If the kidneys are to be grilled, slice them almost but not quite through, so that the two halves of each kidney open out flat. Wash the kidneys in cold, salted water and dry thoroughly with paper towels before using.

Cooking: Brush with melted butter before grilling, or shallow fry in half butter and half oil. Cook for about 6 minutes, turning them once.

Sweetbreads

Sweetbread is the culinary name for the neck (thymus) and the stomach (pancreas) glands of lamb, calves and bullocks. They have a delicate flavour, a close, smooth

77

texture and are rich and filling to eat. Allow between 125–175 grams (4–6 ounces).

Lamb sweetbreads are considered the finest in texture; calf sweetbreads are more economical, and also have a good texture; bullock sweetbreads, although larger and coarser, can be made tender by cooking them for 3–4 hours. They are ideal for dishes with sauces. Neck and stomach sweetbreads are both readily available, but stomach sweetbreads are more sought after because they have a smoother texture and are regular in shape.

Preparation: Place the sweetbreads in a mixing bowl and nearly fill it with cold water. Soak for 3 hours, drain and discard the water. Remove the sweetbreads from the bowl and drain them on paper towels. Remove and discard the skin and any membranes. Place the sweetbreads in a large saucepan and cover with cold water. Place the pan over moderately high heat and bring the water to the boil. Remove the pan from the heat and set aside for 10 minutes. Remove the sweetbreads from the pan and drain them on paper towels.

Cooking: Sweetbreads may be either cooked whole, sliced or chopped into pieces. They can be braised in butter and stock, shallow fried in butter or poached in various sauces.

Brains

The brains of calves, sheep and pigs are considered culinary delicacies. Calves' brains are the most popular. They are bland and need a sauce with a definite flavour. Allow 450 grams (1 pound) for four people.

Preparation: Soak the brains in cold water for at least 4 hours, changing the water frequently. Remove and discard any loose skin. Rinse the brains in tepid water to remove any clots of blood.

Cooking: Poach the brains in well-flavoured stock. Sheep's brains 15 minutes; calf's and pig's brains, 20–25 minutes. Once poached and drained, brains may be cooked in a variety of ways. One popular way is to dip them in seasoned flour, beaten egg and breadcrumbs and shallow fry until golden.

Heart

The hearts of calves, oxen, sheep and pigs can be used for economical and tasty dishes. The meat is firm, lean and close in texture.

Ox hearts weigh between 1½–2 kilograms (3–4 pounds) and serve four to six people. A calf's heart is usually enough for two and a sheep's heart will serve one. Since hearts are a lean, dry meat they are best cooked by braising, though they can also be baked, stewed and fried. When cooked whole, they are usually stuffed.

Preparation: Cut away the veins, membranes and gristle. Wash thoroughly in cold running water to remove all blood. Soak the heart in cold, salted water, or water and vinegar (1 tablespoon of vinegar to 600 millilitres [1 pint] of water). Soak a sheep's heart for 2 hours, calf's heart for 4 hours and ox heart for 8 hours or overnight. Cooking time: ox heart, 2 hours; calf's heart, 1–1½ hours; sheep's heart 45 minutes–1 hour.

Ox tongue

Ox tongue may be bought either fresh or salted from most butchers, and weighs between 2–2¾ kilograms (4–6 pounds).

Preparation: To prepare a fresh tongue for cooking, place the tongue in a large mixing bowl, cover with water and set aside for 3 hours. Drain the tongue. Scrape the skin and remove any surplus gristle. Wash the tongue and drain it.

Cooking: To cook a tongue, place it in a large saucepan and add enough water just to cover. Place the pan over moderate heat and bring the water to the boil, removing the scum as it rises to the surface. When the water boils, cover the pan and reduce the heat to low. Simmer the tongue for 5–6 hours or until the bones can be pulled away easily, and the tongue is tender when the thickest part is pierced with the point of a sharp knife. Remove from the heat and allow the tongue to cool 30 minutes in the cooking liquid. Drain and discard the cooking liquid. Place the tongue on a board and remove the skin, bones and gristle from the meat. To serve the tongue hot, serve it whole or sliced with mushrooms or madeira sauce.

Salted tongue: To prepare a salted tongue for cooking, place the tongue in a large mixing bowl, cover with water and soak for 24 hours, changing the water twice. Drain the tongue, scrape the skin and remove any surplus gristle. Wash the tongue with fresh water and drain it thoroughly again. Cook following the instructions given above for unsalted ox tongue.

Tripe

Tripe comes from the stomach linings of cattle and oxen. This lining is made up of four different parts, only three of which are sold as tripe. This explains the varied appearance of the meat. The most common varieties are honeycomb, which resembles a honeycomb, and blanket, which is fairly smooth with a slightly velvet surface.

Preparation and cooking: Tripe requires prolonged cooking, but is usually sold partly cooked, so cooking time varies according to the tripe bought. Ask the butcher for advice on its cooking time. Wash under cold running water until the water runs clear.

In general, if the tripe is bought completely uncooked, it will require 3–3½ hours simmering in salted water and or milk, or, if prepared, 1–1½ hours cooking.

Oxtail

Oxtail has a strong, meaty taste. Allow one tail for four people.

Preparation: Oxtail is sold already skinned and chopped into serving pieces.

Cooking: It is best cooked by 'moist' methods of cooking—such as braising and stewing. Prepare the day before eating, so that all excess fat may be removed. It also makes a rich meaty soup.

Trotters or feet

Pig's trotters are nutritious and inexpensive. They are generally sold cleaned and prepared for cooking.

They come in two main sizes, medium or large. (The very small trotters, called pettitoes, come from suckling pig.) Pig's trotters are usually cooked whole, but they are sometimes split in half if they are very large. Allow two medium trotters per person.

Calves' feet are also used in cooking and prepared the same way as pig's trotters. They are especially rich in gelatine and are therefore added to any savoury you want to gel, especially aspic.

Preparation: If the pig's trotters have been split, tie them together.

Cooking: To boil pig's trotters, pour 3¾ litres (6 pints) of water into a large saucepan and add flavourings such as scraped and sliced carrots, a large chopped onion, a bouquet garni, a few black peppercorns and salt to taste. Bring the water to the boil and add the trotters. Reduce the heat to low, cover the pan and simmer for 3–4 hours (depending on the

78

size of the trotters), or until they are very tender. Drain in a colander and discard the cooking liquid. The trotters are now ready to be eaten. They can also be cooked further—fry, grill or cut them into pieces to use in stews.

Head

The head of animals—ox, calf, sheep, and pig—is a source of much well-flavoured nutritious meat, such as tongue and brains. Pickled and boiled heads make very good pies and casseroles. Brawn is jellied head, usually made with calf's or pig's head, and is known as *fromage de tête* in France.

Sausage

There are two major categories of sausage: 'dry' sausages, that is sausages that, generally, may be eaten uncooked, and 'wet' sausages, which need to be cooked in some way before they are eaten.

Most sausages are made from minced pork, fat or lean, and usually seasonings and preservatives as well—the ingredients that make up commercially sold sausages are, by law, required to be stated on the label.

'Dry' sausages include salami, mortadella, garlic sausage and liver sausage. 'Wet' include frankfurters, bratwurst, Italian sausages and chorizo. Wet sausages may be boiled, grilled, baked or fried.

Poultry and Game

Poultry is the collective term used to describe domestic birds which are reared for the table. Game, on the other hand, is defined as being wild animals and birds which are hunted for sport and then prepared for eating.

Poultry includes chicken, turkey, duck, goose, guinea fowl and pigeon. Game includes grouse, partridge, pheasant, rabbit, hare and deer (which provides venison).

Poultry must be plucked, hung and drawn before cooking—jobs usually done these days by the butcher before the poultry is sold. Game is usually hung after it has been shot to allow the flesh to mature—the length of time depends on the game in question and, to some extent, the time of the year. Game is plucked and gutted immediately before it is sold—a service again usually performed by the butcher.

When you are buying fresh poultry, look for chickens with tender, firm flesh and plump breasts. Ducks should have rich, fatty flesh, while good-quality turkeys can be recognized by their firm white flesh. When you are buying fresh game, look for hare with dark flesh and plump rabbits with pale meat. Venison should be dark red with creamy white fat.

Frozen poultry and game should be thoroughly thawed before cooking. The best method for poultry is to thaw it in the refrigerator, unwrapped, which takes from 12 hours to 3 days, depending on size. Poultry giblets are usually found in a bag in the neck cavity, and the neck is placed in the body cavity.

Roasting times for individual poultry or game is given in the chart on page 98.

Chicken

Chicken is the most frequently served poultry and the most versatile. It goes well with many different sauces and vegetables and can be cooked by all the dry and moist heat methods described earlier.

Two types of chicken are on the market. **Battery** chickens have been raised indoors on a controlled diet that puts on maximum weight in minimum time, but they do not develop much flavour. However, this does not matter if the chicken is being sauced and strongly flavoured. They are the least expensive sort to buy. **Free-range** chickens mature more slowly, living outdoors, and supplement their diet by whatever they find about them to eat. They have a stronger, more interesting flavour which is suitable for simple unadorned cooking—roasting, grilling, etc. They are, however, more expensive.

Chickens have a number of other names which denote size and age. A **poussin** is a very small chicken, aged between 6–8 weeks, and weighing between 350–700g ($\frac{3}{4}$–1$\frac{1}{2}$ lb). It can be roasted, fried or grilled and is generally served either whole or split in half. **Spring** chickens are 3 months old and weigh between 1–1$\frac{1}{4}$ kg (2–2$\frac{1}{2}$ lb). **Roasting** chickens are up to 9 months old and weigh 1$\frac{1}{2}$–2 kg (3–4 lb). They are also called *cockerels, pullets* and *fat fowls*. **Capons** are castrated young cocks which have been specially fattened. Their flesh is white and delicate and they usually weigh from 2$\frac{1}{2}$–4$\frac{1}{2}$ kg (6–10 lb) and are no more than 10 months of age. **Boiling**

fowl are larger, older birds which are tougher and therefore require longer, slower cooking.

Even though the poultry you buy is supposedly oven-ready, a number of things need to be done. First, remove from the skin all remaining feathers and feather sacs. Next, cut out the oil sac at the base of the tail (it is the bump on the tail) by making a semi-circular cut above it and scraping out the yellowish oily substance, which can give the flesh an unpleasant flavour. Finally, with your fingers explore the body cavity, removing excess fat, blood vessels and soft, dark red matter from between the ribs, Sometimes the lungs have not been removed. Inspect the neck cavity. If you wash the bird, make sure the skin is thoroughly dry before roasting, or it will not brown well. Never soak it in water.

Remember that stuffing should be put into poultry only at the last minute to preclude the possibility of spoiling. Poultry placed on a high roasting rack need not be turned in order to brown evenly, although sometimes the pan needs to be turned around. To turn unstuffed poultry thrust a large wooden spoon into the cavity, lift, and rotate.

No poultry should be overcooked, because it dries out, loses flavour and become stringy. Therefore, knowing how to test for doneness is important. A boiled chicken is done when the meat feels tender when pierced with a skewer. Other chickens are done if their juices run a clear yellow rather than rosy when pierced deeply. With a whole chicken, pierce the thickest part of the thigh, since this is the slowest cooking part. A meat thermometer inserted into the thigh should read 80°–82°C (175°–180°F).

While the poultry is cooking, make stock for the gravy. Use the neck, gizzard, which should have been cut open and contents discarded (if the butcher has not done this, do the cutting well away from other cooking), feet (ask the butcher for them) and wing tips. Cut the wing tips off at the first joint before cooking; they lack meat and are not worth eating, yet they will give flavour to stock. Simmer for an hour or more with the usual ingredients (see stock page 111).

Turkey

What has been said about chicken—cleaning, doneness, stock—also applies to turkey. Modern turkeys differ from those of a generation ago in having much smaller body cavities in relation to total weight and in being more tender. The effect of this is that they hold much less stuffing than formerly. For families who like stuffing, the bird never holds enough. Therefore place extra stuffing in a small casserole, moisten it with a little strong turkey stock, cover tightly with aluminium foil, and put in the oven for the last hour of roasting.

More tender turkeys also mean they cook more quickly than formerly, so be prepared to stop the cooking a little early.

A loosely covered turkey will keep warm for a half hour or more. A warning: sometimes at Christmas so many people are cooking at the same time that gas pressure falls and oven heat is reduced. If this regularly happens in your neighbourhood, you ought to plan for it.

Duck

Duck is prized for its rich, succulent, fatty flesh. It has far less meat in relation to weight than a chicken, however. A 2 kilogram (4 pound) duck is only enough for two people, and a 2½ kilogram (6 pound) one will do for four or five.

To prepare a duck for roasting, clip the wing ends and neck, and truss it so that the wings and legs are close to the body. Prick the skin around the thighs, back and lower breast so that during roasting excess fat can run out.

Ducks are usually stuffed before roasting. After stuffing, close the cavity with a trussing needle and string or with a skewer.

Goose

Choose a goose which is not more than one year old and which has yellow feet. Since goose is not meaty allow a 3½

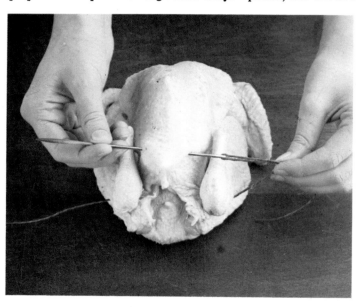

Push the needle through the lower part of the carcass. Pass the string over one drumstick, through the tip of the breastbone and over the other drumstick. Tie firmly.

Then re-thread the needle and thrust it through the top of the carcass, above the wings, where the drumstick and the second joint meet, and then out the other side.

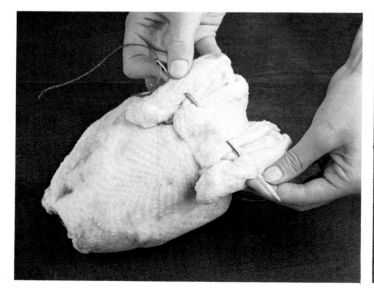

Turn the bird over and carefully push the needle through the wing, then the neck flap and finally, the other wing. Tie the string very firmly.

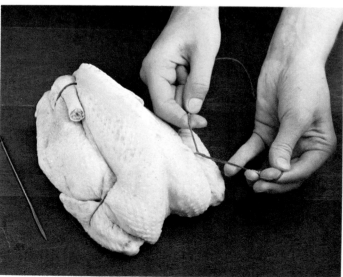

Tie the string ends together firmly. Rub salt and pepper (and any other herb of your choice) over the skin of the bird. It is now ready to be cooked.

80.

kilogram (8 pound) goose for four people, and a 4½ kilogram (10 pound) goose for six people.

Geese are usually roasted, but most methods of cooking turkey can be applied to goose. The basic method of roasting is to prick the bird all over with a fork and rub it with lemon juice, salt and pepper. The goose is placed on its breast on a rack in a roasting pan. Remove the fat from the roasting pan frequently. When the goose is half cooked, turn it over on to its back. To test if the goose is cooked, prick the thigh with the point of a sharp knife. The juices that run out should be clear.

Game

The classic way of cooking game birds is to roast them in the oven. Bard, that is, cover them well with salt pork or streaky bacon and baste them frequently during cooking because they are generally rather lean and can be dry. Often, because of their uncertain age and tenderness it is best to cook them slowly in moist heat. Braising either whole or cut into pieces is often the most satisfactory method.

Trussing Poultry

Poultry is trussed so that it keeps its shape during cooking and is therefore easier to carve.

The simplest way to truss a bird is with a skewer and a piece of string. Push the skewer through the bird just below the thigh bone. Turn the bird on to its breast. Catch in the wing pinions with the string, pass the string under the ends of the skewer and cross it over the back. Turn the bird over, pass the string over the drumsticks and tie under the parson's nose (tail).

To truss poultry in the traditional way you need to have a long trussing needle and strong fine string or trussing thread.

Carving Meat and Poultry

Carving, the cutting or slicing of large cuts of meat or whole game, is a necessary skill. Correctly carved meat prevents waste, improves presentation, saves time (thus avoiding bringing cold meat to table), and helps make the most of leftovers.

If you have any doubts about your

Pull the leg away from the body and sever it through the joint.

Carve the breast meat in slices, parallel to the breastbone.

Or cut the breast off in one piece with scissors, then halve.

81

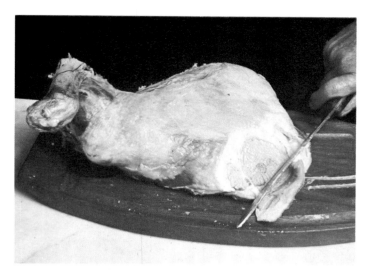

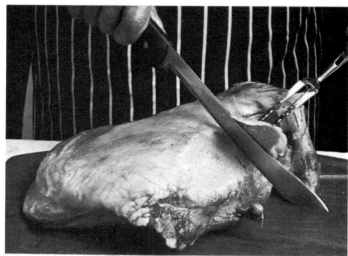

Carve the shoulder of lamb from the blade end, cutting the slices as thinly as possible, with the grain.

Turn the shoulder over and carve it into thin slices, across the thicker end of the meat.

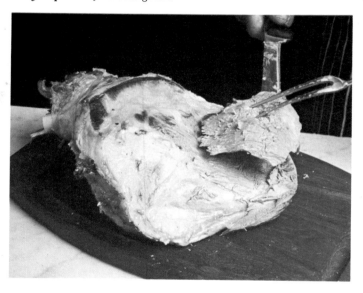

Turn the shoulder over once more, fatty side down, and cut the meat, with the grain, into thin slices.

Leg of lamb, on the bone. Begin carving from the shorter, or knuckle end in short, thick slices.

prowess as a carver, or if you are relatively new to the craft, test your expertise (or conduct your experiments, depending on how confident you are of your prowess!) in the safety and privacy of the kitchen. To make a first attempt at the table, with all hungry eyes upon you, takes courage, and in such circumstances even the strongest nerve can fail.

The most important point to remember is that each type of meat has a particular grain which, generally speaking, runs lengthways along the carcass. The meat is usually carved against the grain, because this shortens the length of the fibres and produces more tender slices. One of the few exceptions to this rule is loin of veal, which is carved with the grain.

82

Before carving the meat, remove and discard any trussing thread, string or skewers.

Avoid cutting the meat in short or deep cuts—aim for large, thin, even slices.

The pictures and directions shown are a guide to carving cuts of meat which have been cooked with the bone. Directions for boned or rolled cuts of meat are not given, because carving is simple—just remember that slices should be fairly thin.

Game

Small game birds such as pheasant, grouse and partridge are served in three different ways, according to the szie and toughness of the bird—whole (very small birds only), jointed, before or after cooking, or carved in the same way as

poultry, although sometimes only the breast is eaten.

To carve poultry

With the exception of very small birds, the legs are removed first before you carve. To do this, pull the leg away from the body with a two-pronged fork and sever through the thigh joint. Separate the drumstick from the thigh by cutting through the knee joint. To remove the wings, use the fork to hold down the pinion and cut through the shoulder joint. If the fowl is large the breast may be carved in thin slices, parallel to the breast-bone. With a smaller bird, the breast is removed in one piece and then cut in half.

If the bird has been stuffed, then this

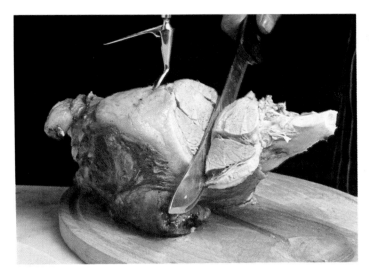

Continue carving the leg from the knuckle, graduating to longer, thinner slices, towards the aitch bone.

For loin of veal, turn the meat on to its side and steady it with a carving fork. Cut off the chine bone.

Now turn the loin over so that the fatty side is upper most and carve towards the knuckle end.

To carve gammon, grasp the knuckle bone and carve thinly towards the knuckle end, down to the leg bone.

is removed after carving and a small amount is served with the meat. When you're serving poultry, especially chicken and turkey, it is traditional to serve a little white meat (meat from the breast area) plus a little dark (from around the thighs, wings and legs) per serving— always allowing for personal preferences. of course.

Fish and shellfish

Fish

Fish is a readily available source of protein, vitamins and minerals. It is classified by its source, either fresh or salt water, and by type, white, oily or shellfish.

Since fish is extremely perishable, it must be cooked as quickly as possible after being caught, and in the interim must be kept cold.

Packets of frozen fish are a convenient way of buying. Frozen fish is often fresher than that bought from the fishmonger, because it was quick-frozen as soon as it was caught. Fish from the fishmonger can be recognized as fresh if it has a clear, shining eye and fresh-smelling flesh, and is firm when pressed gently with the fingertip.

Fish can be bought whole, in steaks or in fillets. A fishmonger will usually clean, dress and cut the fish. However, if you catch your own fish, preparation at home is not difficult.

Scaling: To scale a fish, dip it first in cold water and lay it on a board. Grasp the fish by the tail and, with a sharp knife, scrape from tail to head against the grain of the scales. Wash the fish thoroughly in cold water.

Cleaning or gutting: To clean the fish, cut off the head (if the recipe does not specify leaving it on) and make one long cut down the underside. Using a spoon, scrape out the intestines, which should come out in one piece. Wash the inside of the fish well, holding it under cold water to get rid of any remaining blood.

To clean a fish which is to be kept whole, the easy way is to slit the fish along the belly from under the head to the anus, or you can remove the intestines through the gills. Next, cut away all the fins—the pelvic fins on the underside next to the head, the pectoral fins on either side behind the gills, the dorsal fin on the back and the ventral fin, which is on the underside of the back. The fish is now ready to be cooked.

Filleting: To fillet a fish is to remove the flesh from the backbone in lengthways pieces. Some fish provide two fillets, some four. First make an incision right down the backbone. Then with short, sharp cuts, separate the flesh from the bone and carefully work the flesh away. Drop the fillets into a bowl of cold water and dry them with a clean cloth or on paper towels.

To skin the fillets, place, skin side down, on a board with the tail towards you. Put some salt on the board. Start at the tail and scrape the flesh loose with a heavy knife. Hold the salted tail with your left hand and, keeping the knife blade perpendicular to the board, push down and toward the head end while moving the knife slowly back and forth in a sawing motion. Always grasp the skin close where the knife is.

Cut fish is usually improved if the fillets or steaks are sprinkled with a little salt and left for a few minutes before cooking. They should also be rinsed in cold water to reduce cooking odours. If they are to be fried, dry them well with paper towels. As a general rule, you will require between 175–225 grams (6–8 ounces) of fish steaks or fish fillets or 450 grams (1 pound) of whole fish per person.

Cooking fish

Fish can be cooked in numerous ways – frying, grilling and poaching are perhaps best known, but steaming and baking are also suitable. The most popular method of cooking fish is shallow or deep-frying.

The length of the cooking time varies according to the method used and the type of fish, but generally the fish is cooked if it flakes easily when tested with a fork, and the flesh has turned white and opaque. Try not to overcook fish because it becomes dry and tasteless.

Fish which is to be fried is usually coated in seasoned flour, egg and breadcrumbs, or batter. It is best to deep-fry fish in vegetable oils, since they are lighter and leave the surface of the fish crisp and dry. The thinner the fish, the higher the temperature of the fat should be. Fill a large saucepan one-third full of oil. Heat the oil over moderate heat

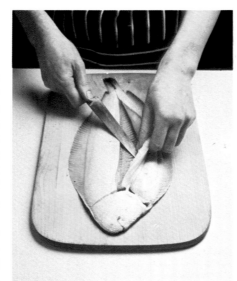

Make an incision down the backbone and carefully ease the flesh away.

Turn round so the head is facing you and remove the other fillet in the same way.

Turn the fish on to its front and remove the remaining fillets, with roes.

Carefully ease the flesh off the skin in one piece.

until it reaches 188°C (370°F) on a deep-fat thermometer, or until a cube of stale bread dropped in to the oil browns in 45 seconds. Successful deep-frying requires a frying basket which fits easily into the pan. This should be heated before the fish is put in so that the fish does not stick to the basket. Depending on the size, the coated pieces of fish will take about 3–7 minutes to cook through. The breadcrumbs should turn a light golden brown in colour. Drain the fried fish on paper towels before serving.

To grill, preheat the grill to high. Brush the fish with melted butter and place under the grill. Cook for 10–15 minutes, depending on the thickness of

the fish. Fish steaks and fillets only need to be grilled on one side until cooked through whereas whole fish must be turned to brown evenly on both sides. Whole fish should be scored with three shallow slits on each side to speed up the cooking process and to prevent curling.

Fish is poached in milk, court bouillon, fish stock, wine and water. It can be done on top of the stove or in the oven. To poach in the oven, preheat it to moderate 180°C (Gas Mark 4, 350°F). Lay the fish in a shallow baking dish. Heat the poaching liquid until it is boiling and pour it over the fish. Cover the dish loosely and place it in the oven. When poaching on top of the stove, place the fish in warm, not boiling, liquid and bring it to near the boil. Reduce the heat to low and poach the fish until it is cooked. Allow 10–12 minutes per half kilo (8–10 minutes per pound) for large whole fish, 15–20 minutes in all for small whole fish like plaice, flounder or sole, 8–12 minutes for fillets and 10–15 minutes for steaks lying in a single layer in the dish. An onion, lemon slices, chopped carrots and celery may be put in the poaching liquid to add flavour to the fish. For the jug method of poaching smoked fish fillets, see page 74.

Steaming is the best way of retaining flavour in a delicate lean fish. Put the fish on an ovenproof plate or dish and moisten with water, court bouillon, etc. Either put into the top part of a double boiler or put into a colander set over a pan half full of simmering water. Cover tightly and cook for the same time as for poaching.

To bake a whole fish, lay the fish on a large piece of aluminium foil. Place a bay leaf, salt, pepper and thin slices of onion and lemon inside the fish. Rub the fish all over with oil, if you are eating it cold, or butter if it is to be served hot. Wrap the fish like a parcel, leaving space inside for the air to circulate, and carefully fold the edges to seal. Place the fish in a roasting pan and bake it in the oven preheated to 150°C (Gas Mark 2, 300°F). A 1–1½ kilograms (2–3 pound) fish will take about 1 hour. Carefully remove the fish from the foil and, while it is still hot, remove the skin gently with a knife. This is a particularly good way of cooking salmon and salmon trout.

Shellfish

Shellfish is the collective term for all edible crustacea and molluscs. Among these are clams, crabs, lobsters, mussels, oysters, prawns and shrimps. Overheating and overcooking both ruin the delicate flavour and texture of shellfish. Therefore use low heat and cook the minimum possible time. Serve hot dishes at once.

Bivalves

Bivalves, or two-shelled molluscs, include clams, cockles, mussels and oysters. All are prepared in the same way, and all can be eaten raw or cooked.

To prepare bivalves, wash thoroughly in several changes of cold water and scrub with a stiff brush to remove all

Types of Fish (or categories of fish)		
White Fish	**Oily Fish**	**Other**
Bass (sea wolf, sea perch, sea salmon, white salmon)	Carp	Salted:
	Conger eel	Bloater (herring)
Bream	Eel	Buckling (herring)
Brill	Herring (sprat, whitebait)	Kipper (herring)
Catfish	Mackerel	Smoked:
Cod	Mullet (red, grey)	Cod
Coley (coal fish, saithe)	Perch	Haddock
Dab	Pilchard	Mackerel
Dogfish (rock eel)	Salmon	Salmon
(Flounder)	Sardine	Trout
Haddock	Smelt	
Hake (stockfish)	Trout (brown, salmon or sea, lake)	Octopus
Halibut		Squid
Lemon sole	Tuna, tunny	
Pike		
Plaice		
Rock Salmon		
Skate (ray)		
Sole (common, Dover or black)		
Turbot		
Whiting		

mud and seaweed from the shells. On mussels, use a sharp knife to scrape off the tufts of hair, or beards, that protrude from between the closed shells. Discard any shells that are not shut tightly or do not close when tapped; also discard those with broken shells.

After cleaning place the bivalves in a bowl of lightly salted cold water and let them stand for an hour. If they are to stand longer than this some people add a little cornmeal, oatmeal or flour to the water.

Opening the shells is something of an art, since you must slide a knife between the shells and break the hinge. If you do this often a special oyster knife is a great help. Always open bivalves over a basin in which to catch the juice, which should be kept frozen to add to, or use in place of, fish stock.

To steam, pour barely enough water into a large saucepan to cover the bottom. Add a teaspoon of salt, bouquet garni, and any other flavourings, depending on the ultimate use. Place the bivalves in the pan, cover tightly and place over high heat. Shake the pan frequently so that the shells move around. Cook until the shells open, which is generally 6–10 minutes. If any shells are still closed, discard them. Either serve the cooking

liquid with the bivalves or save it for another use.

Prawns

The prawn family—shrimps, prawns and scampi or Dublin Bay prawns—are free-swimming crustacea with soft, translucent shells. They come in sizes ranging from about 2½ centimetres (1 inch) shelled to more than 10–12 centimetres (4–5 inches), and have flavours that differ somewhat depending on variety and location. Cold-water prawns are supposed to have more flavour than those from tropical waters.

Prawns are available throughout the year. They are sold fresh, canned, frozen, dried, potted and cooked and peeled. Unfortunately uncooked prawns are hard to find in many areas.

Raw prawns can be cooked either before or after shelling. If they are to be used cold they are cooked in the shell.

To cook, first rinse the prawns well under cold water, which not only cleans them but will virtually eliminate cooking odours. Bring water to the boil, add the prawns and simmer for 3–6 minutes, depending on size. Stop the cooking as soon as they have changed colour. Do not overcook, for this makes them rubbery. Drain, cool and peel.

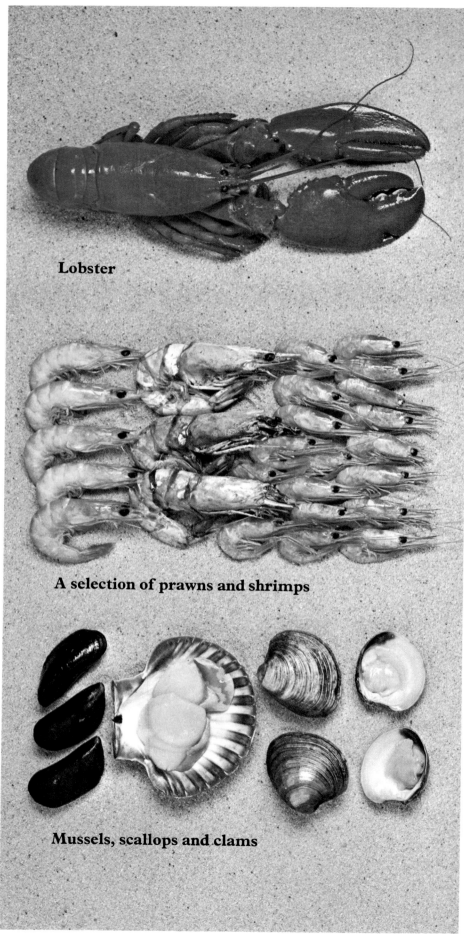

Lobster

A selection of prawns and shrimps

Mussels, scallops and clams

To peel either cooked or raw prawns, pull the head end off gently with the fingers, remove the legs and then the back shell. Depending on the recipe leave the tail on or gently pull it off. Unless the vein running along the top of the back is black, do not remove it. If it must be removed, scrape it out with the sharp point of a knife. Cooked prawns should be added to sauces at the last minute and cooked only long enough to heat them through.

Scallops

Scallops *(pectens maximus)*, also known as Coquilles St Jacques, are shellfish found around the coasts of France and the United States. They have two shells, one flat and the other concave, which contain the edible muscle flesh. Fresh scallops should have white flesh and a vivid orange or coral roe. Scallops are in season from November to March and reach their peak in January and February.

Scallops are usually sold already opened. If this has not been done, however, treat as you would any other bivalve. Remove the flat shells with a knife or place them with the flat shell uppermost in a warm place, where they will open of their own accord. Using a sharp knife, remove the flesh from the shell and cut away the black gristly fibre attached to the flesh. The scallops are now ready for cooking. Do not discard the scallop shells; they may be washed, scrubbed and used as containers for scalloped dishes.

Poach in court bouillon or lightly salted water, for 8–10 minutes or until the flesh is firm. To fry scallops, either marinate them in a mixture of olive oil and lemon juice for 30 minutes or poach and drain them. Coat the scallops in either case with beaten egg and bread-crumbs or batter and fry them for 8–10 minutes or until they are lightly browned all over.

Lobsters and crabs

Lobsters and crabs may differ in appearance, but both can be treated in the same manner. Also given similar treatment are crawfish and crayfish. The crawfish, or spiny lobster *(langouste* in France), differs from the lobster in that its front legs do not have enlarged pincers. Crayfish are small fresh-water creatures resembling lobsters.

If you are buying live lobsters or crabs, see that they are active. A dead or dying one should never be cooked. The most usual way of cooking lobster is to boil it. There are several ways of doing this. The first, and reputedly more humane, method is to place the lobster or crab in a large saucepan. Cover it with cold salted water and bring it to the boil very slowly over moderately low heat. When the water comes to the boil, increase the heat to moderately high and boil the lobster for 20 minutes, the crab for 10–15 minutes per half kilo or pound.

The second method is to plunge the lobster head-first into boiling water and then cook it for 20 minutes. Cool the lobster in the cooking liquid. This is not suitable for crab.

Alternatively, it may be killed before cooking. Tie the claws together and lay on a chopping board. With a towel wrapped around one hand for protection, grasp the lobster firmly. With a large, heavy, sharp knife, cut through behind the head to sever the spinal cord. Then sever the spinal column just behind the eyes.

Lobster may also be grilled. First kill the lobster, then slit it in two lengthwise. Remove the sac and the intestines. Brush the lobster halves with butter or oil and season with salt and pepper. Preheat the grill to high. Place the lobster in the grill pan, shell side down, and grill for 12–15 minutes or until it is cooked through. Serve the lobster halves in their shells, garnished with parsley and lemon wedges.

To prepare a boiled lobster for the table, first twist off the large claws. Crack them with a nutcracker or a light hammer through the centre and at the joint. Remove the smaller claws which are used for garnishing. Using a large pointed knife, split the lobster from head to tail down the middle. Remove the sac, intestines and gills. Retain the liver. To serve, arrange it with the head upright and the split tail and claws around it. Garnish with parsley and lemon wedges.

To prepare the crab, follow the step by step instructions on the right.

Crabmeat is generally mashed and seasoned with salt, pepper, mustard and vinegar. The meat can then be piled back into the shell and garnished. Most fishmongers will 'dress' a crab in this way if given adequate notice.

Fresh crayfish are green or brown, but turn bright red in cooking. If they are very fresh and have recently been in flowing water they do not need to be

To extract meat from a crab, remove the legs and pincers, then pull the body away.

Pull off any gills or 'dead mans fingers' and scoop out meat from the claws.

Carefully remove the stomach bag and any spongy matter from the shell.

Scoop out the flesh from the shell and add it to the claw meat.

gutted before boiling. Otherwise they should be washed under cold running water before cooking, and the bitter-flavoured intestinal tube beneath the tail should be removed. Then place them in salted water or court bouillon, bring to the boil and simmer for 5–7 minutes.

To gut the crayfish, hold it firmly in the left hand and with the fingers of the right hand pull the middle fin on the tail with a sharp twist, removing the stomach and intestines with it. Wash the crayfish well in running water.

Snails

Both land and sea snails are eaten throughout the world. In size they range from the giant conch of tropical waters to small periwinkles.

Periwinkle, also called **winkle,** is the common name of small edible sea snails. There are 80 species but the Common Periwinkle is the largest in size and the one found in the greatest numbers around the coasts of Northern Europe and Northeastern North America. Periwinkles are known as **vignots** in France, where they are sold cooked on the streets or made into soup. To cook periwinkles, first wash them in plenty of water. Soak them for 10 minutes and wash them again to remove any sand. Drain the periwinkles and cook them in plenty of boiling, salted water for 20 minutes.

The **whelk** is another small marine mollusc found along the Atlantic coasts of Europe and North America. They are a popular food, especially in parts of northern Europe, and have a hard, chewy texture, even when they are cooked. To prepare whelks, wash them thoroughly several times in clean water to remove all the sand, then simmer them in boiling salted or sea water for 30 minutes. Drain them and remove the flesh from the shell by inserting a pin and pulling.

Vegetables and fruits

Vegetables and fruits require far more careful handling than other foods. Many are delicate, bruise easily, and must be used as soon after purchase or picking as possible. Both contain a high percentage of water, many vitamins and minerals but little fat. Thus they supply essential nutrients and some roughage without many calories and so make good between-meal snacks.

Vegetables

Vegetables are probably the most neglected and badly prepared items in our diet. They often seem less interesting and more fussy to cook than other parts of the meal, because they must be done quickly at the last minute when other things also need attention.

Vegetables are versatile; they can be served alone or in combination, raw or cooked, sauced or plain. Some, like aubergines, dried beans and onions, are notable for blending well with other ingredients and are used in casseroles, flans and other cooked dishes; others, like fresh peas, French and runner beans, do best on their own. Most vegetables can be cooked by several methods. Almost all can be either boiled or steamed, most root and non-green vegetables can also be braised and sometimes fried, baked and roasted. For specific information on cooking methods and times see the chart on pages 100–107.

Always check vegetables for doneness before the minimum suggested cooking time is up, and stop the cooking if they seem done. Timing is difficult to judge because so many variables are involved: age, freshness, variety (for instance, maincrop potatoes take longer than new ones of the same diameter), size and thickness. Even weather plays a part. Often, owing to plant breeding, modern vegetables (like modern poultry) take less time to cook than the old varieties.

Ideally, vegetables should be eaten immediately after picking, though some, especially roots, store well. Since this is not possible for most people you should search out a supplier—corner green-grocer, supermarket—with good produce and get to know the days when fresh supplies arrive; for those are the days on which to shop. Vegetables with a lot of natural sugars need to be eaten most quickly; foremost among these are sweetcorn and peas followed by leafy vegetables like spinach, spring greens, asparagus, French and other fresh beans, courgettes and aubergines. Green vegetables should be stored unwashed in a polythene bag to retain moisture. Keep them at a temperature of about 7°C (45°F), which generally means the vegetable bin in the refrigerator. Certain thick-skinned vegetables like potatoes, turnips and onions should be stored in a cool dark place between 12°–18°C (55°–65°F). But remember that onions hasten the spoilage of potatoes; likewise apples cause carrots to take on a bitter taste.

Other things to remember are:

1. Never wash vegetables until you are ready to use them, because water dissolves away water-soluble vitamins.
2. Never soak vegetables in water after preparing them for the same reason; instead place in a polythene bag if you have to prepare them in advance. A few exceptions are noted in the table on pages 100–107.
3. Make sure the entire top of root vegetables has been removed before storage, or the root will continue to supply the stem with nutrients. One exception is red beetroot, whose skin should not be damaged in any way or the root will 'bleed' and lose its colour during cooking.
4. Try to use vegetable cooking water when making sauces or soups; in this way nutrients that are leached out can still be used.

Preparation differs greatly from vegetable to vegetable (see pages 100–107 for details). Most should be carried out as close to cooking time as possible. Invest in a good peeler, and peel vegetables thinly, since flavour and nutrients are just under the skin. Do not bother to peel young carrots, especially for stews; potatoes can be roasted cut but unpeeled, and baked. When you top and tail (take off ends of vegetables such as French beans) or cut off dried up surfaces (like the bases of sprouts), remove as little as possible. Cut vegetables into uniform lengths or chunks, so that all will cook in the same length of time. Do not salt the water until the cooking process is under way.

Boiling is the most common method of cooking vegetables, but you are unlikely to find much agreement about methods. The major controversy is how much water to use. On one side stand those who believe in a minimum: they claim that fewer vitamins are lost in this way and in fact since this method requires that the pan be tightly covered, the vegetables are as much steamed as boiled.

On the other side are arrayed believers in the French method, which uses large pans and lots of boiling water. They claim the vegetables are in the water for less time, since the water returns to a boil more quickly after the vegetables are added. A third school uses just enough water to cover the vegetables. The last method, most agree, is suited for long-cooking, starchy vegetables.

Faced with this conflicting advice, you need to take into account your own preferences and equipment. If your saucepans are small, opt for the first method, or for the third if you tend to burn things. You may find that you prefer to cook different vegetables by different methods.

A second area with many opinions is whether to start in cold or boiling water. One general rule followed by some says root vegetables, because they grow underground, should be started in cold water with a lid on the pan, whereas above ground vegetables, which grow in the sun, should be put into boiling water and cooked uncovered or partly covered. When you consult cookbooks, you will find each one has its own unique exceptions to this general rule. So it's probably best to try the various methods amd decide which one gives *you* the best results.

Vegetables should be cooked at just above the simmer after being brought rapidly to the boil. Many deteriorate with fierce or prolonged heat.

Agreement is closer to universal on when vegetables are done: tender but still firm, not soft and mushy. Ideally, at the point of doneness, you should drain the vegetables and serve them at once. Even if they must wait a few minutes, drain them immediately, since as long as they are in hot water they continue to cook. Here the sequence becomes drain, refresh in (that is, place under) cold running water for a brief minute to reduce the temperature just to below the cooking point, and put in a warmed serving dish in a warm place, no more than partly covered to allow steam to escape. Remember the longer your vegetable waits, the more tired and less delectable it becomes.

If your vegetables are going to have a long wait, refresh them until cool while they are still slightly underdone. This will stop the cooking completely. Then just before serving either plunge them into lots of rapidly boiling water for just long enough to heat through, or toss them over moderate heat in melted butter until they are hot and well coated.

Steaming vegetables takes a little longer than boiling them. They are placed in a steaming basket or pan and set over boiling water, tightly covered. This method gives consistently good results and is supposed to retain more nutrients than boiling.

Other cooking methods are braising, baking, roasting and frying. These are not suitable for all vegetables but are useful. Braising requires a frying pan with a tightly fitted lid. You begin by coating uniformly sized and preferably thin vegetables with a minimum of hot fat, then adding a little liquid, covering tightly and bringing to the boil. Reduce heat and steam the vegetables. Shake the pan regularly to prevent sticking. An alternative but slower method is to place the covered vegetables in the oven after they have come to the boil.

Roasting and baking are used mostly for root vegetables such as potato, onion, parsnip and turnip. In roasting, the peeled vegetables are coated with hot dripping either under a joint of meat or poultry or in a seperate pan. They are then cooked in the oven for 45 minutes to 1 hour or more depending on oven temperature and vegetable size. Baste several times with dripping and turn over to ensure even browning. Sometimes to achieve faster cooking and greater heat penetration, the vegetable is first parboiled (partly cooked) for 5–15 minutes. Baking is done with the skin still on (although it is often pricked with a fork) and in dry heat. The vegetables are placed on a rack so air can circulate around them and cooked for about an hour, timing depending on size and temperature. They are done when they feel soft when squeezed (pick them up in a potholder). Sometimes skin is removed before serving (onions); at other times it is left on (potatoes).

Frying of many sorts is popular. Deep-frying is used mainly for potatoes, parsnips and other hard vegetables. The requirements are the same as for meat and fish—fat heated to the correct temperature, vegetables absolutely free of water, and batter coating left to dry for about 10 minutes.

Stir-frying is an oriental method of quick cooking which has become popular in the west. A little oil is heated until very hot, then thinly sliced vegetables are added. These are stirred and turned constantly using two spoons or spatulas. With mixed vegetables, longer cooking types are added first, shorter cooking ones later. When the vegetables are barely tender, about 150 millilitres (5 fluid ounces) of stock is added and the pan tightly covered, allowing the vegetables to steam for 2–8 minutes. The pan is uncovered and a teaspoon of cornflour mixed with water or soya sauce is stirred in to thicken the liquid. The vegetables should be only crisp tender.

Vegetables are also excellent raw. Indeed far more vegetables than most people realize can be enjoyed in this way, and these are listed in the vegetable table (pages 100–107). Raw vegetables can be used in salads and as garnishes. They can also be served with pre-dinner drinks as a healthy substitute for crisps, and as between meal snacks. As a drink accompaniment, raw vegetables should be chilled and cut into bite-sized pieces. Serve them alone or follow the North American custom by supplying dips. However, if you base your dips on soured cream both the fat and calorie intake are increased. By substituting yogurt for soured cream, you can make a healthier dip.

Dried legumes

Dozens of varieties of dried beans and peas are available, often from foreign countries and with foreign names. This and the frequent lack of information on the package cause inhibitions about cooking them. But as the price of meat goes up, they are going to become a more important part of our diet.

Beans are a good source of vegetable protein, though none contains all the essential amino acids (see page 140) and therefore they should not be your only protein source. They benefit from good seasoning including tomatoes, onions, garlic and chilli.

Soya beans are a particularly useful form of protein for vegetarians: the beans are extruded to form soya protein (TVP) which can be used as a meat substitute.

Cooking times for beans are difficult to determine because they depend on so many variables: where they were grown, weather during the growing season, time elapsed since drying, length of soaking. Most of these are unknown to the cook. Also significant is how you are using them. If they are for a purée or soup you will cook them longer than if they are to be served whole as a vegetable.

Unless the beans are preprocessed (which is more common in North

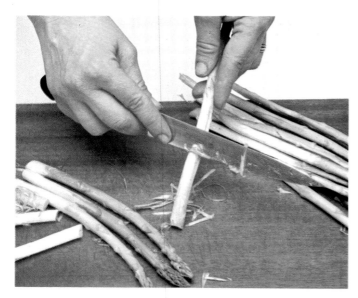

Top left: to prepare asparagus, peel and scrape the stalks thickly at the butt end and very thinly towards the tip.

Bottom left: wash the stalks and tie them into neat bundles with string – not more than 10 stalks to a bundle. Trim to even sizes.

Above: stand in a jar of boiling water and cover with pierced foil. Boil in a pan of boiling water for 15-20 minutes or until tender.

America than elsewhere), they need to be washed and then soaked in three to four times their volume of water for at least six hours but for less than 12 – a longer soaking period leads to fermentation. Discard any that float. As an alternative to soaking put the washed beans in cold water to cover, bring them to the boil and simmer for 2 minutes. Cover and remove from the heat: then let stand for 1 hour. The beans are then ready for cooking. Lentils need little or no soaking.

Unless the soaking water has become bitter, use it for the long slow simmering, since it contains nutrients leached from the beans. Remember 1 cup of dried beans expands to 2–2½ cups while cooking Therefore start with the pan less than half full.

Frozen vegetables

Frozen vegetables, with the exception of spinach, should not be thawed before cooking. Drop into a minimum of boiling water and cook, covered, for only a short time—indeed, generally less time than the package suggests. Spinach as it thaws produces a lot of water, so you need add no more. Cook it uncovered to heat it through and allow most of the moisture to evaporate.

Preparing vegetables

Certain techniques are used time and again in cooking, for instance mincing and dicing vegetables and parsley, preparing mushrooms, peeling and seeding tomatoes, and parboiling, blanching and refreshing vegetables.

Mincing or dicing: Mincing or dicing means cutting into small cubes. This technique is used especially for onions, garlic, carrots, celery and sometimes green or red peppers. Mincing parsley means a much finer preparation.

Minced onion is the most frequently called for in recipes. First cut off the brown tip of the onion and peel off the skin; do nothing to the root end where the tear-inducing oils are located. Next cut the onion in half through the root end and tip. Place the onion, cut side down, on a cutting board with root to your left. Make many parallel cuts from root to tip without cutting through the root. Hold the onion together with your fingers while you make several slices parallel to the cutting board. Again, make sure not to cut through the root end. Finally, starting at the tip end and

To prepare artichoke hearts, bend back the lower leaves of each artichoke until they snap off.

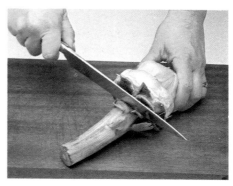
Remove all the outer leaves until you reach those bending inwards. With a sharp knife slice off the stalk.

Arrange the artichoke on its side and cut off the remaining leaves just above the white heart.

Rotating the base of the artichoke against the knife blade, trim off all the green leaf bases.

still holding the onion together with your left hand, cut down towards the board. Discard the root. The fineness of the mincing depends on how close to each other the cuts are. To slice an onion, cut the onion in half and then make cuts at right angles to the board.

Garlic and shallots are minced in the same manner, though fewer cuts can be made. To remove onion and garlic smells from your hands, wash them in cold water, sprinkle with salt and rub into the skin well, rinse again in cold water. Repeat if necessary. Avoid getting salt in open cuts, since it burns them.

Carrots and celery use a modified versions of the onion technique. Hold one end in the left hand and make lengthwise cuts through the vegetable. With the carrot or thick celery, slice through parallel to the table once or twice. Lastly, slice down starting at the right end and working to the left. Use the parsley technique below to turn diced celery into a finer mince. Minced or chopped parsley implies flakes so fine you can't see the leaf structure. It is advisable to wash parsley well ahead so that the leaves will be dry when you be-

gin chopping. Break off the stems (save them in the freezer for *bouquets garnis*) and gather the rest into a small pile. With a very sharp knife make many cuts through the leaves.

The technique is to hold the knife point loosely in the left hand and move the handle up and down with the right hand. Slightly change the location of the handle with each stroke. Frequently regather the parsley and cut some more.

Preparing mushrooms: Cultivated mushrooms are sorted in to three grades: button (small unopened), cup (slightly opened), and flat (completely opened). The cups and flats can be large or small. Both the caps and the stalks are used in cooking.

Mushrooms that are to be fried or grilled should not be washed under running water. Instead they should be wiped clean with dampened fingers or a cloth. Washing affects those which are to be boiled or put in stews less adversely.

Mushrooms should be peeled only if a very white surface is needed or if the peelings are needed for another purpose (perhaps a stuffing for tomatoes or mushrooms). Under no circumstances

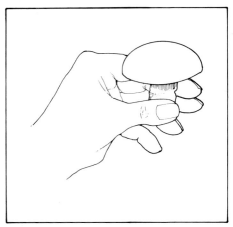

To peel a mushroom, hold the stem in your hand, gill side down.

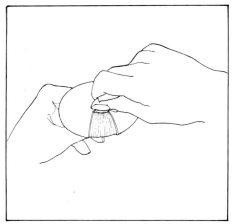

Put your thumb under the edge of the cap and pull gently towards the centre.

Chinese mushrooms need to be soaked gently before being used.

To peel a tomato, put it into a pan of boiling water and leave for a little.

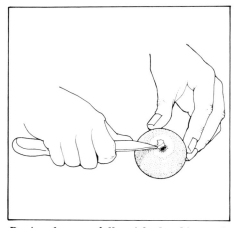

Drain, then carefully nick the skin at the stem end with a knife.

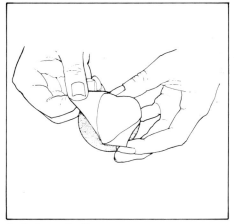

Pull the peel off gently with your fingers — it should come away easily.

Dried mushrooms of both the European and Chinese type require a preliminary soaking in cold water for 30 minutes before they can be used. Often the stem does not soften and must be cut off. Use the soaking water with discretion, since it is strongly flavoured.

Peeling and seeding tomatoes: The skin and seeds are removed from tomatoes because they tend to be tough and bitter. Do the seeding over a small strainer and bowl so that the juice is conserved for adding to stews or sauces.

Either put the tomatoes into a heat-proof bowl and pour over boiling water to cover; leave for 1 minute. Drain. Or half fill a saucepan with water and bring to the boil. Drop one tomato at a time into the boiling water to cover completely and count to eight slowly. Remove it with the slotted spoon and drop it into a bowl of cold water. Now nick the skin at the stem end with a knife, and with the fingers pull off the peel. If the tomatoes are to be cut into strips or left in pieces, cut into quarters With your thumb, scoop out the seeds. If the tomato is to be used whole, cut off the top (which is the end opposite where the stem was attached) and use a spoon to scoop out the seeds.

Parboiling, blanching and refreshing: Parboiling and blanching both refer to the partial cooking of foods, usually vegetables. Parboiling means the cooking process is begun in boiling water and continues only for a short time, usually no more than 10 minutes. The food is then drained and finished by another method, usually roasting or baking. Vegetables receiving this process are long-cooking ones, such as potatoes.

Blanching means to plunge a vegetable or fruit into boiling water to harden it or partly to cook it. Most vegetables must be blanched before freezing to retard enzyme action and prevent 'off' flavours. Blanching is also used to remove too strong a taste, such as for cabbage, onions and smoked bacon.

Generally, after vegetables have been blanched, they are refreshed. To refresh means to plunge hot foods into cold water, thus stopping the cooking process. In some cases refreshing means thoroughly to cool the food, in others it means only to reduce temperature below the cooking point but to leave it hot. In the latter case putting the vegetables under running water is usually enough.

should peelings be discarded, because they are flavourful.

The peeling technique is simple for flats and rather open cups. Hold the mushroom in the left hand with the gill side down. Place the right thumb under

the edge of the cap, grasping the black edging found on many mushrooms. Pull up and toward the centre, and the skin will peel off in thin strips. To mince the peels and stems as well, use the parsley technique.

Salad greens

Salad greens consist mainly of lettuces, which range from crisp in texture to soft, but also include watercress, endive, chicory and spinach. All should be washed in a minimum amount of water and then dried thoroughly before use, so that the dressing will adhere well. Sometimes salads are made from whole leaves, but large leaves can make serving awkward. Always tear salad greens into pieces rather than cut them.

If you are preparing in advance, the washed, torn greens can be stored in the refrigerator for up to four hours in a polythene bag, and for up to two in the salad bowl. Other vegetables, except tomatoes and olives, can be added at preparation time. Incorporate non-vegetables and olives just before dressing, tomatoes after dressing. The salad dressing can be made in advance too, but it should be added only at the last minute. (Dressing added in advance makes the lettuce go limp.)

Tossing the salad means lifting the lettuce up with two forks or a salad serving set, and letting it fall back into the bowl. This should be done until the dressing lightly coats the surface of the leaves. There should be no excess in the bottom of the bowl. Allow about two tablespoons of made dressing for four people. (See also salad dressing on page 120.)

Fruit

Fruits are one of the most versatile and enjoyable elements in our diet. Most contain necessary vitamins and minerals, and with a few exceptions they are low in calories but have enough carbohydrates (sugars) to assuage hunger and provide pick-up energy. They are welcome at the end of a heavy meal, because they are light and easy to eat. Fruits can be used in starters and in summer luncheon salads. Some are also used as accompaniments to meat and fish.

All fruits are at their best when tree or vine ripened and freshly picked. Then they are unsurpassed eaten raw and virtually unadorned. But fruit is also good cooked and processed in other ways.

Storage

Fruits differ greatly in how they should be stored and how long they will keep. Most fruits when fully ripe should be refrigerated or placed in a cold larder to retard spoilage. Fruits that need to ripen should be kept at about 20°C (68°F) in a dark place. Avocados and bananas both ripen more quickly in a paper bag. The major exception to refrigeration is bananas, which blacken when chilled. Under normal kitchen conditions few fruits will keep more than a week.

The following points are worth remembering.
1. Store under-ripe fruit at a warm room temperature in a dark place. Examine twice a day for ripeness and refrigerate when ripe.
2. To test large fruits for ripeness, gently press the flesh at the stem end; when ripe it will feel soft.
3. Handle all fruits with care because bruised areas spoil. Buy fruit last so it will be at the top of your shopping bag; never drop fruit into a bag.
4. Berries and other small, soft fruits spoil rapidly, so refrigerate and use within 36 hours. Spread highly perishable fruits, like raspberries and blackberries, in a single layer on a tray to retard mould; inspect carefully before using.
5. Some fruits, notably melons and pineapple, have a lovely aroma when ripe.

A varied selection of succulent fresh fruit in season.

To prepare a fresh pineapple, first cut off a 2½cm (1in) slice from both the top and the bottom.

Stand the pineapple upright on a board and, using a sawing motion, cut thick strips downwards.

Turn the pineapple on its side and cut out the prickly pieces in a spiral, following the shape of the fruit.

Using a small pastry cutter or knife, remove the centre core as this is hard and unpleasant to eat.

To prepare a fresh pineapple as a container, cut between the flesh and the peel, following the fruit's contours.

Carefully ease the flesh from inside the peel. The flesh can now be chopped with other fruit and returned.

6. Citrus fruit and pineapple do not continue ripening further after picking; green peaches will soften but won't ripen.

Many raw fruits become quickly discoloured when peeled and sliced, unless counter measures are taken; namely placing in acidulated water (which will lead to some loss of nutrients) or sprinkling with lemon or pineapple juice. The quickest to discolour are apples, avocado, bananas and pears. Be sure to use a stainless steel knife which does not discolour fruits.

Frozen fruits tend to become mushy and lose their shape when thawed. They are fine for cooking or sauces, but if you want to use a few for garnishes be sure they are still partly frozen. Chill tinned fruits before serving for a more attractive taste.

Cooking fruit

Cook fruit by poaching (see page 74) rather than boiling or simmering. Drop the fruit into the boiling liquid and reduce the heat to low. Do not allow the fruit to overcook; it should remain firm but tender. Remove from the liquid the instant it has cooked enough. If the fruit is to be served in the cooking liquid cool it rapidly by putting the saucepan bottom into cold water. Cooking time will depend on the hardness of the fruit and its size. Not surprisingly, ripe peaches need only a few minutes whereas apples take much longer.

Puréed fruits are cut into small pieces and cooked in only enough water to cover the bottom of the pan to 1–2 centimetres (½–1 inch), depending on the amount of moisture in the fruit. Again, cooking should be over low heat. The fruit should be stirred several times during cooking since that on the bottom will soften first. The fruit is cooked when it is very tender and mashes easily. Add sugar at this point rather than earlier; less will be needed to achieve the same amount of sweetness.

If you wish to remove the skin from fruit, such as peaches, plunge into hot water and follow the instructions given for tomatoes (page 92).

Dried fruits

Many common fruits can be dried at home, while others are easily bought. Most dried fruits can be used either before or after soaking and cooking. Soaking should not be for longer than necessary for softening, since the water-soluble nutrients are being leached out. With experience you can learn to use just enough water so that all but a little has been absorbed when the soaking period is up. Try to use any remaining water in the recipe. If you are stewing the fruit use the soaking liquid, adding more if needed.

Store dried fruits, tightly covered, in a cool, dark cupboard. Once opened, packages of dried fruits will begin to deteriorate after a few months. Keep them in a tightly closed polythene bag or other air-tight container.

If the fruit becomes too dried out, it can be 'revived' by steaming. One method is to put the fruit in the top of a double saucepan, sprinkle with a liquid, cover tightly and place over hot, not boiling, water for 10–15 minutes. Alternatively the fruit can be placed in a steamer over a little boiling water, which also tenderizes.

Raisins can be plumped by washing briefly, draining and spreading them in a single layer in a tightly covered pan. Put the pan in a 180°C (Gas Mark 4 350°F) oven for 10 minutes or more until they are fat and unwrinkled. Or soak them for 10–15 minutes in the cooking liquid.

Meat chart

Meat	Suitable for	Cut
Beef	**Roasting**	Ribs (top, fore, back), sirloin, top rump, fillet
	Braising or pot roasting	Brisket, silverside, thick flank, topside
	Stewing	Chuck (also called shoulder, blade bone), leg, neck, oxtail, shin, skirt, thick flank, salted brisket or silverside.
	Frying or grilling	Fillet, entrecote, rump, porterhouse and sirloin steaks, minute steak
Lamb	**Roasting**	All cuts except scrag end and chops or cutlets
	Braising	Leg, boned and stuffed, shoulder, stuffed breast
	Boiling	Leg (bone-in or boned and stuffed)
	Stewing	Breast, scrag and middle neck, shoulder
	Frying or grilling	Loin, chump, best end of neck chops, cutlets
Pork	**Roasting**	Leg, loin, blade, hand and spring, spare ribs, chops, head
	Braising	Spare ribs, cutlets, neck chops
	Stewing	Fillet (has no fat) or braising cuts (fatty so cook a day in advance).
	Boiling	All cuts especially salt belly of pork

Preparation	Cooking Time	Internal Temperature
Preheat oven to 220°C (Gas Mark 7, 425°F). After cooking for 15 minutes reduce temp. to 180°C (Gas Mark 4, 350°F)	Rare: 16 minutes to the half kilo (15 „ „ „ pound) Medium: 27 minutes to the half kilo (25 „ „ „ pound) Boned and rolled: 32 minutes to the half kilo (30 „ „ „ pound) plus 32 (30) minutes over.	60°C (140°F) 72°C (160°F) 80°C (175°F)
Preheat oven to 180°C (Gas Mark 4, 350°F)	For thinner cuts 44 minutes to the half kilo (40 minutes to the pound). For thicker or stuffed cuts 48 minutes to the half kilo (40 minutes to the pound).	
Preheat oven to 150°C (Gas Mark 2, 300°F) or cook on top of stove over low heat	Most require at least $2\frac{1}{2}$ hours	
Preheat grill for 3-5 minutes. Add a little butter and oil to frying pan and heat. Add meat when butter foams.	4-8 minutes on each side depending on thickness and degree of doneness required: rare, 3-4 minutes each side, medium, 5-6 minutes each side, well done, 7-8 minutes each side. Minute steak, 1 minute each side.	
Preheat oven to 200°C (Gas Mark 6, 400°F). After cooking for 20 mins reduce temp to 170°C (Gas Mark 3, 325°F)	22 minutes to the half kilo (20 „ „ „ pound) and plus 22 (20) minutes over	80°-82°C (175°-180°F)
Preheat oven to 180°C (Gas Mark 4, 350°F)	Leg and shoulder: 22 minutes to the half kilo (20 minutes to the pound) Breast: 16 minutes to the half kilo (15 minutes to the pound)	
Bring salted water to boil before adding lamb. Maintain at a slow simmer during cooking.	16 minutes to the half kilo (15 mins to the pound) plus 16 (15) mins.	Well-done: 72°-74°C (160°-165°F) Medium: 62°-64°C (145°-150°F)
Preheat oven to 150°C (Gas Mark 2, 300°F) or cook on top of stove over low heat.	At least 2 hours.	
Preheat grill for 3-5 minutes. Add a little butter and oil to frying pan and heat. Add meat when butter foams.	10-20 minutes for chops 7-10 mins for cutlets. Reduce heat to medium after cooking each side for 2 minutes.	
Preheat oven to 190°C (Gas Mark 5, 375°F).	For bone-in joints: 38 minutes to the half kilo (35 minutes to the pound) plus 32 (30) minutes over. For boned and rolled joints: 44 mins to the half kilo (40 minutes to the pound) plus 44 (40) minutes over.	88°C (190°F)
Preheat oven to 180°C (Gas Mark 4, 350°F).	For spare ribs: 27-32 minutes to the half kilo (25-30 mins to the pound). For cutlets and chops: 22-27 mins to the half kilo (20-25 mins to the pound).	
Preheat oven to 150°C (Gas Mark 2, 300°F), or cook on top of stove over low heat.	At least $1-1\frac{1}{4}$ hours	
	32 minutes to the half kilo (30 mins to the pound) plus 32 (30) mins over.	

Meat	Suitable for	Cut
Pork	**Frying or grilling**	All chops and cutlets, fillet, leg steaks
Bacon, Ham and Gammon	**Baking and boiling**	All gammon, including middle gammon, corner gammon, gammon slipper and gammon hock. Collar cuts of bacon, including prime collar and forehock.
	Frying or grilling	Prime leg or top back bacon; gammon and collar rashers, gammon steaks
Veal	**Roasting**	Leg, fillet, loin, saddle, breast, neck, hock and knuckle
	Braising	Breast, neck, hock and knuckle
	Boiling	Cheaper cuts
	Stewing	Cheaper cuts and more fatty cuts
	Frying or grilling	Loin and chump chops, cutlets, escalopes

Poultry	Suitable for	Cut
Chicken	**Roasting**	Whole; poussin, roasting chicken, capon
	Braising	Roasting chicken, capon
	Stewing (fricassé)	Roasting or young boiling fowl cut into 4 or 8 pieces.
	Sautéing (stewed in butter)	Spring or roasting chicken pieces.

Preparation	Cooking Time	Internal Temperature
Preheat grill for 3-5 mins. Add a little butter and oil to frying pan and heat. Add meat when butter foams.	Grill for 15-20 mins on each side depending on thickness. Fry for 5 mins on each side or until well browned. Cover pan and reduce heat to low simmer for 25-35 mins depending on thickness of chops.	
Soak gammon or ham for at least 6 hours or overnight to reduce saltiness, or put in saucepan of water and bring slowly to boil. Drain, add fresh water and bring to boil again; simmer required time. Unsmoked gammon soak 2 hrs. To bake: simmer for half the cooking time, wrap in foil and bake in oven preheated to 190°C (Gas Mark 5, 375°F). A half hour before done, remove foil and peel off skin, Make a diamond pattern in the fat, insert whole cloves and cover with brown sugar to glaze. Bake for last half hour at 220°C (Gas Mark 7, 425°F).	Boiling or baking time: 22 minutes to the half kilo (20 minutes to the pound) plus 22 (20) minutes over.	
Heat frying pan without fat for bacon; add a little fat for gammon and collar rashers. Preheat grill for 3-5 minutes.	Fry until fat has entirely lost its transparency. Grill steaks for 5 minutes on each side.	
Preheat oven to 200°C (Gas Mark 6, 400°F). After cooking for 20 mins reduce to 170°C (Gas Mark 3, 325°F). Baste every 20 minutes.	Bone-in; 22 mins to the half kilo (20 mins to the pound) plus 22 (20) mins. Boned and rolled; 32 mins to the ½ kilo (30 mins to the pound) plus 32 (30) minutes.	85°C (185°F)
Preheat oven to 190°C (Gas Mark 5, 375°F).	32 minutes to the half kilo (30 mins to the pound).	
Start in cold water and bring to the boil. Maintain at a slow simmer.	16 minutes to the half kilo (15 mins to the pound) plus 15 minutes.	
Preheat oven to 150°C (Gas Mark 2, 300°F) or cook on top of stove over low heat.	At least 1 hour	
Preheat grill for more than 5 minutes, melt butter and oil in frying pan until it foams, then add meat.	Grill for 3-5 mins on each side, reduce heat and cook till done. Fry over moderate heat for 3-5 mins on each side, reduce heat to low and cook till done. Total time; 15-30 mins for chops and cutlets; 6-8 mins for escalopes.	
Preparation	Cooking Time	Internal Temperature
Preheat oven to 220°C (Gas Mark 7, 425°F). After cooking 15 mins reduce temp. to 180°C (Gas Mark 4, 350°F).	Unstuffed ready-to-cook weight; 1kg (2lb) – 50-60 mins 1½kg (3lb) – 1hr + 10-20 mins 2kg (4½lb) – 1hr + 15-30 mins Stuffed; add 10-30 mins to roasting time.	82°C (180°F)
Preheat oven to 170°C (Gas Mark 3, 325°F). Brown chicken in casserole in hot fat.	Same cooking times as for roasting.	82°C (180°F)
Brown pieces in butter and oil, add hot liquid and simmer.	Simmer 1 hour or longer, until tender. Time depends on size of pieces and age. Place leg and thigh meat below breast and wing.	
Heat 2 tbsp butter and 1 tbsp of oil in frying pan or casserole until it foams.	Cook in butter for 8-10 mins, until lightly browned. Cover and simmer 20-25 mins until tender.	

Poultry	Suitable for	Cut
Chicken	**Boiling**	Fowl
	Grilling	Pieces, or halved spring chicken or poussin.
	Frying	Spring or roasting chicken cut in 8 pieces off bone.
Duck	**Roasting**	Whole
	Braising	Whole, halved or quartered
Goose	**Roasting**	Whole
Turkey	**Roasting**	Whole
	Grilling, sautéing, frying	Pieces

Vegetable chart

Vegetable	Description	Preparation
Artichoke, Globe	Large, thistle-like head of closely packed leaves. Where bud joins stem is fleshy area called the heart.	See page 91. Rub cut edges with lemon juice to maintain colour.
Artichoke, Jerusalem	Thin skinned, knobbly either purple or white skin, white flesh. Distinctive, delicate flavour.	Wash well. Peel under running water. Drop into acidulated water (vinegar or lemon juice) until ready to use.
Asparagus	Either white or green in colour. Older stalks will be tougher than young ones.	See page 90.
Aubergine	Mainly pear-shaped and purple, but from dark purple to mauve and yellow to white, and from long and thin to quite round. Select firm, smooth, shiny ones of uniform colour – no wrinkles.	Slice thinly across, arrange flat on plate and sprinkle with salt. Leave 20 min for excess moisture to come out. Squeeze and pat dry.

100

Preparation	Cooking Time	Internal Temperature
Place fowl in cold water and bring to the boil.	Simmer 1½-2 hours until tender.	
Preheat grill for 3-5 mins. Reduce heat to mod after 2 mins. Butter skin, baste.	Legs: 10-15 mins each side. Breast: 8-10 mins each side.	
Heat 75 g (3 oz) butter and oil in frying pan until it foams. Reduce heat to low.	With bone: cook pieces for 20 mins, turning several times. Off bone: cook 5-10 minutes.	
Preheat oven to 230°C (Gas Mark 8, 450°F). After cooking for 15 mins reduce temp. to 180°C (Gas Mark 4, 350°F).	Unstuffed ready to cook weight: 　1½kg (3½lb) – 1hr + 15-20 mins 　2kg (4½lb) – 1hr + 25-35 mins 　2½kg (5½lb) – 1hr + 35-45 mins Stuffed; add 20-30 mins to time	82°-85°C (180°-185°F)
Preheat oven to 170°C (Gas Mark 3, 325°F). Brown duck in casserole in hot fat.	Same cooking time as for roasting.	As for roasting
Preheat oven to 230°C (Gas Mark 8, 450°F). After cooking for 15 mins, reduce temp. to 180°C (Gas Mark 4, 350°F).	Stuffed: 22-27 mins to the half kilo (20-25 mins to the pound).	85°C (185°F)
Preheat oven to 230°C etc as above.	Weight as purchased, then stuffed: 　2¾-3½kg (6-8lb) – 2½-3 hrs 　3½-4½kg (8-10lb) – 3-3½ hrs Reduce cooking time by ¼ hour for each ½ kilo or pound unstuffed.	82°-85°C (180°-185°F)
Follow directions for chicken.	Increase cooking time, depending on size and thickness.	

Boiling Time	Other Methods	Other Comments
Cook whole in plenty of salted water to cover – 30 min; choke removed – 15 min. Leaf pulls away easily from heart when done. Flesh soft.	Steam – 50 min whole 　　　25 min choke removed.	Do not use aluminium or iron saucepan, which will discolour flesh. Choke can be removed before cooking: spread top leaves apart and pull out prickly leaves surrounding hairy choke and with teaspoon scrape out choke. Squeeze on lemon juice, press leaves back together again. Rich in Vitamin C.
30 min in acidulated water.	Steam – 35 min Deep-fry – parboil 15 min; dry, cut into sticks, dip in batter. Fry for 3 min.	Good for soups. Rich in iron, thiamine, niacin.
Stand upright in pan so stems are in water, tips out – cover loosely with aluminium foil and steam 15-20 min or use glass jar method (see page 90).	Sauté, quartered, over moderate heat for 30 min.	Average serving is six stalks per person. Use tough stalks in soup stock. Serve hot with melted butter or hollandaise sauce; cold with vinaigrette. Good alone as a first course or as a vegetable accompaniment to meat, fish and chicken dishes. Rich in Vitamin A, thiamine, riboflavin, Vitamin C.
	Sauté – in butter and oil; turn occasionally cook 10 min. Deep-fry in batter for 3 min. Grill after dotting with butter and oil.	Skin can be bitter and tough. To remove place aubergine directly on gas or electric burner and char skin, turn often; skin will peel off easily with knife and fingers. Absorbs great quantities of fats. Combines well with meat, cheese and tomato.

Vegetable	Description	Preparation
Beans, Broad	Have either long pods with kidney-shaped beans or shorter pods and round seeds.	Young beans: cook in pods after topping and tailing (removing ends). Older beans: remove seeds from pods (and use pods for soup).
Beans, French and Runner	Many shapes and colours. Most common has long thin pod, dark green in colour.	Remove stringy edges if necessary. Top and tail. Leave whole if young; halve or cut into lengths if large.
Beetroot	Red bulbous root, also a white variety.	Remove leaf stalk 5cm (2in) above root so it won't bleed. Do not trim off root ends. Wash carefully so skin is not damaged.
Broccoli, Calabrese or Italian green sprouting, purple, green, white	Some types mostly stem with a few flowering shoots, other types mostly a head of flowerets. Purple types turn green on cooking.	Cut off lower tough part of stalks; remove wilted leaves. Peel stalks if old from butt upwards. Separate flowerets from old stalks, cut stalks into lengths.
Brussels Sprouts	A variety of miniature cabbage – choose small, solid heads with tightly folded leaves, green and very fresh.	Cut off old-looking base, with sharp, knife make deep cross in centre of large ones – do not split circumference of base. Remove yellowed leaves.
Cabbage, Savoy and White	Savoy has green wrinkled leaves, is milder in flavour than white which has smooth leaves and a tight head.	Remove coarse outer leaves, cut into quarters and remove hard core. Either cook quarters or finely shred.
Cabbage, Red		Cut into quarters and shred.
Carrot	Orange variety most popular, also white, yellow and purple varieties.	Scrape rather than peel since vitamins and flavour are close to skin, or for casseroles just scrub well. Cut large ones into quarters, sticks or rings.
Cauliflower	Hard white head made up of many flowerets. Should be white and firm with fresh green leaves.	Cut off green leaves, trim stalk. Either leave whole or separate into flowerets – cut from base to outside.
Celery	Long white or green stalks rising from a base and ending in curly yellow-green leaves. Best when young.	Remove outer stalks if old and tough. Trim off top and base. Peel off strings with a knife if necessary. Cut into quarters lengthwise or separate stalks.
Chicory	Conical white head of crisp tightly packed leaves. Best heads are tightly closed at top.	Remove damaged or wilted leaves. Leave white, quarter or separate into leaves.
Courgette	Best young, no more than 2½cm (1in) in diameter and 15cm (6in) long. Has edible light green skin.	Trim ends and wipe clean. Leave small ones whole – slice larger ones into rounds or cut lengthwise into sticks. Sprinkle with salt and let stand for 20 min to remove excess water.
Cucumber	Most popular type is long and thin with bright, dark green skin and seeded core.	Peeling optional. Sprinkle with salt and let stand 20 min before cooking to remove excess water.
Kale	Member of cabbage family with green curly leaves.	Discard coarse outer leaves. Chop and place in saucepan with just enough water to cover.

Boiling Time	Other Methods	Other Comments
15-30 min depending on age and size.	Steam – 15 min or more depending on size.	Rich in iron, thiamine, riboflavin, niacin and Vitamin C.
5-15 min.	Steam – 10-20 min.	Rich in Vitamins A and C.
Simmer 1-2 hours, depending on size. Do not pierce with fork. Cooked when skin peels off easily.	Steam – 2 hours.	Often sold ready cooked. Often sold marinated in vinegar.
10-15 min – cook tough stem longer than tender top.	Steam – 20 min.	Flowerets also good eaten raw. Member of cauliflower family. Rich in Vitamin A, riboflavin and Vitamin C.
10 min. Long cooking brings out cabbage smell.	Steam – 15 min.	Member of cabbage family. Also good eaten raw. Good source of Vitamin C if not over-cooked. Rich in iron, Vitamins A and C.
Quarters – 10-15 min. Shredded – 5 min.	Steam – quarters 20 min. Shredded – 10 min. Braise – parboil 10 min, braise 1 hour.	Used raw in salads when shredded. Short cooking and crisp texture enhance Vitamin content and improve flavour. Rich in Vitamin C.
	Parboil 10 min. Layer in casserole with apple slices and sliced onion, sprinkle with vinegar and sugar. Add stock and braise 1 hour or more.	Benefits from long slow cooking. Vinegar added to maintain the red colour. Rich in Vitamin C.
Simmer 10-20 min. Add sugar if old.	Steam – 15-30 min. Oven braise. Braise on top of stove in butter, stock, and sugar for 10-20 min. Liquid should just evaporate.	Excellent raw. Very rich in Vitamin A.
Whole – 15-20 min. Flowerets – 8-12 min. Be careful not to overcook.	Steam – whole 25 min. flowerets 15 min.	Excellent raw. Rich in Vitamin C.
Blanch for 10 min before cooking by any other method. Boil 18 min. Pan-fry, tightly covered, in butter for 15 min.	Braise in white stock with herbs for about 45 min.	Excellent raw – keep prepared in polythene bag, or iced water in refrigerator until ready to use. Use leaves and outer stalks in stocks and sauces; also in soups and stews. Rich in Vitamin C.
20 min for whole heads.	Braise in butter for 1-1¼ hours.	Frequently used raw in salads. Boiled chicory is usually served with béchamel or cheese sauce.
10-15 min if whole.	Steam – whole for 20 min. sliced 10 min. Sauté – 7-10 min over moderate heat.	Excellent combined with onions, tomatoes, aubergines and cheese; makes good soup.
Not recommended.	Sauté – 7-10 min over moderate heat. Bake – in butter in 190°C (Gas Mark 5, 375°F) oven for 1 hour or until crisp tender.	Used mostly raw in a variety of salads. Rich in Vitamin C; also A if not peeled.
10-15 min or until tender but still slightly crunchy. Drain and squeeze out all water.		Finish off with sauce (velouté, cheese) or serve with knob of butter. Combine with cooked onions and Italian sausages and serve hot. Rich in calcium, iron, Vitamins A and C.

Vegetable	Description	Preparation
Leek	Smaller paler varieties are often more tender.	Cut off roots and remove tops 8cm (3in) above white stem. Remove coarse outer leaves, wash well to remove grit between layers.
Lettuce family (also curly endive)	Many varieties from tight crisp heads, to soft open leaves. Most are green but some varieties are red or copper coloured.	Remove coarse or damaged outer leaves. Wash well and drain thoroughly.
Marrow	Colour of skin ranges from off-white and yellow to dark green, many shapes. Smaller sizes are better than large.	Peel, halve lengthwise and scoop out the seeds. Slice or dice, sprinkle with salt and let stand 10 min if braising or sautéing to remove some water, dry.
Mushroom	Comes in 3 grades: button – small unopened cup – slightly opened flat – completely opened	Wipe clean rather than washing under water. Trim off dry base of stem. See page 91 for peeling and chopping.
Okra	The long thin green pods can reach 20cm (8in) in length. When over-cooked become gummy, therefore are used to bind stews, sauces and soups.	Leave small pods whole; if large cut into pieces. For braising cut crossways into thin slices.
Onion	Comes in various sizes from pickling (tiny, used whole) to large Spanish.	Remove outer skin and brown top end; do not cut off root end before all other preparations are done because it contains the eye-irritating oils. See page 91.
Parsnip	Carrot-shaped root with a pale yellow exterior.	Trim off both ends and peel off coarse outer skin. Cut in half lengthwise and and remove hard centre core.
Pea	Young small freshly picked peas are sweetest.	Shell peas.
Pepper, sweet or bell	Green (unripe) or red or yellow (ripe). Choose those with shiny smooth skins.	Cut off stalk end and remove white pith and all seeds, which are painful to eyes and lips.
Pepper, Chilli	Small and elongated, either green (unripe) or red (ripe). Seeds are very hot. Red chillis are hotter than green.	Chillis can burn so wear rubber gloves or touch only with fork and knife. Cut off stalk end and remove seeds and pith.

Boiling Time	Other Methods	Other Comments
Whole – 12 min. 5cm (2in) lengths – 8 min.	Steam – 20 min whole. Braise – cover with white stock and cook for 30 min in 180°C (350°F, Gas Mark 4) oven.	Allow 2 per person. Rich in iron and Vitamin A.
Not suitable. Blanch old, opened-out endive for 10 min.	Braise – blanch for 5 min, refresh under cold water. Place leaves in baking dish with a little white stock and onions, parsley and cloves. Cook 45 min at 190°C (375°F, Gas Mark 5) oven.	Sometimes cooked with fresh peas. Most frequently used raw in salads. Loose headed varieties rich in iron, Vitamins A and C. Curly endive high in Vitamins A and C.
10 min.	Steam – 20 min. Braise – half cover with white stock and cook for 40 min. Sauté – over moderate heat for 15 min.	Combines well with other ingredients, especially onions and tomatoes. Rich in Vitamin C, though amount varies with variety.
In butter and 1-2 tbsp water, tightly covered, for 5 min.	Grill – brush with melted butter and grill for 5 min. Sauté – for 3 min using 25g (1oz) butter for 125g (4oz) of mushrooms. Steam – 10 min.	Wild mushrooms need to be gathered by experts who can distinguish between safe and poisonous. Lemon juice helps to keep white. Cooked mushrooms give off a lot of moisture – do not overcook. Can be used raw in salads, marinated in oil, vinegar and herbs. Rich in iron, thiamine, riboflavin and niacin.
Whole – 8 min. Cut – 5 min. Cook, covered, in a layer no more than ½cm (1in) thick.	Braise in frying pan with tight fitting lid for 10 min, stirring frequently. Remove cover and cook until tender and golden brown.	Less sap is released by whole okras. Used in Indian and Creole cooking. Rich in Vitamin A, thiamine, riboflavin and Vitamin C.
5–30 min at very low heat.	Steam – 30-35 min. Sauté – sliced or chopped, for 5-7 min or until translucent. Braise – whole small onions are browned in a little butter, a small amount of beef stock is added and onions are cooked 30-40 min. Bake – peeled at 180°C (350°F, Gas Mark 4) oven for 2 hours or until tender. Cut off root and gently squeeze out onion.	See page 63 for description of various members of onion family and other uses. Frequently used as a seasoning to flavour casseroles and other dishes; large ones can be stuffed. *Spring onion:* a very young onion with a fresh, tender long green top. Both bulb and stalk are used in salads and as a garnish. They can also be used in cooking. Rich in Vitamin C if green tops are used.
–30 min.	Steam – 35 min – use only young parsnips. Roast – parboil for 5 min, then roast with joint. Deep-fry as for potatoes.	Root discolours when exposed to air – drop into acidulated water as soon as peeled and cut. Rich in Vitamin C.
–12 min.	Steam – 20 min. Braise – line casserole with lettuce leaves add peas, chopped onion, and enough white stock just to cover. Bake for 35 min at 180°C (350°F, Gas Mark 4) oven.	The mange-tout or snow pea has an edible pod. Cook whole or quartered like French beans; serve while still crisp. Rich in iron, Vitamin A, thiamine, niacin and Vitamin C.
ot suitable. lanch for 5 min before stuffing with t pre-cooked food. auté – in hot oil for 10 min.	Bake – blanched stuffed peppers at 180°C (350°F, Gas Mark 4) oven for 10-15 min. Grill – blanched, stuffed peppers to brown topping.	Used raw in salads. To peel, put under grill and turn often until skin blisters then pull off. Overcooking causes bitterness. Can be frozen without blanching. Red and yellow ones go bad quickly. Rich in Vitamin C (green); very rich in Vitamins A and C (red).
		Seeds are far hotter than pod. Oils cause burning so touch as little as possible with hands, avoid putting hands to face. Rich in Vitamins A and C, niacin (green); very rich in Vitamin A and C, niacin (red, seedless); seeds very rich in thiamine, riboflavin and niacin.

Vegetable	Description	Preparation
Potato	Many varieties, some best for boiling, others for baking. New potatoes are small early potatoes often boiled in jackets.	Scrub but do not peel new potatoes; peel all potatoes thinly. Baked – prick each deeply with a fork to allow steam to escape during baking.
Pumpkin	Can have green or orange skin.	Cut open and remove seeds and pith. Cut flesh from skin.
Radish	Most common types have red or red and white skins; others are all white or black skinned.	Cut off tops just above bulge, remove hairy roots.
Spinach	Leaves range in colour from pale to dark green; dark type is slightly coarser.	Remove wilted leaves, cut off discoloured bases of stem. Cut off stems at base of leaf. Always wash thoroughly before cooking.
Swede (also known as rutabaga)	Closely resembles turnip in shape, but is larger, has purplish-brown skin; flesh is yellow in colour.	Peel and slice off skin. Wash flesh and slice or chop it.
Sweetcorn	Sweetcorn should be cooked within a few minutes or hours of picking. Look for ears whose husks are green and fresh.	Just before cooking pull off husk and remove silk.
Sweet Potato and Yam	Both are tubers with reddish skin and either white or yellow flesh. They are both tropical plants, but are not related.	Before boiling, peel and halve or quarter or remove skin afterwards for other methods, blanch for 10 min, cool and slip off skin with knife and fingers.
Tomato	Red or golden in colour when fully ripe. Salad variety is round, cooking variety is oval.	For peeling, seeding, juicing, see page 92.
Turnip	Bulbous white root with a smooth leafy green top. Both root and top are edible.	Prepare and cook roots like swedes. Prepare and cook tops like cabbage or kale.

Note: "Rich in Vitamins" means that at least 10 per cent of the recommended daily intake is supplied by 125 grams (4 ounces) of the cooked vegetable. In many cases the amount supplied is far higher.

Boiling Time	Other Methods	Other Comments
15–20 min. Mashed – cook and drain potatoes – mash with a fork or masher. Just before serving add 300ml (½pt) boiling milk to 1kg (2lb) potato. Beat in till light and fluffy.	Steam – 15-20 min. Bake – arrange in hot oven so they do not touch. Bake 45 min-1½ hours, depending on size and oven temperature; 190°C (375°F, Gas Mark 5) is best. Roast – either under meat for 1 hour turning and basting twice or in seperate pan (preheat tin with ½cm (¼in) of oil until very hot) rolling potatoes in oil – turn and baste several times. Deep-fried – cut into chips and cook 5 min in hot oil; use baking potatoes. Sauté – add single layer of potatoes, sliced or diced, to hot butter and oil. Fry, turning frequently, for 10-15 min.	Potato skin is good to eat and unpeeled potatoes are more nutritious since most vitamins and minerals lie just under the skin. Baked potatoes cook faster when a metal skewer is thrust through the centre before cooking. To have fluffy boiled potatoes return drained potatoes to saucepan and shake over heat until a film begins to form on pan and potato surface is no longer moist. For baked in skin: rich in thiamine, niacin and Vitamin C, boiled peeled reduces vitamin content though it still remains high.
20 min or until tender.	Bake – place halves face down on baking sheet, add 1cm (½in) water and bake 30 min in 190°C (375°F, Gas Mark 5) oven.	Serve seeds, wash and dry thoroughly, fry and salt; use as a snack. Pumpkin is seldom served alone as a vegetable but is used in casseroles or other prepared dishes and as pie filling.
6-8 min depending on size.		Mainly eaten raw alone or in salads. Rich in Vitamin C. Serve cooked with béchamel or parsley sauce.
Use no water at all or only enough to cover bottom of pan. Boil 10 min. Drain, press down hard with wooden spoon to get all liquid out.		Allow 225g (8oz) of fresh spinach per person since it cooks down greatly. After draining, purée spinach in electric blender or force through a coarse sieve. Spinach can be mixed with a béchamel or cheese sauce; blends well with many things, especially eggs. Good raw in salads. Rich in iron, Vitamins A and C.
20-30 min.	Roast – parboil thick slices for 12 min, drain. Arrange around a joint of meat for last hour of cooking.	Boiled swedes are usually mashed with butter, salt and pepper. Rich in Vitamins A and C.
For older corn only, add 1 tbsp sugar to the water. 10-20 min depending on age and size. Done when kernels turn bright yellow.	Steam – for young fresh corn – 5-7 min, or until kernels take on bright translucence. Roast – for young sweetcorn, remove silk but leave on husk, wash under running water. Roast over hot coals for 20-25 min, turning occasionally or bake on rack in 200°C (400°F, Gas Mark 6) oven.	Overcooking makes sweetcorn tough. Has many uses and combines well with other vegetables. Rich in thiamine and Vitamin C.
30-40 min if peeled use a minimum of water.	Baked – see potatoes Sauté – see potatoes Roast – see potatoes	Sweet potatoes have a sweet flavour and are rich in Vitamin A and C. They spoil rapidly. Yams keep well but are low in nutrients and relatively high in carbohydrates.
Not suitable.	Bake – whole, placed stalk end down on baking sheet, brush with oil, bake 15 min in 190°C (375°F, Gas Mark 5) oven. Grill – halve, place cut side up on grill pan and place under moderate heat for 5-10 min.	Baked and grilled tomatoes should not be overcooked or they will collapse. Goes well with many herbs and other vegetables, cheese. Excellent raw, seeds if in a green 'jelly' can be bitter, so discard. Oval (or plum) tomatoes make more flavourful sauces.
		Roots can be eaten raw, peeled or unpeeled. Rich in Vitamin C.

Chapter Six

Stocks

Your own stock makes a world of difference in the flavour and texture of many basic dishes. Soups, gravies, gelatines and aspics all take on memorable new dimensions.

Stock is worth making on a large scale because of its many uses and any surplus can be frozen in suitably sized containers. When estimating final results, remember that stock is always reduced by at least half and sometimes more to concentrate the flavour. Although stock may take up to five hours to cook, cooking can be stopped at any time and continued again when it suits you.

Stocks are made from a variety of ingredients, depending on how they are to be used. The four major categories are meat, chicken, fish and vegetable. It is important to keep in mind how you are going to use a particular stock and to select your stock ingredients to complement those dishes.

Choosing ingredients

The best are made from fresh bones (or fish trimmings), fresh meat (or fish) and vegetables bought specifically for the purpose. A more economical stock can be made from leftover or surplus ingredients which might otherwise be wasted. For instance, chicken carcasses and meat bones can be wrapped and stored in the refrigerator until you have enough to make stock, and certain vegetable peelings and some vegetable cooking liquids are also worth saving. But be selective: the stockpot is not a dustbin; throwing all your scraps into it indiscriminately will only produce poor results.

Meat and bones

When the butcher bones and trims meat for you, be sure to take everything home.

After all, you have paid for the bones and trimmings and most of them are ideal for the stockpot. Have the butcher cut large bones into short convenient pieces. Wash all bones well before use.

Beef and veal bones make the best all-purpose stock. Ham, gammon, pork and lamb bones all have distinctive flavours. They are excellent for specific purposes, but don't use many in a general-purpose stock. If you have a freezer, make pork or lamb stock with bones left when the joint is eaten, freeze and use for gravy stock next time you have the same type of meat. Veal bones, pigs' trotters and calves' heads produce gelatinous stocks, so include one if you want to make aspics and jellied soups.

The addition of raw meat gives stocks a stronger flavour and makes them nourishing. The cheapest cuts such as shin and neck are suitable, especially for long cooking. Sometimes better cuts are simmered in the stock and then used to provide a family-meal.

The vegetables most commonly used in meat and fish stocks are onions, leeks, carrots and celery. Always use fresh vegetables and especially avoid old celery stalks which have an unpleasant flavour. Mushroom peelings add colour as well as flavour as do tomatoes, though the latter can sour stock that is kept for more than a day. Parsnips should be used sparingly. Turnips, cauliflowers and members of the cabbage family can be used for vegetable stock, but their flavour is too strong for meat or fish stock. Cooked vegetables make stock cloudy, as do potatoes and other starchy vegetables such as peas and beans.

Parsley, marjoram, thyme and bay leaf (either fresh or dried) are used to flavour most stocks. Salt and peppercorns are also used, and occasionally mace. Never season stock heavily, however. Wait until the liquid has been reduced or add when you are making the final dish.

Basic methods

Meat stock, white or brown

Simple meat stock is made from a collection of meat and bones consisting mainly of beef, veal and chicken, though a small amount of pork could be added. For white stock, the meat and bones are placed in water and brought to the boil. When the liquid comes to the boil, skim away fat and scum with a slotted spoon (you may need to skim again during cooking). Reduce heat, add herbs, salt and peppercorns. Add vegetables and half-cover the pan with a lid. For brown stock an additional step is needed. The meat, bones and vegetables are placed in a roasting pan and browned in a hot oven for about 40 minutes. They are then transferred to the stockpot. Pour off the accumulated fat, add some water to the roasting pan and scrape up the brown juices. Add these to the stockpot. Fill the pot with cold water and bring to the boil.

Simmering: Never let the stock boil; if it does, fat and scum amalgamate with the stock and make it cloudy. Simmer gently until the liquid has reduced by one-third and you feel maximum flavour has been extracted from the ingredients. This may take up to five hours, but cooking can be stopped at any time and continued later. Never cover airtight unless the contents have cooled completely, or the stock will sour. Skim as necessary during cooking and top up with boiling water if the liquid has evaporated below the level of the ingredients.

Degreasing: When the stock has cooked enough, strain through a fine sieve into a bowl. Discard bones, vegetables and herbs. Keep the meat to use for potting, making into a cottage pie or Bolognese sauce if it has any flavour left.

If the stock is not for immediate use, refrigerate it as soon as it has cooled. Leave the bowl uncovered until the fat has hardened and formed a seal which

To make basic white stock, first chop the vegetables. Put them into a heavy saucepan with meat or fish bones.

Add water and bring to the boil very slowly. When the foam forms a definite scum, remove it with a spoon or skimmer.

When the scum has stopped rising in large quantities, add herbs (bouquet garni, for instance as here) and seasonings.

Half-cover the saucepan, then simmer the stock for the amount of time specified in the recipe being used.

Skim and top up with boiling water if the liquid falls below the ingredients. Then pour through a colander into a clean bowl.

If the stock is to be used immediately, mop up the fat with kitchen paper towels, or a slice of bread.

Or cool it a little then skim off fat with a skimmer. Or leave it until completely cold (as above) and scrape off solid fat.

Strain the de-greased stock through a sieve lined with fine muslin or cheesecloth back into a clean saucepan.

Reheat the stock. If the flavouring seems weak, boil rapidly to reduce and concentrate the flavour. Season to taste.

helps the stock to stay fresh longer. Scrape the fat off only when the stock is needed. Then cover the bowl with foil to prevent the stock absorbing or passing on smells and flavours to other foods. Stock kept in the refrigerator must be brought to the boil every three or four days.

Straining and final flavouring: Strain degreased stock through a sieve lined with fine muslin. Reheat and, if the flavour is too weak, boil down to concentrate its strength. Correct seasoning if necessary by adding salt or pepper.

Meat glaze: At this point a meat glaze can be made by reducing 3 litres (5 pints) of stock to about 400 millilitres ($\frac{3}{4}$ pint) of glaze. Boil slowly until most of the liquid is gone and it becomes a syrup which coats a spoon nicely – watch closely at the end so it doesn't burn.

Meat glaze will keep for weeks in the refrigerator. If a mould should develop, wash it off with warm water then simmer the glaze with a spoonful of water until a syrup forms. It can also be frozen. A spoonful of glaze dissolved in hot water will take the place of a stock cube. A half teaspoon stirred into soups and sauces boosts flavour mervellously.

Clarifying: Stock for aspic or clear soup should be sparkling and clear. Clarifying is quite simple when both stock and whisk are absolutely grease free. Turn the cold stock into a pan set over low heat. When the stock is liquid but still cool, whisk in one large egg white for every litre (2 pints) of stock. Continue whisking until frothy white globules form on the surface. Boil for 2–3 minutes, then turn off the heat and leave for about 10 minutes. The egg whites, acting as a magnet for all the minute cloudy particles, turn a dirty brownish-gray and leave a clear stock below.

Line a sieve with a double layer of damp butter muslin and place over a large bowl. Slowly pour the stock through the sieve to strain off the scum. Repeat the process until the stock is clear.

Other stocks

Chicken stocks can also be either white or brown. However, never brown chicken parts in the oven, where they tend to burn. Instead, brown the chicken and vegetables, cut into small pieces, in hot oil or drippings.

Fish stock is a white stock made with fresh fish, fish heads, bones and trimmings. It needs only a short simmering.

110

Storage

Most meat and chicken stocks can be kept in the refrigerator for up to 10 days, but must be degreased and brought to the boil after four days and boiled up again every three or four days thereafter. Meat or vegetable stocks that includes cabbage, lots of onion or other strongly flavoured vegetables will not keep as long as meat stock without such ingredients. Fish stock should always be used within a few days, or frozen.

White beef stock

There is really no substitute for a well-flavoured, home-made beef stock. It is an essential ingredient in many dishes, sauces and soups.

Makes $1\frac{3}{4}$ litres (3 pints)

1 kg (2 lb) beef shin bones, cut into pieces
1 marrow bone
$3\frac{1}{2}$ litres (6 pints) water
1 large onion, cut in half
2 carrots, scraped and cut in big pieces
1 large leek, washed thoroughly and cut in half
1 celery stalk, trimmed
8 peppercorns
4 cloves
1 bouquet garni
1 tablespoon salt

In a large saucepan, cover the bones with the water and bring slowly to the boil. Skim the surface with a slotted spoon to remove the scum. Continue to remove the scum as it rises.

When the scum stops rising, add the remaining ingredients, partly cover and simmer gently for 4 hours, or until the liquid is reduced by half.

Strain the stock through a sieve lined with two layers of muslin into a large bowl. Set the stock aside to cool, then store it in the refrigerator or use as required.

Brown Stock

Brown stock is the base for sauces and gravies.

Makes $2\frac{1}{2}$ litres (4 pints)

$2\frac{3}{4}$ kg (6 lb) veal and beef shin and marrow bones, broken or sawn into short pieces
$4\frac{3}{4}$ litres (8 pints) cold water
6 peppercorns
6 cloves

1 bouquet garni
1 carrot, scraped and diced
1 turnip, peeled and diced

Preheat the oven to moderate 180°C (Gas Mark 4, 350°F).

Place the bones on a baking sheet and put them in the oven to brown for about 40 minutes.

Remove the baking sheet from the oven and transfer the bones to a large stockpot or saucepan. Add all the remaining ingredients. Place the pot over high heat and bring the liquid to the boil. Skim the surface with a slotted spoon to remove the scum.

After the stock has reached boiling point reduce the heat and simmer, partly covered with the lid at an angle, for $2\frac{1}{2}$-3 hours, or until the stock has reduced to half the original quantity.

Strain the stock into a large bowl. Set the stock aside to cool, then store it in the refrigerator or use as required.

Veal Stock

Veal stock is an essential part of many classic recipes. Make the stock the day before it is needed, so that it may be chilled, the fat removed and the stock reheated as required.

Makes $1\frac{3}{4}$ litres (3 pints)

1 kg (2 lb) veal bones, cut into 5 cm (2 in) pieces
$\frac{1}{2}$ kg (1 lb) knuckle of veal, cut into $2\frac{1}{2}$ cm (1 in) pieces
2 onions, sliced
1 small turnip, peeled and chopped
4 carrots, scraped and chopped
125 g (4 oz) button mushrooms, sliced or 125 g (4 oz) mushroom stalks, chopped
1 bouquet garni
2 fresh marjoram sprays
8 peppercorns, crushed
1 strip lemon rind
3 litres (5 pints) water

In a large saucepan, blanch the veal for 5 minutes, drain and rinse. Wash out the saucepan. Return the veal to the pan along with the rest of the ingredients. Bring to the boil. Partly cover the pan, reduce the heat and simmer the stock for 3 hours.

Remove the lid, increase the heat and boil the stock for 15-20 minutes or until it has reduced by one-third of its original quantity. Remove the pan from the heat. Pour the stock through a sieve into a mixing bowl. Discard the contents of the sieve.

Set the bowl aside to cool. Chill the stock in the refrigerator for at least 3 hours or until the fat has risen to the surface and set.

Remove the bowl from the refrigerator. Remove and discard the fat and reheat the stock as required.

Chicken Stock

A well-flavoured home-made chicken stock is invaluable. It forms the basis for many sauces and soups and is used in a wide variety of other dishes.
Makes 1½ litres (2½ pints)

Carcass, bones and giblets (excluding the liver) of a cooked or raw chicken
1 carrot, scraped and sliced
4 celery stalks, trimmed and sliced
1 onion, stuck with 2 cloves
1 bouquet garni
Grated rind of ½ lemon
1 teaspoon salt
10 peppercorns
1¾ litres (3 pints) water

In a large saucepan, bring all the ingredients to the boil. Remove any scum that rises to the surface with a slotted spoon.

Half-cover the pan with the lid, reduce the heat and simmer the stock gently for about 2 hours.

Strain the liquid into a bowl. Set the stock aside to cool. Store it in the refrigerator or use as required.

Fish Stock

To make a good fish stock, it is preferable to use the bones and trimmings from a firm-fleshed fish, such as sole or plaice. Shells of prawns, shrimps and lobster may also be added.
Makes 1¼ litres (2 pints)

1¼ kg (3 lb) fish bones and trimmings, washed thoroughly
1 bouquet garni
1 celery stalk, trimmed and chopped
1 large onion, sliced
2 carrots, scraped and sliced
Salt
6 peppercorns
Juice of ½ lemon
2½ litres (4 pints) water
225 millilitres (8 fl oz) white wine

In a large saucepan, bring all the ingredients to the boil. The liquid should cover the bones and vegetables, so add more if necessary. Remove any scum that rises to the surface with a slotted spoon. Simmer the stock for 30-40 minutes.

Remove the pan from the heat and strain the stock into a large mixing bowl. Use it immediately or allow it to cool and store in the refrigerator until required.

Vegetable Stock

For this recipe, whole vegetables have been used. For a more economical stock replace some of them with celery leaves and trimmings, and peelings from root vegetables. Vegetable stock makes a nourishing thin soup when served with grated cheese.
Makes 1¾ litres (3 pints)

50 g (2 oz) vegetable fat
1 large onion, finely chopped
3 large carrots, scraped and chopped
3 celery stalks with leaves, trimmed and chopped
1 large turnip or parsnip, peeled and chopped
1 teaspoon soft brown sugar
2½ litres (4 pints) hot water
1 bouquet garni
6 white peppercorns
1½ teaspoons salt
2 whole cloves

In a large saucepan, melt the vegetable fat. Add the onion, carrots, celery, turnip or parsnip and sugar and cook, stirring frequently, for 8-10 minutes or until the onion is golden brown. Pour in the hot water and add the remaining ingredients, stirring frequently. Reduce the heat to moderately low and simmer, stirring occasionally, for 45 minutes.

Remove the pan from the heat and pour the stock through a fine wire sieve into a large mixing bowl. Press down on the vegetables to extract all the juices.

Set the stock aside to cool. Store it in the refrigerator or use as required.

Court Bouillon

Court bouillon is an acidulated stock, which is used for poaching fish. It can be reused, providing it is strained after use and stored in the refrigerator.
Makes about 2½ litres (4 pints)

2½ l (4 pints) water, or water and wine mixed
½ kg (1 lb) carrots, scraped and sliced
2 medium-sized onions, sliced
4 celery stalks, chopped
1 bouquet garni
2 teaspoons salt
150 ml (5 fl oz) cider or wine vinegar

Pour the water or water and wine mixture into a saucepan and add the vegetables, bouquet garni, salt and vinegar. Bring the liquid to the boil. Reduce the heat to low and simmer the mixture for 1 hour.

Remove the pan from the heat and strain the mixture through muslin or a fine sieve set over a large bowl or pan. Use immediately, or allow it to cool and store in the refrigerator until required.

Types of stocks and their uses

Brown stock: So-called because ingredients are coloured by browning before water is added. It is usually made exclusively with beef bones and meat (but sometimes includes veal and/or chicken) plus celery, root vegetables and herbs. Ideal choice for brown sauces. Also kidney, tomato and other vegetable soups requiring good colour and strong flavour, for moistening red meat casseroles and pies. A very strong meaty stock (aspic) is used for clear hot and cold jellied soups.

Game stock: This is made from game carcasses and meat scraps plus beef bones (fresh or saved from making brown stock) plus a few vegetables, notably celery and herbs. Distinctive gamey flavour, medium colour. Use for game soups, sauces to serve with game, to moisten game patês, pies and casseroles.

White stock: This is usually made from the bones and meat scraps of one or several of the following: veal, chicken, rabbit, pork, mutton, lamb and ham (occasionally beef is used), plus celery, root vegetables and herbs. Omit mutton, lamb and ham for a general purpose stock and only use pork sparingly. Delicate meaty flavour and pale colour if based on veal and/or chicken. Use for cream soups, fine white sauces and aspics. The predominance of lamb or mutton makes stock ideal for Scotch and barley broths. Use ham stock for purées and soups made with pulses.

Chicken stock★: This is made with boiling fowl and knuckle of veal for maximum flavour; or chicken carcass, skin and giblets plus poultry scraps; or giblets only. Always includes celery, a few root vegetables and herbs. Poultry flavour pale colour. Excellent general-purpose stock for all types of soups, sauces for vegetables and white meat dishes, moistening white meat casseroles and pies, and boiling rice for savoury dishes.

Fish stock★: Use fish heads, bones and

trimmings, lemon, celery, a few root vegetables and herbs. Turbot heads, halibut, sole and plaice bones are best. Add fresh cheap white fish to bolster flavour if bones are few. Almost colourless. Quickly made. Delicately flavoured. Wine can replace some of the water. Use immediately for fish soups, poaching fish, fish aspics and sauces or rice to accompany fish dishes.

Vegetable stock: A good way to use up scraps. Can be made from one or several of the following: celery stalks and leaves, trimmings from leeks and carrots, outer leaves, watercress stalks, mushroom peelings, outer lettuce leaves, young pea or broad bean pods and some vegetable cooking liquids. Mostly used in vegetarian cookery. Colour and flavour can be strengthened by lightly browning vegetables in butter before water is added. Blend all ingredients in a blender to make an instant soup. Or strain off vegetables and use liquid for soups, braising vegetables, cooking pulses and rice.

*NB Strictly speaking, chicken stock and fish stock are types of white stock.

Soups

Soup is normally served as the first course, in which case it should stimulate the appetite rather than satisfy it. The richer and heavier the main course, the lighter the soup should be. Conversely, creamy soups with a lot of body to them are most suitable when a plain, light main course is planned.

Very substantial soups, such as bouillabaisse or minestrone, are really more like stews than soups and can be a meal in themselves. Use them for informal occasions, to replace the first and main course and follow with something light. On average allow 150 millilitres (5 fluid ounces) of soup per person or a generous 300 millilitres (10 fluid ounces) when the soup is the main part of your meal.

Soups can be divided into two types – thick soups and thin soups.

Enriching soup

This is an optional extra, done just before serving to add creamy flavour and improve texture. Simply stir in small pats of butter or a little cream or soured

112

cream. Cook over gentle heat until warmed through but on no account allow to boil.

An egg yolk beaten into cream will thicken as well as enrich the soup. Allow 1 egg yolk and 3 tablespoons cream per 600 millilitres (1 pint) soup. Blend the yolk and cream in a small bowl. Stir in a spoonful of hot soup. When blended, add another spoonful. Continue adding and blending in the hot soup until the bowl is full. Remove the soup pan from the heat and gradually stir the contents of the bowl into the soup. Pour into warmed soup plates or a tureen and serve immediately.

Making thick soups

Thick soups can be divided into three categories: purées, creams and veloutés. The basic difference between them is the thickening agent used.

Purées are made with fruit or vegetables and are usually substantial enough to need no additional thickening. Ingredients are simply reduced to a purée in a blender or rubbed through a sieve with the cooking liquid.

Cream soups can be made from fish, shellfish, poultry or vegetables. The flavoured cooking liquid is strained off after the basic ingredients have been cooked. The liquid is then thickened with a mixture of butter and a cereal product (usually flour). Often some of the original ingredients are stirred into the soup just before serving for added flavour.

Veloutés are velvety smooth and thick luxurious soups usually made with a vegetable, though sometimes white fish or poultry are used. They are made by a combination of puréeing and thickening.

Basic method for purée soups

This is the simplest method of making a soup and is used exclusively for vegetables and fruit. Potatoes, Jerusalem artichokes, carrots, parsnips and pulses (peas, beans and lentils) will all purée to a thick soup after cooking.

Vegetables such as mushrooms, lettuce and watercress do not have much substance in themselves. If used alone, large quantities would be needed to create the right consistency for a purée soup. Therefore, a vegetable, such as potato is usually added to give the starchy ingredient necessary for thickening.

Fruit soups usually produce a slightly

thinner purée, which can be thickened with a little arrowroot or cornflour if wished or simply enriched with a little cream or soured cream just before serving.

It is difficult to approximate the proportions of vegetable or fruit, butter and liquid needed to make a purée soup because they vary so much depending on chosen ingredients and consistency required. As a rough guide, allow 25 grams (1 ounce) butter and 600 millilitres (1 pint) liquid for 450 grams (1 pound) vegetables or fruit.

Sweating the vegetables: Clean and dice or slice the vegetables. Put them in a saucepan with a little melted butter over very low heat. Shake the pan or stir to coat the vegetables all over with the butter. Cover and cook very gently for 5-10 minutes to soften the vegetables and let them absorb the butter without browning. This process is called sweating and must be done very slowly over gentle heat. Fast cooking will fry the vegetables, giving them a hard outer skin so the butter cannot be absorbed. Frying will also spoil the colour of the soup.

Adding the liquid: After 5-10 minutes, add the liquid. For vegetable soups, chicken or other white stock is generally used. Vegetable stock or vegetable cooking water are other possibilities or for a creamy vegetable soup, milk diluted with a little stock. Season lightly with salt, pepper and complementary herbs and spices.

For fruit soups, use fruit juice or water with sugar, lemon zest and spices such as cinnamon or cloves for added flavour.

Bring to the boil and simmer, covered, until the ingredients are quite tender, about 15-25 minutes depending on varieties used. Do not overcook, especially when green vegetables are used, or flavour and colour will be lost. In plain and chilled soups, fat tends to coagulate when cold, spoiling texture and appearance, so sweating is usually omitted when the soup is to be served chilled. It may also be omitted when a plain, easily digested soup is being prepared. In this case, the vegetables or fruit are cooked directly with the liquid.

Making the purée: Purée vegetables or fruit with their cooking liquid, using a sieve or a blender.

Place a large sieve over a bowl or clean saucepan. Pour on the contents of the soup pan, pressing the vegetables through with a wooden spoon. Discard any fibrous pieces remaining in the sieve. Scrape the purée from the under side into the soup bowl. In some cases, a nylon sieve is necessary to avoid discolouration of ingredients.

Using a blender is the quickest and easiest way to reduce fruit or vegetables to a purée with their cooking liquid (although it may be necessary to sieve the soup after blending to remove fibres). A blender produces consistently smooth results which are ideal for a velouté or cream soup but, can be too textureless for a purée soup.

Serving: If the soup is to be served

Potage Parmentier.

hot, reheat gently after puréeing and adjust seasoning to taste. Add more liquid if the consistency is too thick. If too thin, the soup can be simmered to reduce the quantity of liquid by evaporation – but this process is not effective when a lot of thickening is needed. Enrich, as already described, if wished.

If the soup is to be served cold, the consistency can be slightly thinner, and the seasoning should be a little stronger since flavours appear to diminish when ingredients are chilled. Cool the soups, cover and chill thoroughly before serving.

Potage Parmentier
This traditional purée soup proves you don't need exotic or expensive ingred-

ients to make a really delicious and nourishing soup. It tastes just as good served cold as hot—when cold it is called Vichysoisse.

6 servings

125 g (4 oz) butter
1 kg (2 lb) leeks, washed, trimmed and chopped
$\frac{1}{2}$ kg (1lb) potatoes, peeled and chopped
2 celery stalks, trimmed and chopped
600 ml (1 pint) chicken stock
600 ml (1 pint) milk
Salt and pepper
$\frac{1}{2}$ teaspoon sugar
$\frac{1}{4}$ teaspoon grated nutmeg
300 ml (10 fl oz) double cream

In a large saucepan, melt the butter, add the leeks, potatoes and celery and fry for 8 minutes, stirring occasionally.

Pour on the stock and milk and bring to the boil. Season with salt, pepper, sugar and nutmeg. Cover the pan and simmer for 30 to 40 minutes, or until the vegetables are soft. Reduce to a purée in a blender or rub through a sieve.

If serving hot, return the purée to the pan. Reheat and enrich with the cream. If serving cold, put the purée into a bowl and stir in half the cream. Chill in the refrigerator for 4 hours and stir in the remaining cream before serving.

Basic methods for cream soups

Cream soups are finer in texture and richer than purée soups. They can be made from fish, shellfish, poultry or vegetables. A higher percentage of the basic ingredient is needed since only the cooking liquid is used for the final soup, although reserved pieces are sometimes used to garnish it.

Any vegetables used are sweated in butter as described for purée soups (page 112), then simmered in liquid (usually a suitable stock or milk diluted with stock). Fish or poultry, if used, are added to the simmering liquid; they are never sweated. Cooking is longer than for a purée soup, to extract maximum flavour from the ingredients. The flavoured liquid is then strained off and thickened.

Thickening cream soups: A cereal product (usually flour) and butter are used to thicken cream soups, using the roux method, beurre manié, or blended flour.

The roux method of thickening is also widely used in sauce-making. (See page 117 for a detailed description.)

Beurre manié is flour and butter mixed together before cooking. Use a fork or palette knife to blend butter and flour to a paste, using the same amounts as for a roux. Form the mixture into small pellets and stir into the soup, a few at a time, until the desired consistency is achieved. The flour thickens the soup as it disperses. Bring the soup to simmering point.

Blended flour is the easiest method and particularly suitable when a plain soup is wanted or if the soup is to be enriched before serving. Mix plain flour (allow 25 grams [1 ounce] flour for 600 millilitres [1 pint] soup) to a smooth paste with 1-2 tablespoons of cold liquid in a small bowl.

114

Gradually blend in a ladle of hot soup, then slowly stir the contents of the bowl into the soup pan. Bring to the boil, stirring until thickened.

Cornflour or arrowroot can be used in place of plain flour; they are useful when a very smooth result is required. Arrowroot, in particular, is ideal for fish soups and fruit soups since it remains clear and uncloudy on thickening.

Serving: Check seasoning and consistency as for purée soups and enrich just before serving if wished.

Cream of Chicken Soup

This is a good way to produce a cheap meaty soup.

4 servings

½ onion, diced
½ carrot, scraped and diced
60 g (2½ oz) butter
1 chicken joint, weighing about 225-275 g (8-10 oz)
1 bay leaf
2 whole cloves
2 peppercorns
900 ml (1½ pints) chicken stock
40 g (1½ oz) flour
300 ml (10 fl oz) milk, warmed
Salt and pepper

Sweat the onion and carrot in 15 grams (½ ounce) butter for 5 minutes. Add the chicken, bay leaf, cloves, peppercorns and stock. Bring to the boil, cover and simmer for 30 minutes. Strain off the stock and reserve. Discard the seasonings. Skin and bone the chicken. Cut the flesh into bite-sized pieces and reserve.

Melt the remaining butter in a clean saucepan. Stir in the flour and cook without browning. Blend in the milk, stirring, and bring to the boil. Add the strained stock, stirring well. Adjust seasoning to taste.

Stir in the chicken just before serving.

Basic method for velouté soups

Veloutés are made by combining the methods used for purée soups and cream soups. In addition they can be enriched and thickened with egg yolks and cream.

Poultry or white fish can be used but vegetables are the usual main ingredient. Those with a distinctive flavour (such as asparagus, Jerusalem artichokes, celeriac, leeks and Florence fennel) are particularly suitable.

Sweat the vegetables (see page 112), add the liquid (and poultry or fish if used) and

simmer as for a purée soup. Because several thickening agents will be used, a smaller than usual quantity of the basic ingredient will be needed but those chosen need to be well flavoured. Reduce to a purée (in a blender for really smooth results), sieve if fibrous and then thicken with a roux or, for the finest results, with blended cornflour as described for cream soups. Check seasoning and enrich with cream and egg yolks just before serving.

Fennel Velouté

The smoky aromatic flavour of Florence fennel makes it an ideal vegetable for a luxurious velouté soup.

4-5 servings

40 g (1½ oz) butter
350 g (12 oz) Florence fennel, thinly sliced, green fronds reserved for garnish
1 small onion, chopped
900 ml (1½ pints) chicken or white stock
Salt and pepper
1½ tablespoons cornflour
2 egg yolks
4 tablespoons cream

Melt the butter and sweat the vegetables for 5 minutes. Stir in the stock. Season, cover and simmer for 15-20 minutes.

Pour off about half the cooking liquid into a clean saucepan. Reduce the vegetables with the remaining cooking liquid to a purée in a blender. Pour through a sieve, to remove fibres, into the saucepan.

Blend the cornflour with 2 tablespoons of cold water in a small bowl. Gradually stir in a ladle of hot soup, then stir the contents of the bowl into the saucepan. Bring to the boil and cook for 1 minute. Adjust seasoning to taste.

Blend the egg yolks with the cream, stir in a ladle of hot soup and then stir back into the pan. Heat through gently but do not boil. Serve at once, garnished with green fennel fronds.

Making thin soups

Thin soups, like thick soups, can be divided into three categories – broths, thin soups and clear soups.

Basic methods for broths

Broths are made with water and meaty bones, and given long slow cooking to extract maximum flavour from the ingredients. The liquid is not thickened in any way, but meat is picked off the bones, which are then discarded, and the meat (and often vegetables) are stirred into the broth before serving. A well-known broth is cock-a-leekie which is made with chicken, veal knuckle and leek.

Broths can also be made using fish as the main ingredient (*bouillabaisse* and *moules à la marinière* are two examples). If a lot of fish is included, supplementary vegetables, pulses and cereals are quite unnecessary. Fish broths are more quickly cooked than meat broths because fish bones give off a bitter flavour if cooking is prolonged.

Cooking: Dice or slice a few firm vegetables, such as carrots, turnips, a potato and onion or leek for flavouring. You can sweat them in butter, although this is not essential. If a richly coloured soup is required, let them fry to a golden brown.

Add a meaty bone, raw, to the pan. Cover the ingredients with water, add barley and any pre-soaked dried vegetables (about 25 grams [1 ounce] to 600 millilitres [1 pint]), such as lentils, haricot beans and split peas. Season lightly with salt, pepper and suitable herbs, such as thyme, basil, oregano or mixed herbs.

Bring slowly to the boil, skim the surface if any scum rises, then cover the saucepan and simmer for 2-3 hours. Lift out the bone, take off any meat and cut it into bite-sized pieces. Discard the bone. Skim off any fat from the soup and return the meat to the pan. Add any fresh green vegetables such as peas or cabbage which need only a short cooking time (they would lose colour, texture and freshness if added earlier) and complete cooking.

Scotch Broth

A filling, meaty soup, Scotch Broth is thickened with pearl barley and dried peas. If you wish to remove all the fat from the broth, allow the broth to cool for at least 8 hours or overnight. Remove and discard the fat that rises to the surface. Reheat the broth before serving.

4-6 servings

1¼ kg (3 lb) neck of mutton or lamb, chined and trimmed of excess fat
1¾ l (3 pints) water
Salt and black pepper
50 g (2 oz) pearl barley, blanched
50 g (2 oz) green split peas, soaked overnight in cold water and drained

1 large carrot, scraped and chopped
1 large onion, chopped
2 leeks, washed thoroughly and diced
2 celery stalks trimmed and diced
1 large turnip, peeled and diced
2 tablespoons chopped fresh parsley

Cut the meat into 10-13 centimetre (4-5 inch) pieces. Place the meat in a large saucepan and pour over the water. Set the pan over moderately high heat and bring the liquid to the boil. Skim off and discard any scum which rises to the surface. Add the salt, pepper, barley and peas. Reduce the heat to low, cover and simmer 1½ hours. Add the carrot, onion, leeks, celery and turnip. Re-cover the pan and continue cooking for a further 1 hour or until the vegetables are very tender. Remove the pan from the heat. Using tongs, transfer the meat to a chopping board and slice the meat from the bones. Discard the bones and return the meat to the pan.

Return the pan to moderate heat and cook for a further 5 minutes. Taste and add more salt and pepper if necessary. Sprinkle with parsley and serve.

Basic methods for thin soups

Thin soups are made by cooking ingredients in stock, but there is no need to clarify the stock. The liquid is not thickened, except when added ingredients do this naturally (as when a potato disintegrates). Chicken, meat, game, fish or shellfish stock can be used.

Thin soups give plenty of scope for your own recipe ideas. The soup can have a variety of ingredients added to give bulk and substance: for example, rice or pasta, grated or diced cheese, slivers of ham or bacon, eggs, bread and vegetables.

Both broths and thin soups tend to be substantial. Although it sounds contradictory to describe, say, minestrone as a thin soup, this is technically correct. While a bowl of minestrone is full of vegetables and pasta, the liquid element is thin. The consistency of the liquid and not the other ingredients differentiates a thin soup from a thick one.

Thin soups containing fish or shellfish are often called chowders. Pork or bacon is sometimes added too.

Cooking: The success of a thin soup lies in the quality of the stock from which it is made. It is essential to have a well flavoured stock, since cooking time is considerably shorter than for a broth.

This means that ingredients added either during the cooking or at the end do not impart as much flavour to the liquid as they would with longer, slower cooking.

The basic method is much the same as for broth, and a wide range of vegetables can be used. Quickly cooked vegetables such as peas and beans should be added towards the end of the cooking time, so that they remain whole.

Minestrone

6-8 servings

50 g (2 oz) dried haricot beans, soaked in cold water overnight
1¼ l (2 pints) beef stock
1 large carrot, scraped and diced
1 onion, sliced
2 rashers streaky bacon, sliced (optional)
1 garlic clove, finely crushed
Salt and pepper
1 celery stalk, trimmed and sliced
1 leek, washed thoroughly and sliced
3 tomatoes, blanched, skinned and quartered
25 g (1 oz) spaghetti, broken into short lengths
Freshly grated Parmesan cheese

Drain and cook the beans in fresh water until tender (do not add salt). Drain and turn the beans into a large clean saucepan. Add stock, carrot, onion, bacon, garlic and seasoning. Cover and simmer over low heat for 20 minutes. Add the celery, leek and tomatoes and continue cooking for 10 minutes. Taste and adjust seasoning.

Bring the soup to the boil and add the spaghetti. Lower the heat and simmer for 10-12 minutes.

Stir in 2 tablespoons of grated Parmesan cheese and serve with additional Parmesan in a separate serving bowl.

Basic method for clear soups

Clear soups, or consommés, make excellent appetizers. They are not too filling, but because the flavour is savoury and strong, you only need a little for each person – about 150 millilitres (5 fluid ounces). They can be served hot or cold.

When cold, consommé is a soft jelly which is usually chopped before serving. It should not be ice-cold, and can be garnished with lemon quarters or chopped anchovy fillets and soured cream. When hot, consommés are often garnished with croutons or strips of meat, or blanched julienne strips of vegetables. To blanch the julienne strips, put the prepared vegetables into a sieve or frying basket. Plunge into boiling water for 30 seconds, then refresh in cold water. Drain and dry.

Since clear soups are essentially twice refined stocks, they are, in fact, very simple. But like all simple things they must be perfect to be really good. Flavour, colour, clarity and texture (if the soup is to be served cold) are all important. Clear soup is simply not worth making if you are going to rely on a commercial stock cube. Home-made stock is the essential ingredient of a consommé. Use a really good beef or chicken stock. Be sure to include chicken or veal bones, a pig's trotter or half a calf's foot when making the stock, since these ingredients provide a gelatinous texture. Browning the bones is also important, for it gives the rich colour so characteristic of a good consommé.

In addition, after the initial browning, you can add a little sugar and cook, stirring, for a few minutes before pouring on the liquid. The sugar will caramelize giving the stock an extra rich golden colour. Finally, remember to strain, degrease and clarify the stock thoroughly (see pages 108–110).

Cooking: Your stock should be further

To make minestrone (a thin soup), first cook the dried, soaked haricot beans in fresh water until tender.

Drain, then add the beans to a saucepan with the other long-cooking vegetables (carrot, onion), bacon, stock and seasoning.

Cover and simmer for 20 minutes. Add the short-cooking vegetables (celery, leek, tomatoes) and cook for 10 minutes.

Finally, bring to the boil, add the spaghetti and simmer for 12 minutes. Stir in 2 tablespoons grated cheese before serving.

116

enriched by cooking fresh meat and vegetables in it, clarifying it again and, finally, flavouring it with sherry or Madeira.

For beef consommé, use lean meat to impart a strong flavour and mince or dice it so that all the nourishment is drawn out during the cooking. Economical cuts, such as shin or stewing steak are just as suitable as a more expensive joint. The higher the proportion of meat to liquid the better the flavour of the consommé. (The meat itself can be used afterwards, but since little flavour is left in it choose a recipe such as cottage pie or spaghetti sauce and add plenty of extra spices and flavourings.) For chicken consommé, use fresh uncooked chicken legs or thigh joints to give maximum flavour.

Beef Consommé

This is just a basic guide – add more or less vegetables if you like. Chicken consommé is made in the same way.

6-8 *servings*

350 g (12 oz) lean beef, minced
1¾ l (3 pints) bouillon (clarified beef stock)
1 small carrot, scraped and diced
1 small onion, diced
1 celery stalk, trimmed and diced
1 bay leaf
1 whole clove
6 peppercorns
Salt
2 egg whites and shells
3 tablespoons sherry or Madeira

Place the meat in a large saucepan with the stock and set over low heat. Add the vegetables together with the bay leaf, clove, peppercorns and a little salt.

Lightly beat the egg whites to a soft foam, slide into the soup and add the crushed shells. Whisk with a balloon whisk until the soup comes to the boil. Set the whisk aside and allow soup to rise slowly to the top of the saucepan. Carefully remove the pan from the heat and let the soup subside – but do not break up the foam covering the surface. Return the pan to very low heat, and leave to simmer gently, uncovered, for 1 hour.

Strain the soup through a fine cloth or jelly bag into a clean bowl, sliding foam, egg shells and other ingredients out of the saucepan. Let the liquid drip through by itself. Do not press the bag at all or the consommé may become cloudy.

If time permits, allow the clear soup to become quite cold then lift off hardened fat from the surface. Alternatively, skim as much fat as possible off the hot soup with a spoon, and draw paper towels across the surface: they will act like blotting paper, absorbing any remaining small globules or grease.

Reheat but do not boil. Taste and adjust seasoning. Stir in sherry or Madeira and garnish if wished immediately before serving.

Sauces

A sauce is a liquid, seasoning or relish, served with food in order to complement, coat, contrast with or garnish it. A sauce can be made separately from the food it is seasoning or used in the actual preparation to bind the various ingredients together. This section comprises only savoury sauces; sweet ones are discussed on pages 136–139.

Types of sauces

Sauces may be roughly divided into five categories: white, brown, egg-based, tomato and other (which includes mint, apple and bread). Additionally, there are pan gravy and *vinaigrette* or French dressing. Each of these groups has dozens of variations, so learn to recognize the basic type when you see such names as sauce mornay and béarnaise.

Both white and brown sauces have a roux base. White roux is cooked only long enough to eliminate the raw taste of the flour and only 'white' liquids such as milk, chicken and fish stocks, and wine are added. In brown sauces, the roux is cooked until it browns slightly and 'brown' liquids such as brown stock and red wine are added.

Egg-based sauces combine egg yolks and a high proportion of butter or oil, whisked together to become thick and glossy. The two most famous are hollandaise and mayonnaise, which both have numerous variations.

Several general points about sauces are worth emphasizing. Never economize on time or ingredients. Use home-made stock instead of a stock cube if possible. Use a heavy-based saucepan, which will distribute the heat more evenly, thus preventing burning. Avoid aluminium pans which tend to discolour white sauces.

Many sauces can be prepared in advance and stored in the refrigerator, covered closely with a disc of dampened greaseproof or waxed paper. Always re-heat a sauce which has been kept in the refrigerator in a bain-marie or double-boiler, because this helps to prevent the sauce going lumpy or burning.

Making a roux: The term roux comes from the French and means specifically equal weights of butter and flour cooked slowly together before a liquid is added. This cooking eliminates the raw taste of flour, which can spoil a sauce. Roux are either white or brown. A white roux is cooked over low heat. First the butter is put in a medium-sized saucepan. When it has melted, slowly blend in the flour. Stir the roux with the back of a metal spoon as it bubbles gently without colouring for 2 minutes. Remove from the heat and cool to well below boiling point before adding liquid. A cool roux reduces the likelihood of a lumpy sauce. Add the liquid and blend well, making sure that all the roux is off the bottom of the pan. Return the pan to the heat, bring the sauce to the boil, stirring constantly, and simmer for about 5 minutes. Season to taste.

The quantities given below are for three consistencies of white sauce. Be a little more generous with butter than flour, and you will find the liquid blends in more easily.

	Butter and flour Consistency to 300ml (10 fl oz) liquid
Thin, pouring	15 g (½ oz)
Medium, Coating	25 g (1 oz)
Thick, Panade	50 g (2 oz)

A brown roux is made with cooking oil, vegetable fat or dripping instead of butter, unless it is for a delicate dish. Heat the fat over low heat and blend in the flour. Cook, stirring, for 8–10 minutes or until the flour has turned a pale golden nut brown. It will keep cooking for a few minutes after it is removed from the heat. Cool and add liquid as for white sauce. A brown sauce should simmer for 1 hour or more to bring out its full flavour.

Blending method: Blended sauces tend to contain little or no fat, so the thickening agent, which may be flour, cornflour or arrowroot is first blended with a little of the cold liquid to make a smooth paste.

For a 300 millilitre (10 fluid ounce) sauce: in a small bowl blend together

117

25 grams (1 ounce) plain flour or 15 grams ($\frac{1}{2}$ ounce) cornflour with 3–4 tablespoons of the cold liquid. Bring the rest of the liquid to the boil and pour this into the bowl containing the paste mixture. Return the mixture to the saucepan, bring the sauce to the boil, stirring constantly, and simmer for about 3 minutes, until thick. Season to taste.

Brown sauces

Brown sauces take more time to make than white sauces because they require long, slow cooking. Therefore it pays to make large quantities of basic brown sauce and to freeze most in 300 or 600 millilitre (10 fluid ounce–1 pint) containers.

Sauce Espagnole (Basic Brown Sauce)

Strong and rich flavoured, Sauce Espagnole can be used as an accompaniment to steak, vegetables, game or eggs, and as a base for other brown sauce variations.

Makes about 300 millilitres (10 fluid ounces)

25 g (1 oz) butter
1 carrot, scraped and diced
1 onion, chopped
50 g (2 oz) green streaky bacon, rinds removed and chopped
25 g (1 oz) flour
450 ml (15 fl oz) brown stock
1 bouquet garni
2 tablespoons tomato purée
Salt and black pepper

Melt the butter in a heavy-based saucepan and cook the vegetables and bacon over a low heat for 10 minutes or until lightly browned. Add the flour, and cook for 2–3 minutes, stirring constantly, until the roux is brown.

Remove the pan from the heat and gradually add 300 millilitres (10 fluid ounces) of stock. When the sauce is smooth, return the pan to the heat and bring to the boil slowly, stirring constantly. Add the bouquet garni, and simmer, covered, for about 30 minutes. Add the rest of the stock and the tomato purée, and simmer, covered, for another 30 minutes, stirring frequently.

Strain the sauce, skim off any fat, adjust the seasoning and serve.

Other sauces based on Sauce Espagnole include **Sauce diable,** a peppery sauce made by adding wine, vinegar,

Rich, creamy, home-made mayonnaise. For a lighter taste, you can use half olive oil and half good-quality vegetable oil.

shallots and cayenne pepper; **Sauce Robert,** with onions, wine and Dijon mustard; and **mushroom.**

Brown deglazing sauce

Brown deglazing sauce is much simpler than brown sauce. Remove most of the fat from the pan, and add about 300 millilitres (10 fluid ounces) of brown stock. Carefully scrape up all the coagulated pan juices with a wooden spoon, and boil the sauce down over high heat until it is reduced by about half. Off the heat, stir in a knob or two of butter before serving.

Egg-based sauces

Egg-based sauces are made by gradually incorporating butter or oil into well-beaten egg yolks. An egg and oil combination is called **mayonnaise,** an egg and butter mixture **hollandaise.** When finished, both sauces have thickened into smooth creams that hold their shape.

Despite their reputation for difficulty, neither sauce is especially hard to make when you understand how egg yolks work. First, in order to absorb a fat the yolks have to be beaten until thick and light in colour. Second, the fat must be added slowly and in tiny quantities at first. If either sauce should curdle, there are tried and true methods of rescuing them.

Mayonnaise

For mayonnaise, the oil is added to the well-beaten egg yolks by droplets until the sauce has the thickness of double cream. About half the oil will have been added. Do not stop beating until this point is reached. The rest of the oil can be added by the tablespoonful, making sure that all of it is incorporated before the next spoonful is added. When the sauce is finished beat in 2 dessertspoons of boiling water as a further insurance against curdling.

A standard egg will absorb no more than 150 millilitres (5 fluid ounces) of oil, and a novice should use slightly less than this maximum. Trying to add more oil than a yolk can absorb causes the mayonnaise to curdle.

Mayonnaise
Makes 300 millilitres (10 fluid ounces)

2 egg yolks, at room temperature
Salt and white pepper
1 teaspoon dry mustard
300 ml (10 fl oz) olive oil, at room temperature
1 tablespoon white wine vinegar or lemon juice

In a medium mixing bowl, whisk together the egg yolks, salt, pepper and mustard until they are thoroughly blended and have thickened. Add the oil, a few drops at a time, whisking constantly with a wire whisk. After the mayonnaise has thickened the oil may be added a little more rapidly.

Beat in a few drops of vinegar or lemon juice from time to time to prevent the mayonnaise from becoming too thick. When all the oil has been added, stir in the remaining vinegar or lemon juice.

If the mayonnaise does curdle, or if after standing for several days in the refrigerator the sauce has thinned and released oil, take the following steps.

First, warm a small basin in hot water and dry it thoroughly. Next, place in it a tablespoon of mayonnaise and a teaspoon of dry mustard. Beat these with a wire whisk until they become thick and creamy. Continue beating in the rest of the sauce by the teaspoonful, allowing each addition to thicken before more is added. Especially at first, add only small quantities.

Other sauces based on mayonnaise are **tartare sauce,** flavoured with double cream, finely minced capers, gherkins, fresh chives and chervil. Mayonnaise with herbs (chopped fresh parsley, basil chives, marjoram, tarragon) makes another variation. To keep for more than a few days, however, the herbs must be blanched for 1 minute before being stirred into the mayonnaise.

Hollandaise

Hollandaise sauce is made over hot water so that the eggs are warmed slightly while the butter is added. The eggs must be thick, smooth and light in colour before the butter is added to them. At first, add the softened butter by the half teaspoonful, making sure that it has been incorporated fully before the next spoonful is added. When the sauce begins to thicken, you can add slightly larger amounts of butter. Never try to hurry the sauce. A standard egg can absorb up to 65 grams (2½ ounces) of butter, but a novice should use no more than 50 grams (2 ounces).

If the sauce must be kept warm for any length of time over hot water, stir in a tablespoon of velouté or béchamel (white) sauce.

Hollandaise sauce

Traditionally served with asparagus and salmon, Hollandaise Sauce can also accompany other vegetables and fish dishes. It is always served warm.
Makes 225 millilitres (8 fluid ounces)

5 tablespoons white wine vinegar
6 peppercorns
1 bay leaf
175 g (6 oz) butter
3 egg yolks
Salt

In a small saucepan, bring the vinegar, peppercorns and bay leaf to the boil over moderate heat. Reduce the heat and simmer the mixture for 10 minutes, or until it is reduced to 2 tablespoons. Pour the vinegar mixture through a sieve into a cup. Set aside. Discard the peppercorns and bay leaf.

To make béarnaise sauce, first strain the vinegar mixture, then cream the butter and beat the egg yolks.

Over warm water, stir the mixture carefully until it thickens. Then stir in the butter, a small piece at a time.

When the mixture is smooth, remove the bowl from the heat and beat in seasonings such as cayenne, tarragon and chervil.

In a small mixing bowl, cream the butter with a wooden spoon until it is soft, beat the egg yolks to blend them together. Beat in the salt and a heaped teaspoon of the softened butter. Stir in the strained vinegar.

Put the bowl with the egg yolk mixture over a medium-sized saucepan one-third full with warm water. Place the pan over the lowest heat. The water should heat gradually but never come to boiling point. Whisk the egg yolk mixture until it begins to thicken.

Add the remaining butter, a teaspoon at a time, stirring constantly. When all the butter has been added, taste the

To make French dressing, measure the vinegar into a bowl or jug.

Then add seasoning and beat gently with a fork to dissolve the salt.

Pour over the oil and beat vigorously to mix and thicken the dressing.

sauce. Add more salt if necessary. If the sauce is too sharp, add a little more butter. Pour the sauce into a warm sauce boat and serve.

If by misfortune the sauce will not thicken, the butter has probably been beaten in too quickly. To remedy, warm a bowl in hot water and dry it. Add a teaspoon of wine vinegar or lemon juice and a tablespoon of the hollandaise and whisk

until it thickens. Beat in the rest, a dessertspoon at a time, making sure each addition has thickened before the next is added.

If a finished sauce begins to separate, resuscitate it by using the above technique.

Béarnaise is probably the most widely used variant of hollandaise. The technique for making it is the same, but the flavourings are sharper: wine vinegar, shallot, bay leaf, tarragon, chervil and peppercorns. Sometimes meat glaze melted in white wine (**Sauce Colbert**) or tomato paste (**Sauce Choron**) are stirred into the **béarnaise. Mousseline sauce** is hollandaise with a small amount of whipped cream stirred in just before serving.

If hollandaise is to be used with fish, the vinegar and peppercorn flavouring is replaced by a white-wine fish stock cooked down to concentrate it.

Salad Dressings

Although there seems to be many types of salad dressing, most are variations on two basic themes: French dressing, also known as **vinaigrette,** and mayonnaise (see egg-based sauces).

The classic French dressing consists of olive oil, vinegar, salt and pepper. Crushed garlic, mustard and/or chopped herbs may also be added, in which case the dressing becomes **vinaigrette.**

Basic French Dressing
Makes about 125 millilitres (4 fluid ounces)

2 tablespoons wine vinegar
1 teaspoon salt
1 teaspoon black pepper
5 tablespoons olive oil

In a small mixing bowl, beat the vinegar, salt and pepper together with a fork. Pour on the oil and beat until well mixed. Use as required.

Other sauces
The category 'other sauces' brings together a necessarily incomplete collection of popular sauces. Given here are tomato sauce and traditional accompaniments for beef, lamb, pork and poultry.

Tomato sauces
Tomato sauces are simple to make and keep well in a screw-top jar in the refrigerator for up to 5 days; they can also be frozen. Sugar is added in the

following basic tomato sauce recipes to counteract the bitterness often found in cooked tomatoes. Dried herbs other than basil can be used, especially marjoram and oregano.

Fresh Tomato Sauce
Makes about 750 millilitres (1¼ pints)

1¼ kg (3 lb) fresh tomatoes, halved
2 teaspoons salt
1 teaspoon sugar
1 teaspoon dried basil
½ teaspoon grated lemon rind

Preheat the oven to warm 170°C (Gas Mark 3, 325°F).

Place the tomatoes in a large ovenproof casserole. Cover the casserole with a well-fitting lid or aluminium foil and place in the oven. Bake for 45 minutes or until the tomatoes are very soft. Remove the casserole from the oven.

Place the tomatoes in a large sieve set over a large saucepan. Rub the tomatoes through the sieve until only a dry pulp is left. Discard the pulp. Add the salt, sugar, basil and lemon rind to the pan. Place the pan over moderate heat and cook, stirring frequently with a wooden spoon, for 10 minutes or until the mixture is fairly thick.

Canned Tomato Sauce
Makes about 750 millilitres (1¼ pints)

1 tablespoon vegetable oil
1 medium-sized onion, chopped
1 large carrot, scraped and finely chopped
1 celery stalk, trimmed and finely chopped
1 garlic clove, crushed
1 x 800 g (28 oz) tin Italian plum tomatoes
3 parsley stalks
1 tablespoon sugar
2 teaspoons salt
1 teaspoon pepper
1 teaspoon dried basil, marjoram or oregano

Heat the oil in a large saucepan and add the onion, carrot and celery. Stir to coat the vegetables in the oil, cover and cook slowly without colouring for 10 minutes. Add the garlic and cook for 2 minutes.

Add the tomatoes and can juice, parsley, sugar, salt and pepper. Bring to the boil and simmer, uncovered, for 30 minutes or more. Stir several times. Add basil, marjoram or oregano for the last 15 minutes of cooking.

If the sauce is not thick enough, raise the heat and slowly boil off any excess. Stir frequently. Correct the seasoning before serving.

Horseradish Sauce

Horseradish sauce is the classic accompaniment to hot or cold roast beef. It is also excellent with smoked trout.

6 servings

1 teaspoon lemon juice
2 teaspoons vinegar
1 teaspoon prepared mustard
Salt and black pepper
1 teaspoon sugar
3 tablespoons grated fresh horseradish
150 ml (5 fl oz) double cream, stiffly whipped

In a medium-sized mixing bowl, combine the lemon juice, vinegar, mustard, salt, pepper, sugar and horseradish. Fold in the cream and spoon the sauce into a sauce boat. Serve cold.

Mint Sauce

The traditional British sauce for roast lamb, this should be made with young, fresh mint, preferably straight from the garden.

6 servings

12 tablespoons finely chopped fresh mint
1½ tablespoons sugar
75 ml (3 fl oz) malt or distilled white vinegar
1 tablespoon hot water

Pound the mint and sugar together in a mortar with a pestle, or combine them together in a small bowl. Add the vinegar and hot water and stir until the sugar has dissolved. Set the bowl aside and leave it for 1–2 hours before serving.

Apple Sauce

Serve this tart apple sauce as a refreshing accompaniment to pork, goose, or duck.

4 servings

700 g (1½ lb) cooking apples
Finely grated rind of 1 lemon
1 tablespoon water
Salt
Sugar to taste
40 g (1½ oz) butter

Peel, core and slice the apples. Place them in a bowl of water with a little salt as they are being prepared, to prevent them from becoming brown. Drain and place them in a large saucepan. Bring the apples, lemon rind, water and salt to the boil. Cover and simmer until the apples are soft. Add sugar to taste, a little at a time, stirring constantly. Allow the apples to cool. Purée the apples in a blender or rub through a sieve. Beat in the butter. If the sauce is to be served hot, return it to a clean saucepan and simmer for 2–3 minutes.

Bread Sauce

Serve with roast turkey, chicken or pheasant.

4 servings

1 medium-sized onion, studded with 2 cloves
1 bay leaf
300 ml (10 fl oz) milk
50 g (2 oz) fresh white breadcrumbs
Salt and pepper
1 tablespoon butter
1 tablespoon single cream

Place the onion, bay leaf and milk in a saucepan. Cover the pan and place over very low heat for 10–15 minutes, to infuse the milk with the flavouring. Remove and discard the onion and bay leaf. Bring the milk to the boil, add the breadcrumbs and simmer for 3–4 minutes, or until the sauce is thick and creamy.

Remove the pan from the heat. Stir in the salt, pepper, butter and cream with a wooden spoon. Gently reheat the sauce, but do not allow it to boil. Serve at once.

Marinades

Marinades are used to give foods more flavour, to change flavour, and to tenderize. Meat and vegetables are most commonly marinated; the soaking periods can be from as little as 15 minutes to add flavour, to a week for a large leg of pork or venison to tenderize and improve flavour, to even longer for salting and brining a piece of beef.

Fruit is also marinated, in which case the term used is **macerate.** Macerated fruit is soaked in a liqueur or liqueur and juice combined.

Most but not all marinades are liquid based. (One exception is a herb and salt combination rubbed on meat.) Marinades are generally composed of an acid liquid such as wine, beer, wine vinegar, lemon juice and yogurt. To this base is added salt, a variety of herbs and spices (garlic, pepper, thyme, bay leaf, sage, juniper berries, cloves, allspice, mace, etc.) and sometimes aromatic vegetables (onion, carrot, celery). Oil is often included to help the mixture adhere to the meat or vegetable.

Short-term marinades (those left for less than 36 hours) are frequently uncooked. Marinades to be used for more than 36 hours are usually cooked; this keeps the vegetables in the marinade from souring. Cooking also makes flavour more available to the food placed in it, and therefore is sometimes also used for short marinades, especially for vegetables. Cooked marinades should be chilled before meat is placed in them unless the recipe specifies otherwise. Sometimes raw vegetables are put into a hot marinade which cooks them slightly before it cools, adding to the penetration of flavour.

The length of marination depends on the result you wish to achieve. A short marinade imparts a mild flavour but will not tenderize much, while a longer one adds a stronger flavour and has greater tenderizing powers. Length of marinade also depends on the size of the food being marinated. Thus cubes of stewing steak would soak for 2–3 hours, whereas a whole piece of stewing steak of about 2 kilograms (4 pounds) would require 12 hours or more. Meat can be braised in its marinade, or if the meat is grilled as in the case of kebabs, the marinade may be used in making a sauce or for basting. So never throw a marinade away until you decide whether it will be needed at a later stage in cooking.

Since marinades are acid based, the most suitable containers are earthenware, china, glass and enamel. Avoid aluminium and cast iron, which the acid affects.

Stuffing or forcemeat

Stuffing, or forcemeat, is any sweet or savoury mixture which is put inside another food such as poultry, rolled joints of meat, fish and vegetables to add flavour and maintain shape. Frequently stuffings are a preparation of minced meat, fish, shellfish, vegetables or fruit, mixed with spices and herbs, which are bound with egg, milk, cream or stock. A breadcrumb or flour mixture, called a *panade*, is sometimes added to give more body.

Stuffing is usually flavoured according to its use or accompaniment – for example chestnuts for turkey, sage and onion for loin of pork, orange or apple for duck, truffle and *fois gras* for game, fish, rice or mushrooms for large fish.

A stuffing should not be soggy; do not therefore add all the liquid called for at once. Handle the mixture gently, so it does not become compacted, then pack into the bird or joint lightly, leaving room for expansionduring cooking.

Although stuffings can be made in advance, they should never be put in the bird or joint until just before cooking because of the possibility of bacterial contamination.

Thyme Stuffing

Thyme Stuffing is simple to make and reasonably economical too. It tastes particularly good with fish, veal or poultry. The amount given below is sufficient to stuff a 2 kg (4 lb) fish or chicken.

Makes about 225 grams (8 ounces)

125 g (4 oz) fresh white breadcrumbs
2 dessert apples, peeled, cored and finely chopped
1medium-sized onion, finely chopped
75 g (3 oz) sultanas or seedless raisins
2 teaspoons finely chopped fresh thyme
2 teaspoons finely chopped fresh lemon thyme
Salt and black pepper
1 egg, lightly beaten

Place all the stuffing ingredients in a medium–sized mixing bowl and stir until they are thoroughly combined. If the mixture is still slightly crumbly, add a little water or lemon juice.

The stuffing is now ready to use.

Chestnut and Sausage Stuffing

This is the traditional stuffing for turkey. It is simple to make and adds a delicious flavour to the bird. The amount given below is sufficient for one 4–5 kg (10–12 lb) turkey.

700 g (1½ lb) chestnuts, peeled
600 ml (1 pint) beef stock
1 celery stalk, trimmed and chopped
Salt and black pepper
2 tablespoons butter
1 large onion, finely chopped
225 g (8 oz) pork sausagemeat
75 g (3 oz) fresh white breadcrumbs
2 eggs, lightly beaten

Put the chestnuts, stock, celery, salt and pepper in a saucepan. Simmer for 1 hour, or until the chestnuts are tender and have absorbed all the stock. Transfer the chestnuts and celery to a mixing bowl and allow to cool. Crumble the chestnuts into small pieces, or mash through a coarse sieve.

In a small saucepan, melt the butter. Add the onion and sausagemeat and cook for 8 minutes. Allow the sausage mixture to cool, then add the breadcrumbs and eggs to the chestnuts along with the onion and sausagemeat and mix well with a spoon.

The stuffing is now ready to be used.

Bread

Bread is one of our cheapest sources of food energy since it contains proteins, iron, calcium and B vitamins. It is easy to buy a commercially made loaf of bread or even freshly baked bread from a bakery, but neither of these gives the satisfaction of bread you have made yourself.

Making bread is an art, but contrary to opinion, it can be easily mastered. Bread recipes vary considerably and the guidelines set out here will not fit all of them exactly, but if you understand what each ingredient is meant to do and what the techniques are, you will be well on your way to successful bread-making.

The techniques discussed below are for yeast-based bread only. Soda and other breads based upon bicarbonate of soda, or other raising agents, are much simpler to make, require no raising and only one kneading before cooking.

Ingredients

Flour: The best flours for both bread and yeast doughs are milled from hard wheat. These flours have a high gluten content which produces an elastic, springy dough; whereas soft-wheat flours make a rather sticky dough. Try to use strong plain or baker's white flour which contains more hard wheat and is particularly good for bread-making. When making bread, it is best if the flour and liquid are at room temperature. Warm flour that is too cold in the oven.

Yeast: The most important thing to remember about yeast is that it is a living cell which must be provided with a 'friendly' environment if it is to do its job properly. Yeast is destroyed by extreme heat – over 45°C (11°F). If you add hot water to it, or try to speed up the rising process by leaving the dough in a very hot place, it will be killed. You can use cold water to dissolve the yeast and leave the dough to rise in the refrigerator overnight (this prolongs the rising process), but it will develop most satisfactorily if the room temperature and the temperature of the liquid are between 24°C (75°F) and 30°C (85°F).

Sugar: Sugar provides food for the yeast and also adds flavour to the bread. Sugar also plays a part in browning the crust. If there is not very much sugar in the dough, the yeast will use it all in making carbon dioxide and alcohol, and the baked bread will not be golden brown. Too much sugar, however, retards the yeast's activity and the dough will take longer to rise.

Liquid: The moisture in the dough is supplied by water or milk, or a mixture of the two. It may be added cold: the ideal temperature, however, is lukewarm 27°C (80°F) to 30°C (85°F). Test the milk on the inside of your wrist. Milk should be scalded (brought to just under the boiling point) and then cooled to lukewarm before being combined with flour. Scalding destroys certain bacteria which can sour the dough and also makes the dough easier to handle.

Salt: Salt should never be mixed directly with yeast because it slows down the fermentation process. But a sufficient amount of salt must be added to the dough or the bread will have an uninteresting flavour.

Eggs and butter or oil are variables. When eggs are added to dough, as in sweet breads or French **brioches**, the finished bread is richer and more yellow. Butter or oil increase the volume of the baked bread because the gluten network of the dough is lubricated so that it expands more smoothly and easily. Butter or oil also improves the flavour and keeping qualities of the bread.

Dissolving the yeast: Crumble fresh yeast into a small bowl. Using a fork, cream a small amount of sugar with the yeast and then add a little lukewarm water 30°C (85°F). Mix to a paste and set aside in a warm, draught-free place to ferment. At the end of 15–20 minutes the yeast will be puffed up, bubbling slightly and frothy.

To make bread put the flour and salt into a warmed bowl. Make a well in the centre and pour in the liquid ingredients.

Using your hands or a spatula, mix all the ingredients together until all of the flour is incorporated.

Turn the dough on to a floured board and knead it for about 10 minutes, or until it feels smooth and elastic.

Return the dough to the bowl, cover and leave it in a warm place for about 1 hour, or until it has doubled in bulk.

Turn on to the floured board again and punch down the dough to break up the air pockets. Knead for a further 5 minutes.

Shape the dough into the shape required and either arrange in a loaf pan or on a greased baking sheet. Leave to rise again.

If you are using dried yeast, dissolve a small quantity of sugar in hand-hot water 38°–42°C (100°–110°F) in a small bowl or breakfast cup and sprinkle on the yeast. Leave it for 10 minutes to allow the yeast cells to separate, swell and become active. It should double in volume. The yeast is now ready to begin its work as soon as it is added to the dough.

Mixing the dough: Put the dry ingredients – flour, salt and sugar – in a large, warmed bowl. Make a well in the centre and pour in the liquid ingredients – dissolved yeast, milk and/or water, butter melted in the milk, or oil. Then, using your fingers or a spatula, gradually draw the dry ingredients into the liquids and continue mixing until all the flour is incorporated and the dough comes away from the side of the bowl. If the dough is too soft and wet, more flour may be worked in.

Kneading: Turn the dough out of the bowl on to a floured board or marble slab to knead. This will thoroughly mix the flour with the liquid. The kneaded dough will hold in the gas bubbles manufactured by the yeast. Fold the dough over on to itself towards you and then press it down away from yourself with the heels of your hands. Turn the dough slightly and fold and process it again. Continue kneading for about 5–10 minutes until the dough feels smooth and elastic. Dough made with hard-wheat flours requires a little more kneading than dough made with soft flour. If the dough feels sticky while you are kneading, you can work in a little more flour, but be careful not to add too much or the dough will become stiff.

Rising: Shape the kneaded dough into a ball and place it in a lightly greased bowl. Sprinkle the surface of the dough with a little flour and cover the bowl with a damp cloth. The flour prevents the dough from sticking to the cloth as it rises and the cloth is dampened to increase the humidity. Do not cover the

bowl tightly because to grow the yeast needs air as well as moisture, warmth and food.

Place the bowl in a warm, draught-free place until the dough has almost doubled in bulk. Rising times vary greatly depending on room temperature, the amount of yeast in the dough and the kind of flour used; generally speaking 1–1½ hours is adequate. The longer the fermentation, the better-flavoured and better-textured the bread will be. However, the dough should not be left to rise in a warm place for too long or it will become tough. You can tell if this is happening because a crust will form on top of the dough. If you want to speed up the rising process, place the covered bowl on an oven rack over a pan of boiling water. But be sure that the bottom of the bowl is not too close to the water or the heat will kill the yeast.

To test if the dough has risen sufficiently, press two fingers deep into the dough and withdraw them quickly. If the indentations remain the dough has risen enough.

If you are preparing the dough the day before the bread is to be baked, you can prolong the rising process by putting the covered bowl in a cool place or in the refrigerator for 8–10 hours or overnight. When the dough is fully risen it will be lighter and more spongy than dough which has risen in a warm place. It will require more kneading the second time as well as a longer proving. This slow rising method will, however, produce an excellent bread which will keep well.

Second kneading: Push your fist into the centre of the dough and fold the edges to the centre. This punching down breaks up the large gas pockets and makes available a new supply of oxygen for the yeast plants. Turn the dough out of the bowl on to the floured work surface. Knead it thoroughly and vigorously for 2–3 minutes (a larger batch of dough requires a longer kneading). This second kneading is more important than the first because it temporarily checks the action of the yeast. Use a sharp knife to cut the dough into the number of loaves you are baking. With your hands, shape these pieces into balls.

Proving: What you are proving is that the yeast is still active. To do this the balls of dough are put into the greased tins and pushed out slightly so that they are roughly the shape of the tins. The tins should be only about half full. Sprinkle the surfaces of the loaves with a little flour. Cover the tins with a damp cloth and return them to a warm place for 45–60 minutes. During this time the dough will rise to the tops of the tins.

The proving may be done on an oven rack over a pan of boiling water, but be careful not to place the bottom of the tins too close to the hot water. If you want your bread to have a shiny crust, instead of sprinkling the dough with flour, just before baking brush the tops of the loaves with a mixture of beaten eggs and milk. A country-style finish can be produced by making a criss-cross gash in the top of the dough with a heated, sharp knife or kitchen scissors.

Baking: The bread must always be started in a hot oven. Therefore, preheat the oven to the correct temperature before the dough is put in to bake. Baking stops the fermentation of the yeast and evaporates the alcohol.

Place the tins in the centre of the oven

124

To make the golden crust on this household bread, brush with egg yolk and milk.

and bake for 15 minutes. In this initial stage the loaf rises dramatically, because the leavening gas is expanding rapidly and the gluten cells are stretching to accommodate it. Transfer the tins to a lower shelf and reduce the oven heat. The gluten cells will graduay be set by the heat, and after 25–30 minutes the bread should be done having shrunk slightly in the tins.

To increase the crustiness of the loaves, brush the tops with lightly beaten egg white or cold water 10 minutes before the end of the baking time. For a soft crust, brush the tops with melted butter 10 minutes before the baking time is completed.

Remove the tins from the oven and turn the bread out, upside-down, on to a wire rack. Rap the bottoms of the loaves with your knuckles. If they sound hollow, like a drum, the bread is cooked. If they feel soft, return them, upside-down to the oven with the heat reduced and bake for a further 10-15 minutes.

A shiny, glazed crust, characteristic of French and Vienna bread or rolls, can be obtained by placing a flat pan of boiling water in the bottom of the oven just before the bread is put in, and leaving it in the oven throughout the baking. The steam from the water forms a coating of moisture on the surface of the dough, which gives it time to expand and develop a crust.

Cooling: Bread should be cooled on a wire rack so that the air can circulate around it and prevent moisture from spoiling the crispness of the crust.

Household Bread

This is ordinary white bread, the type most often seen in shops. But like anything home-made, it certainly looks and tastes better. Bake the bread in different containers, or shape the dough into individual braids, rolls, long French-style loaves or round Italian-style loaves.
Makes 4 450 gram (1 pound) loaves

2 teaspoons butter
25 g (1 oz) fresh yeast or 15 g ($\frac{1}{2}$ oz) dry yeast
1 tablespoon plus 1 teaspoon sugar
900 ml (1$\frac{1}{2}$ pints) plus 4 teaspoons lukewarm water
1$\frac{1}{4}$ kg (3 lb) flour
1 tablespoon salt

Grease the loaf tins with the butter.

Crumble the fresh yeast into a small bowl and mash in 1 teaspoon of sugar. Add 4 teaspoons of water and cream the water and yeast together to form a smooth paste. Set the bowl aside in a warm, draught-free place for 15-20 minutes, or until the yeast has risen and is puffed up and frothy.

Put the flour, the remaining sugar and the salt into a warmed, large mixing bowl. Make a well in the centre of the flour mixture and pour in the yeast and the remaining lukewarm water. Gradually draw the flour into the liquid. Continue mixing until all the flour is incorporated and the dough comes away from the side of the bowl.

Turn the dough on to a floured board or marble-slab and knead for about 10 minutes, reflouring the surface if the dough becomes sticky. The dough should then be elastic and smooth. Rinse, thoroughly dry and lightly grease the large mixing bowl. Shape the dough into a ball and return it to the bowl. Dust the top of the dough with a little flour and cover the bowl with a clean, damp cloth. Set the bowl in a warm, draught-free place and leave it for 1-1½ hours, or until the dough has risen and has almost doubled in bulk.

You can make wholewheat bread this shape by baking it in a clay flower pot.

Turn the risen dough out of the bowl on to a floured surface and knead for about 8-10 minutes. Using a sharp knife, cut the dough into four pieces and roll and shape each piece into a loaf. Place the loaves in the tins, cover with a damp cloth and return to a warm place for about 30-45 minutes, or until the dough has risen to the tops of the tins.

Preheat the oven to 240°C (Gas Mark 9, 475°F). Place the tins in the centre of the oven and bake for 15 minutes. Then lower the temperature to 220°C (Gas Mark 7, 425°F), put the bread on a lower shelf in the oven and bake for another 25-30 minutes.

After removing the bread from the oven, tip the loaves out of the tins and rap the undersides with your knuckles. If they do not sound hollow, lower the oven temperature to 190°C (Gas Mark 5, 375°F), return the loaves, upside-down, to the oven and bake for a further 5-10 minutes.

Cool the loaves on a wire rack.

Wholewheat Bread

Although it is most delicious when freshly baked and spread with butter, honey or cheese, stored correctly this bread keeps extremely well for up to a week after baking. For variation, the loaves may be baked in well-greased clay flower pots, or shaped into cottage loaves on a baking sheet. To make cheese bread, add 350 grams (12 ounces) of finely grated Cheddar or any similar cheese to the flour with the yeast mixture.

Makes 4 450 gram (1 pound) loaves

1½ teaspoons butter
25 g (1 oz) fresh yeast or 15 g (½ oz) dry yeast
1 teaspoon brown sugar
900 ml (1½ pints) plus 4 teaspoons lukewarm water
1¼ kg (3 lb) stone-ground wholewheat flour
1¼ tablespoons rock salt or 1 table-spoon table salt
2 tablespoons clear honey
1 tablespoon vegetable oil

To bake the bread, follow the directions given under Household Bread.

American White Bread

This is a smooth-textured, pleasant-tasting milk bread. It has a shiny, golden brown crust and is excellent for sandwiches. This dough recipe can also be used successfully as a base for fruit or nut loaves. For a fruit loaf, during the second kneading add either 150 grams (5 ounces) of sultanas, raisins or dates; for a nut loaf, 150 grams (5 ounces) of chopped walnuts, hazelnuts or almonds. For a fruit and nut loaf, add 150 grams (5 ounces) of dried fruit and 75 grams (3 ounces) of chopped walnuts, hazelnuts or almonds.

Makes 1 450 gram (1 pound) loaf

50 g (2 oz) plus ½ teaspoon butter
15 g (½ oz) fresh yeast or 2 teaspoons dry yeast
1 tablespoon plus 1 teaspoon sugar
3 teaspoons lukewarm water
300 ml (10 fl oz) milk
450 g (1 lb) flour
1 teaspoon salt
Glaze
1 egg lightly beaten with 1 tablespoon milk

To bake the bread, follow the directions for making Household bread. In addition, scald the milk, add the butter to it and, when it has melted, cool to lukewarm. The second kneading should last only 4 minutes.

Pastry

Pastry is an unleavened dough, generally made from shortening, flour and liquid, which is rolled out and used to line flan and tart tins and to envelope or cover sweet and savoury fillings. The eight basic pastries are: shortcrust, rich shortcrust, puff, rough puff, flaky, suetcrust, hot water crust and choux.

The basic ingredients used to make pastry are:

Flour: In almost every kind of dough, refined plain white wheat flour is used. Self-raising flour is used only when a heavier ingredient such as suet is incorporated.

Salt: In most doughs, salt is added in amounts varying from $\frac{1}{8}$ teaspoon to 1 teaspoon.

Sugar: Sugar is added to sweet pastry doughs.

Shortening: All dough includes shortening (a general term that comprises all fats) in proportions which vary according to the richness of the pastry—the more shortening, the richer the dough. Generally, butter is used, but margarine, suet, lard, vegetable fat or oil, or a combination of shortenings can also be used.

Liquid: A small amount of liquid is added to the flour and shortening mixture to bind it and make it more pliable. Water is most commonly used, but other liquids such as eggs, milk, cream, soured cream and buttermilk may be used.

Flavourings: Cheese, herbs, spices and essences may be added to the basic pastry dough.

Yeast: In some doughs, such as that used for making Danish pastries, yeast is used.

Techniques

The method by which shortening is incorporated into flour determines the texture of finished pastry. In puff, rough puff and flaky pastry, the shortening, generally butter, is added either in one large or several smaller pieces, and rolled and folded into the flour and liquid mixture. The resulting texture is, as the names of the pastries imply, light and flaky. For closer-textured pastries, such as shortcrust, the shortening is cut into small pieces and rubbed into the flour with the fingertips until the mixture resembles fine or coarse breadcrumbs. For even closer-textured pastry doughs, such as choux or hot water crust, the shortening is melted with the liquid and then stirred or beaten into the flour. The eggs in choux pastry open out the texture.

The basic points to remember when making pastry dough are:
1. Unless the dough is made with yeast or cooked, the ingredients and implements should be kept cool.
2. For some pastry doughs, such as puff, the ingredients should also be chilled.
3. Again with the exception of yeast and cooked doughs, a minimum of handling is desirable. When possible, use a table knife or pastry blender to incorporate the shortening into the flour. When rubbing the shortening into the flour, use your fingertips and work quickly and lightly. The more you handle the dough, the stickier and less manageable it becomes.
4. When rolling out dough, place it on a lightly floured working surface and use a floured rolling pin. Make sure that the dough does not stick to the surface as it is rolled out. Roll the dough lightly and evenly away from you. Do not turn the dough over or it will absorb too much flour from the working surface. If the dough is sticky or contains a high proportion of shortening, chill it in the refrigerator before rolling it out to make the handling easier.
5. Generally speaking, pastry should be baked, or at least start its baking time, in a hot oven. Long, slow baking produces hard, flat-tasting pastry.
6. Closer-textured pastry dough, such as shortcrust and rich shortcrust, are more suitable for lining flans and pie dishes and for baking blind. All types of pastry doughs are suitable for covering pies and enveloping sweet or savoury fillings.

If you have a freezer, it is well worth your while to make extra dough and freeze it. Wrap it in quantities that are suitable for use, for example 225 grams (8 ounces) and 450 grams (1 pound). Remember to remove the dough from the freezer at least 30 minutes before using so that it can thaw out thoroughly. Tarts and flan cases can also be frozen. It is best to freeze the pastry dough uncooked. If the pie has a cooked filling, this should be cooked and cooled before covering with the pastry dough.

When a recipe calls for 225 grams (8 ounces) of pastry, it means that that much flour should be used.

Preparing a double crust pie

Divide the pastry dough into two portions, one slightly larger than the other. Roll out the larger portion to a little less than $\frac{1}{2}$ centimetre ($\frac{1}{4}$ inch) and about $2\frac{1}{2}$ centimetres (1 inch) wider than the inverted pie plate.

Lift the dough on the rolling pin and place over the pie plate. Lift up the outside of the dough with one hand and press it gently to the sides of the pie dish with the other, taking care not to stretch the dough. Put the prepared filling into the dish, making a slight mound in the centre.

Roll out the smaller portion of the pastry to about 1 centimetre ($\frac{1}{2}$ inch) larger than the dish. Brush the rim of the dough lining with water, lift the dough lid on the rolling pin and place over the filling. Trim the edges and knock up (see below). Make a small slit in the centre of the dough to allow steam to escape during cooking.

Lining a pie plate for an open pie

Roll out the dough to $\frac{1}{2}$ centimetre ($\frac{1}{4}$ inch) thick and 10 centimetres (4 inches) wider than the plate. Lift the dough on the rolling pin and cover the base and sides of the plate. Trim to 1 centimetre ($\frac{1}{2}$ inch) from the plate edge and fold the dough under the rim of the plate. Decorate the edge by pressing down along the rim with your thumb.

Covering a pie dish

Roll out the dough evenly to about $\frac{1}{2}$ centimetre ($\frac{1}{4}$ inch) thick, and 10 centimetres (4 inches) wider than the pie dish. Place the pie dish upside down on the dough to check for width. Cut a $2\frac{1}{2}$ centimetre (1 inch) wide strip from the outer edge of the dough, place it on the moistened rim of the dish and seal the ends together with a little water. Brush the entire strip with water.

Fill the pie dish to just below the rim of the dish and place a funnel in the centre. Lift the dough circle on to the rolling pin and place it over the pie dish, taking care not to stretch it. Then press the lid to the rim. Cut off any excess dough.

Knocking up

This is done to prevent the pastry edges coming apart during cooking. Hold the back of the knife horizontally towards the pie dish and make a series of shallow cuts or dents in the dough edges. Make a slit in the dough to allow steam to escape

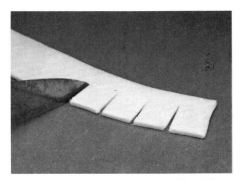

To make pastry roses, make slits, 2½cm (1in) apart, along a strip of dough.

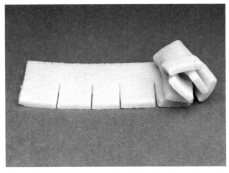

Starting at one end, roll the dough strip up, holding the base firmly.

Using your fingers, pull out the cut dough edges to form petals.

To make leaves, roll out dough trimmings and cut strips about 2½cm (1in) wide.

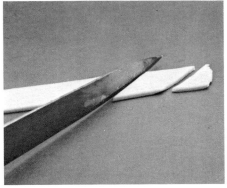

Cut diagonally across the dough strips making diamond patterns.

Now, using a pointed knife, mark veins on the dough leaf.

To decorate the edges, make slits around the rim, then fold back to make a triangle.

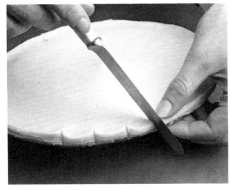

Hold the rim and, with the back of a knife, make indents along the edge.

Press your thumb on to the rim and mark crimps around the edge with two fingers.

Jam tarts – jam filling in baked pastry.

during cooking. Decorate with shapes made from the dough (see photographs on previous page)

Pastry glazes
Dough is usually glazed with beaten egg yolk, lightly beaten egg white, egg white and sugar or whole beaten egg. Of these, egg yolk usually produces the glossiest finish. Brush the glaze on before baking. Sweet dough can be brushed lightly with water and then sprinkled with sugar for a pretty sparkling effect. Milk or a mixture of milk and sugar is also a successful glaze, although the result is not as shiny as egg yolk.

Lining a flan ring
To line a plain flan ring, place the ring on a baking sheet. Roll out the dough thinly to 10 centimetres (4 inches) wider than the ring. Lift the dough on the rolling pin and place it over the ring. Lift up the

128

outside with one hand, and press gently to the sides of the flan ring with the other, taking care not to stretch the dough. Trim the edges by rolling the rolling pin across the flan, away from you first and then back towards you. Gently manipulate the dough to smooth out any air bubbles. Repair any holes or cracks, using pieces of leftover dough as patching material if necessary.

To line a fluted flan ring, press the dough into the shape of the ring, then take off any surplus by running a rolling pin over the top.

Just before baking run your thumbnail between the edge of the ring and the dough. This will ensure the flan case slips out easily after baking. To remove the flan ring, twist it slightly as you lift.

Lining tartlet moulds
Place the moulds closely together on a baking sheet. Roll out the dough until it is thin and large enough to cover the whole area of the tartlet moulds. Lift the

dough on the rolling pin and cover the moulds. Press the dough into the moulds, then take off the surplus with a rolling pin. The moulds should now be baked blind.

Baking blind
Doughs are sometimes cooked before being filled, and this is known as baking blind. Flan cases and individual tartlets are frequently cooked in this way.

Preheat the oven to fairly hot 200°C (Gas Mark 6, 400°F). Prick the base of the dough case all over with a fork. Line the dough case with aluminium foil, greaseproof or waxed paper and half fill it with dried beans or rice. Place the flan ring or tin in the oven and bake for 5 minutes. Remove the beans or rice and foil or paper, and bake 5-10 minutes more, or until the pastry is crisp and golden brown. Remove the pastry case from the oven and allow it to cool. The pastry is now ready to be filled.

(The beans or rice can be stored in a jar

and used again. They will keep for several months.)

Shortcrust Pastry

This is the basic shortcrust pastry used for making sweet or savoury pies and tarts.

Makes 225 grams (8 ounces)

225 g (8 oz) flour
Pinch salt
50 g (2 oz) butter
50 g (2 oz) vegetable fat
3-4 tablespoons iced water

Sift the flour and salt into a medium-sized mixing bowl. Add the butter and vegetable fat and cut them into the flour with a table knife until they form pea-sized globules. Then with your fingertips, rub the fat into the flour until the mixture resembles coarse breadcrumbs.

Sprinkle on 3 tablespoons of the iced water and, using the knife, mix it lightly into the flour mixture. Mix and knead the dough two or three times or until it is smooth. Sprinkle on more water if the dough is too dry. Form the dough into a ball, wrap it in greaseproof or waxed paper and chill in the refrigerator for 30 minutes.

Rich Shortcrust Pastry

Use this pastry as a flan case, for rich or sweet fillings.

Makes 175 grams (6 ounces)

175 g (6 oz) flour
Pinch salt
75 g (3 oz) butter, chilled
1 tablespoon sugar
1 small egg, lightly beaten
1-2 tablespoons iced water

Sift the flour and salt into a medium-sized mixing bowl. Add the butter and cut into small pieces. Rub the butter into the flour until the mixture resembles fine breadcrumbs. Carefully mix in the sugar.

Add the beaten egg with a spoonful of iced water and mix it into the flour mixture with a spatula. Add more water if the dough is too dry.

Knead the dough gently and form it into a ball. Wrap it in greaseproof or waxed paper and chill it in the refrigerator for 30 minutes.

Puff Pastry

This pastry is generally considered to be the best of all the basic pastries in flavour and texture, and the most difficult to make. It should be made with only the finest ingredients: the flour should be of

To make puff pastry, lightly knead the dough with your hands to make it smooth and pliable.

Beat the remaining butter into an oblong. Roll the dough out and place the butter in the centre of the dough.

Fold the four sides of the dough over the butter to enclose it completely and make a neat parcel.

Place the parcel, with the folds facing downwards, on the working surface and roll it out away from you.

Now carefully fold the rolled dough into three and then turn it so that the open end is facing you.

Now roll the dough out again into an oblong, fold it as before and chill it in the refrigerator.

129

good quality and the butter unsalted. The amount of water given in the recipe ingredients is only approximate, since different brands of flour may absorb more or less water. The object in making puff pastry is to produce thin layers of dough interspersed with thin layers of butter. When the dough is cooked, the butter is absorbed by the starch particles when they burst, and the result is a pastry of light horizontal flakes which melt in the mouth.

Puff pastry is used for making bouchées, mille-feuilles, vols-au-vents and small sweet or savoury pastries.

When making puff pastry, it is important that the consistency of the dough and the slab of butter should be the same, that is pliable but not sticky.

When rolling out the dough use an even pressure, avoid stretching the dough and keep the thicknesses of the dough the same all over. Do not use too much flour to prevent the dough from sticking to the working surface or rolling pin, otherwise the proportions of flour to butter will be altered and produce a less satisfactory pastry.

Once the rolling and folding processes have been completed, the puff pastry dough may be covered and chilled in the refrigerator 'for any length of time. Remember to remove it from the refrigerator before it is needed so that it may become pliable and easy to roll into the required shape. Puff pastry may also be frozen for up to 3 months. If you are freezing puff pastry, pack it in 225 gram (8 ounce) 350 gram (12 ounce) or 450 gram (1 pound) portions.

If large quantities of pastry are required it is best to make two batches of 450 grams (1 pound) each.

Makes 450 grams (1 pound)

450 g (1 lb) flour
½ teaspoon salt
450 g (1 lb) butter
225 ml (8 fl oz) iced water

Sift the flour and salt into a large mixing bowl. With a table knife, cut 125 grams (4 ounces) of the butter into the flour. Rub the butter and flour together and mix to a firm dough with the water. Knead the dough to make it pliable and form it into a ball. Cover with greaseproof or waxed paper and place the dough in the refrigerator to chill for 15 minutes.

Put the remaining butter between two pieces of greaseproof or waxed paper and beat it with the back of a wooden spoon or a wooden mallet into a flat oblong slab about 2 centimetres (¾ inch) thick.

On a floured board, roll out the dough into a rectangular shape ½ centimetre (¼ inch) thick. Place the slab of butter in the centre of the dough and fold over it to make a parcel. Place the dough in the refrigerator to chill for a further 10 minutes.

Place the dough, with the folds downwards, on the board and roll out away from you into a rectangle. Fold the rectangle in three. Turn so that the open end is facing you and roll out again. Chill the dough in the refrigerator for 15 minutes. Then repeat this process twice more.

The dough is now ready for use.

Rough Puff Pastry

A rich pastry which is easy and quick to make, Rough Puff Pastry does not rise as well as puff pastry. It is used mainly, therefore, for pie crusts and turnovers.
Makes 225 grams (8 ounces)

225 g (8 oz) flour
½ teaspoon salt
175 g (6 oz) butter
4-6 tablespoons iced water

Sift the flour and salt into a medium-sized mixing bowl. Add the butter and cut into walnut-sized pieces with a table knife. Pour in 4 tablespoons of the iced water and mix quickly with a knife to form a dough, which should be lumpy. Add a little more of the water if the dough looks too dry.

Shape the dough into a ball and place it on a lightly floured working surface. Using a floured rolling pin, roll out the dough into an oblong.

Fold the dough in three, turning it so that the open end faces you. Roll out the dough again into an oblong shape and fold it in three.

Repeat the rolling and folding process once more.

Wrap the dough in greaseproof or waxed paper and chill in the refrigerator for 30 minutes. Remove the dough from the refrigerator. If it looks streaky, roll it out and fold it once more. The dough is now ready to use.

Flaky Pastry

A light, buttery pastry, Flaky Pastry is most often used for mince or fruit pies.

Makes 175 grams (6 ounces)

175 g (6 oz) flour
Pinch salt
50 g (2 oz) butter
50 g (2 oz) lard
3-4 tablespoons cold water

Sift the flour into a mixing bowl and add the salt. Divide the butter into two equal pieces and add one piece to the flour. Rub the fat into the flour until it resembles fine breadcrumbs. With a spatula mix in the water to form a firm dough.

Put the dough on a floured board and shape it into a square. Roll out the dough into an oblong and dot two-thirds of it with small pieces of half the lard. Fold over one-third of the dough and then the other third of the dough to make a neat, square parcel. Press the edges with the rolling-pin to seal.

Turn the dough round so that the sealed ends are facing you and roll out again into an oblong. Dot with pieces of the remaining lard, fold in three, seal the edges, turn the dough and roll out again as before.

Repeat this process with the remaining butter. Wrap the dough in greaseproof or waxed paper and chill in the refrigerator for 10 minutes.

Suetcrust Pastry

A simple-to-make pastry, Suetcrust Pastry may be used in sweet or savoury steamed layer puddings, baked or steamed roly-poly puddings, or as a pastry container for steamed meat puddings. The dough may also be shaped into small balls and cooked in stock to make dumplings.
Makes 225 grams (8 ounces)

225 g (8 oz) self-raising flour
Pinch salt
125 g (4 oz) shredded suet
150 ml (5 fl oz) cold water

Sift the flour and salt into a medium-sized mixing bowl. Stir the suet and water into the flour mixture to form a firm dough. Form the dough into a ball and wrap it in greaseproof or waxed paper.

Place the dough in the refrigerator to chill for 10 minutes.

Hot Water Crust Pastry

This is the traditional pastry for raised pies such as pork, veal, ham and game.

It is essential that the pastry be made as quickly as possible or the fat may

To make a pie case for a raised pie, mould the warm dough around the outside of a lightly greased glass storage jar.

Tie a band of greaseproof paper around the dough to support it. Place on a baking sheet and spoon in the desired filling.

Dampen the edges of the dough case, fit a dough lid on top to cover completely and, finally, crimp to seal the edges.

solidify somewhat.

Makes 350 grams (12 ounces)

350 g (12 oz) flour
1 teaspoon salt
150 ml (5 fl oz) water
125 g (4 oz) vegetable fat or lard
1 egg yolk, lightly beaten

Sift the flour and salt into a large mixing bowl.

In a small saucepan, bring the water and vegetable fat or lard to the boil over high heat, stirring frequently until the fat or lard has melted. Remove the pan from the heat.

Make a well in the centre of the bowl. Pour in the fat and water mixture and the beaten egg. With a wooden spoon stir the mixture around gently. Let flour wash slowly in from the sides. The mixture will not get lumpy if you keep it thick, and the dough will be smooth.

Turn the dough out on to a floured board and knead it well with your hands until it is shiny.

Roll out the dough into the required shape and use at once.

Choux Pastry

This special light pastry is used mostly for éclairs, cream puffs and cheese savouries, but it is also used in such classic French desserts as Gâteau St. Honoré and profiterôles. French in origin, it is named choux because it puffs up during baking and sets in the shape of a cabbage.

Makes 275 grams (10 ounces)

300 ml (10 fl oz) water
75 g (3 oz) butter, cut into small pieces
1 teaspoon salt
275 g (10 oz) flour
5 large eggs

To make pastry for choux puffs, beat the flour into the warm water, melted butter, salt and flavouring.

One by one, beat the eggs into the dough, beating well until the mixture is thick, smooth and glossy.

Fill a piping bag with the mixture and pipe the dough on to greased baking sheets, well apart, in circular mounds.

In a heavy saucepan, bring the water to the boil. Add the butter, and salt. When the butter has melted, remove the pan from the heat and beat in the flour. Continue beating until the mixture pulls away from the sides of the pan.

One by one, beat each egg into the dough until it is well blended, then the next. When the eggs have all been completely absorbed, the mixture should be thick and somewhat glossy.

The dough is now ready for use.

Cakes

Cakes seem to come in an infinite number of varieties, but if you look closely at the recipes you will discover that almost all fall into five categories: creamed butter and sugar; whisked eggs (either whole or separated); rubbed-in fat; melted fat; and yeast. These categories differ from one another in richness, delicacy and keeping qualities.

Cake-making

For the best results when making cakes have all the ingredients at room temperature. Preheat the oven to the specified temperature. If the oven is too cool when you put the cake in, the finished cake will have a heavy texture.

Use the correct size tin or pan as specified in the recipe. If the tin is too large, the cake will be thin and heavy. If it is too small, the mixture may overflow as it rises and the cake's texture will be coarse.

Grease and flour the tin or pan before you begin to mix the cake batter.

To prepare the tin, spread only a thin film of lard, oil or butter over the sides and bottom. Sprinkle in a little flour and tip and rotate the tin to distribute the flour evenly. Shake out any excess by turning the tin upside-down and gently knocking on the bottom. Sometimes sugar is added with the flour. This gives a crisper, crunchier crust, which is especially good on plain cakes.

If the cake requires a long baking, the tin should be greased and then lined with buttered greaseproof or waxed paper. For a rich fruit cake, tie a band of brown paper around the outside of the tin as well.

If the recipe specifies plain flour, do not substitute self-raising, because the texture will be too open and the cake will rise too much. If self-raising flour is called for but not available use plain flour with baking powder in the proportion of 4 level teaspoons baking powder to 450 grams (1 pound) plain flour. Flour and other ingredients should always be sifted before use to remove lumps and aerate the flour.

Measure the ingredients accurately and blend them together thoroughly. Do not beat the batter after the flour has been added or the finished cake will be somewhat heavy.

Folding

Many recipes indicate that the flour, eggs or another ingredient should be folded in. This gentle method keeps a maximum amount of air in the cake batter, which leads to better rising.

Every cook should master the folding technique, which consists of two basic steps. First, cut across the centre of the mixture with a large metal spoon. Second, run the spoon around the perimeter of the bowl, ending with a folding motion towards the centre. Give the bowl a quarter-turn. Repeat these two steps until almost all the substance is incorporated (break up and incorporate the last bits as you pour the batter into the cake tin).

Be sure to get your spoon right down to the bottom of the bowl so that no large pockets of batter or flour remain unincorporated. Be gentle, delicate and even slow in all your motions. For a tender, light cake try to keep the number of folds to eight or ten.

Fill the cake tin only one-half to two-thirds full of batter.

Place the tin in the centre of the oven so the heat can circulate around it. In general, small cakes should be baked near the top of the oven, and large cakes in the middle of the oven.

Bake the cake for the length of time specified in the recipe. Before removing it from the oven, test it to be sure that it is done. If not, continue baking for 5 minutes and test again.

To test if the cake is completely baked, insert a metal skewer or thin knife into the centre of the cake. If it comes out clean, the cake is done. Alternatively, lightly press the top of the cake with a fingertip. The cake will spring back if it is cooked. The cake should also have pulled away slightly from the edges of the tin.

As soon as the baking is completed, remove the cake from the oven and let it stand for a few minutes. Then loosen the sides by running a knife between the cake and sides of the tin (unless the tin has a non-stick finish). Place a clean cloth over the top and turn the cake out on to the cloth. Then transfer it to a wire cake rack (place the rack, inverted on the bottom of the cake and turn it over). The cloth will prevent the top of the cake from being marked by the rack.

If the cake is to be iced or frosted, wait until it has cooled to room temperature before decorating.

Methods of cake making

Creaming butter and sugar

This method is used for richer cakes when the margarine or butter is creamed together with sugar, using a wooden spoon or an electric mixer. The mixture should be beaten until it is light and fluffy, because this incorporates air and dissolves the sugar crystals.

The eggs are then beaten in, one at a time, and the flour is folded into the mixture. If the mixture starts to curdle when the eggs are added, beat in a spoonful of the measured flour as given in the recipe.

Probably the most famous creamed cake is the Victoria Sandwich, though many chocolate and American cakes come in this category. Surprisingly, perhaps, most fruit cakes are based on the creaming method.

Dundee Cake

1 tablespoon melted butter
275 g (10 oz) flour
½ teaspoon baking powder
½ teaspoon ground mixed spice
½ teaspoon ground cinnamon
225 g (8 oz) butter
225 g (8 oz) castor sugar
5 eggs
125 g (4 oz) seedless raisins
125 g (4 oz) currants
125 g (4 oz) sultanas or raisins
50 g (2 oz) mixed candied fruit, coarsely chopped
50 g (2 oz) glacé cherries
grated rind of 1 small orange
grated rind of 1 small lemon
50 g (2 oz) blanched almonds, halved

Preheat the oven to warm 170°C (Gas Mark 3, 325°F). Lightly brush the bottom and sides of a 20 centimetre (8 inch) cake tin with half the melted butter. Line the bottom and sides of the tin with greaseproof or waxed paper. Lightly brush the greaseproof or waxed paper with the remaining melted butter. Set the tin aside.

Sift the flour, baking powder, mixed spice and cinnamon into a large bowl. Set aside.

In a medium-sized mixing bowl, cream the butter with a wooden spoon until it is soft and creamy. Gradually add the sugar and beat until the mixture is pale and fluffy, and drops easily from the spoon when it is tapped against the side

of the bowl. Break one egg into the butter-sugar mixture and beat vigorously until the mixture stiffens and becomes fluffy. Add the remaining eggs in the same manner, beating in 2 tablespoons of the flour mixture before adding the last egg.

Add the raisins, currants, sultanas or raisins, candied fruit, cherries and orange and lemon rinds to the flour mixture. Mix together until all the fruits are coated with flour. Using a metal spoon, fold and cut the flour-and-fruit mixture into the butter-sugar mixture until the ingredients are well blended.

Spoon the cake mixture into the tin, being careful to push the mixture well into the corners. Smooth the top carefully, making it as level as possible. Arrange the halved almonds in concentric circles, their pointed ends towards the centre, on top of the cake.

Bake the cake in the lower part of the oven for 2 hours, or until a skewer inserted into the centre of the cake comes out clean. Cover the top of the cake with brown or greaseproof or waxed paper if it browns too quickly. Turn off the oven heat and leave the cake in the oven for 10–15 minutes before removing it. When it is completely cool remove it from the tin and place it on a wire rack. Peel off the greaseproof or waxed paper.

This cake may be kept for several weeks if it is stored in an airtight tin.

Victorian Orange Buns
Makes 12 buns

125 g (4 oz) plus 1 tablespoon butter
125 g (4 oz) flour
½ teaspoon baking powder
125 g (4 oz) sugar
2 eggs
Grated rind of 1 orange
75 ml (3 fl oz) fresh orange juice
1 tablespoon milk
2 slices candied orange, cut into 12 pieces
1 tablespoon icing sugar

Preheat the oven to fairly hot 190°C (Gas Mark 5, 375°F). With the tablespoon of butter, grease 12 patty tins.

Sift the flour and baking powder into a mixing bowl and set aside.

In a mixing bowl, cream the remaining butter with a wooden spoon until it is soft and creamy. Add the sugar and beat well until the mixture is light and fluffy. Add the eggs, one at a time, adding a

tablespoon of the flour mixture with each egg, and beat well. Stir in the orange rind and juice. Using a large metal spoon, fold in the remaining flour and stir in the milk.

Spoon the mixture into the greased patty tins so that each one is two-thirds full. Place one piece of candied orange on top of each bun mixture.

Place the patty tins on a baking sheet and place the sheet in the oven. Bake for 20–25 minutes or until the centres of the buns spring back when pressed lightly with a finger. Transfer the buns to a wire rack to cool completely.

Place the buns on a serving dish and sift over the icing sugar. Serve at once.

Whisking eggs

Cakes made by this method need not contain fat. The basic ingredients are eggs, castor sugar and flour. The whisking of the eggs and sugar should be done with a wire whisk or electric mixer so that as much air is incorporated into the mixture as possible to produce a light, fluffy cake. In these cakes air is the only leavening agent.

In some recipes the eggs are separated, and only the yolks are whisked with the sugar. The whites are whisked separately until stiff and folded into the sugar mixture along with the flour.

Whisked cakes should be eaten as soon as possible because the omission of fat in the recipe gives them a drier texture. If a sponge cake is to be kept for later use, the same method is used with the addition of melted butter or oil. The best known cake made with this method is called a Genoise Sponge.

Sponge Cake

This is a basic mixture with a high proportion of eggs and no fat, and the result is a very light cake. Serve, sandwiched with whipped cream and strawberry jam.

2 teaspoons butter
75 g (3 oz) plus 2 teaspoons flour
3 eggs
75 g (3 oz) castor sugar
½ teaspoon baking powder

Preheat the oven to moderate 180°C (Gas Mark 4, 350°F). With 1 teaspoon of the butter, grease two 18 centimetre (7 inch) sandwich tins. Line the base of the tins with a circle of greaseproof or waxed paper and grease with the remaining butter. Sprinkle the 2 teaspoons of flour into the tins and tip and rotate them until they are well coated, discarding the excess. Set aside.

Place a large, heatproof mixing bowl over a large saucepan half-filled with simmering water. Place the eggs and sugar in the bowl and set the pan over low heat. Using a wire whisk or rotary beater, whisk the eggs and sugar together for about 10 minutes or until the mixture is pale in colour and thick, and will leave a ribbon trail on itself when the whisk is lifted. Remove the pan from the heat and the bowl from the pan, and continue whisking until the mixture is cool.

Sift the remaining flour and baking powder on to the egg mixture and, using a large metal spoon, fold it in very carefully until the flour is thoroughly combined. Pour the batter into the prepared cake tins and place them in the centre of the oven. Bake the cakes for 25–30 minutes or until the surface springs back when gently pressed with a fingertip.

Remove the tins from the oven and turn the cakes out on to a wire rack. Remove and discard the greaseproof or waxed paper. Set aside to cool completely before serving.

Genoise Sponge
This is a classic French sponge which can be served plain, or filled and iced as here. The mixture is also used to make small shell-shaped **Madeleines** or cut up into small squares or oblongs and made into petits fours.

225 g (8 oz) plus 2 teaspoons unsalted butter, melted
225 g (8 oz) plus 2 tablespoons flour
275 g (10 oz) castor sugar

8 eggs, at room temperature
½ teaspoon vanilla essence

BUTTERCREAM

50 g (2 oz) dark cooking chocolate, broken into pieces
175 g (6 oz) plus 2 teaspoons unsalted butter
350 g (12 oz) icing sugar
2 tablespoons double cream
½ teaspoon vanilla essence

Preheat the oven to fairly hot 190°C (Gas Mark 5, 375°F). Using the 2 teaspoons of butter, grease two 23 centimetre (9 inch) shallow cake tins. Dust them with 2 tablespoons of flour, tipping and rotating the tins so that they are evenly coated. Shake out any excess flour. Set aside.

Place a medium-sized heatproof mixing bowl over a large saucepan half-filled with hot water. Put the sugar, eggs and vanilla essence into the bowl and set the pan over low heat. With a wire whisk or rotary beater, beat the mixture for 20–25 minutes, or until it is thick and pale and will make a ribbon trail on itself when the whisk is lifted.

Remove the pan from the heat and the bowl from the pan. Sift in the remaining flour and, with a metal spoon, lightly fold it into the egg and sugar mixture. Gradually pour in the melted butter, stirring constantly. Pour equal amounts of the batter into each of the prepared cake tins. Place the tins in the centre of the oven and bake for 20–30 minutes, or until the centres of the cakes spring back when lightly pressed with a fingertip.

Remove the tins from the oven and leave for 5 minutes. Then turn the cakes out on to a wire rack to cool completely.

Meanwhile, make the buttercream. Place the chocolate pieces in a small heatproof bowl set over a pan of boiling water. Place the pan over low heat and melt the chocolate, stirring occasionally. As soon as the chocolate has melted, remove the pan from the heat and set aside.

In a medium-sized mixing bowl, cream the butter with a wooden spoon until it is soft. Sift in half of the icing sugar and beat until the mixture is light and fluffy. Add the cream, vanilla essence and the melted chocolate. Sift in the remaining sugar and blend the mixture thoroughly.

Cut the domed top off one of the cakes and discard it. Spread the cake with one-quarter of the buttercream, and place the second cake on top, dome side up. Spread the remaining buttercream over the top and sides of the cake, bringing it up into decorative peaks.

Rubbing in

Plainer cakes, scones and biscuits are made by this method. Usually the proportion of fat is one-quarter to one-half of the flour or dry ingredients. The fat is rubbed into the flour until the mixture resembles breadcrumbs. Fruit and flavourings are added and then the liquid, generally egg and milk.

Shortbread

Shortbread is often formed into shapes in special shortbread moulds. However, if a mould is not available, it may be shaped by hand on a baking sheet.

225 g (8 oz) plus 1 teaspoon butter
225 g (8 oz) flour
125 g (4 oz) rice flour
125 g (4 oz) plus 1 tablespoon castor sugar

Using the teaspoon of butter, grease a large baking sheet and set aside.

Sift the flour and rice flour into a mixing bowl and stir in the 125 grams (4 ounces) of sugar. Add the remaining butter and cut it into small pieces with a knife. With your fingertips, rub the butter into the flour mixture until it resembles coarse breadcrumbs.

Knead the mixture gently until it forms a smooth dough. Turn the dough out on to a floured board and divide the dough in half. Form each piece into a circle about 1 centimetre (½ inch) thick and 15 centimetres (6 inches) in diameter. Transfer the dough circles to the baking sheet, crimping the edges with your fingertips. Prick the top of the dough with a fork. Place the baking sheet in the refrigerator and chill the dough for 20 minutes.

Preheat the oven to moderate 180°C (Gas Mark 4, 350°F).

Place the baking sheet in the centre of the oven and bake the shortbread for 10 minutes. Reduce the oven temperature to cool 150°C (Gas Mark 2, 300°F) and continue to bake the shortbread for a further 35–40 minutes or until it is crisp and lightly browned.

Remove the sheet from the oven and, with a knife, cut the circles into triangles. Allow to cool slightly on the baking sheet. Sprinkle the remaining tablespoon of sugar over the triangles. Transfer the shortbread to a wire rack to cool completely.

Store in an airtight tin if you do not intend to serve immediately.

Melting

This method makes moist cakes that keep well. The fat is melted with the sugar, syrup or treacle and then mixed into the dry ingredients. Most recipes use plain flour with the addition of bicarbonate of soda or baking powder as a raising agent. A better result is obtained if moist brown sugar is used, because this gives the cake a rich dark colour and increases its keeping qualities.

Parkin

Parkin is a moist cake which should be kept for at least a week in an airtight tin before serving.

225 g (8 oz) plus 2 teaspoons butter
450 g (1 lb) flour
1 teaspoon bicarbonate of soda
1 teaspoon salt
2 teaspoons ground ginger
450 g (1 lb) rolled oats
250 ml (8 fl oz) dark treacle
250 ml (8 fl oz) golden syrup
50 ml (2 fl oz) clear honey
2 tablespoons soft brown sugar
350 ml (12 fl oz) milk

Using the 2 teaspoons of butter, grease two 25 centimetre (10 inch) square cake tins. Line with non-stick silicone paper and set aside.

Preheat the oven to warm 170°C (Gas Mark 3, 325°F). Sift the flour, soda, salt and ginger into a large mixing bowl. Add the rolled oats and stir well. Set aside.

In a medium-sized saucepan, melt the remaining butter with the treacle, syrup, honey and sugar over low heat. Cook the mixture, stirring constantly for 1 minute, or until all the ingredients are thoroughly combined.

Make a well in the centre of the flour mixture and pour in the butter and treacle mixture and the milk. Using a wooden spoon or spatula, gradually draw the flour mixture into the liquid.

Continue mixing until all the flour mixture is incorporated. Spoon the batter into the prepared baking tins and place them in the oven. Bake the parkins for 45–50 minutes, or until the cakes are firm when pressed with your fingertips.

Remove the tins from the oven and set the parkins aside to cool in the tins for

for them to rise. Cover them with the cloth or plastic bag and place in a warm place to rise for another 30 minutes.

Brush the top with the sweetened egg and milk mixture and sprinkle with the sugar. Place the buns in the oven and bake for 25–30 minutes.

Cool to warm before serving.

Icings, Fillings and Sauces

This section brings together some ways to put 'finishing touches' on pastry and cakes. The simplest decorations are a dusting of icing sugar, a little jam, whipped or double cream. But these are not suitable for all occasions, and numerous others have therefore evolved.

Icings and Fillings

Icings are sugar-based mixtures that go over the sides and tops of a cake. They can be either firm or soft. Soft icing can also be used as a filling. Fillings go between the layers of a cake or into a pastry case. In general, they are soft. Toppings are usually passed separately and are added by the individual. Most, but not all, are thin enough to pour. Meringue is also a topping, though it fits none of these categories.

Glazes

The term 'glaze' is given both to a thin hot mixture of equal parts of water and sugar which is brushed over yeast cakes and buns to give them a shiny surface, and to a modified jam.

A jam glaze is used in various ways. It can be spread over a blind-baked flan case to prevent a soggy crust. Painted over a fruit flan, it gives a shiny finish. Glaze is also used on the top and sides of cakes before icing to hold crumbs in place so they won't spoil the icing. Sometimes it forms a thin filling between layers.

Glazes are spread most easily with a brush – an ordinary 2½ centimetre (1 inch) pastry brush works quite well.

Apricot jam and redcurrant jelly make the best glazes because they contain sufficient pectin to stiffen the glaze and prevent it from being sticky to the touch. The glaze should be applied while still hot; in the case of a fruit flan while the fruit is still warm. Apricot should be

15 minutes before turning them out on to a wire rack to cool completely.

Yeast

Yeast cakes and buns are made in the same manner as yeast breads, though the dough is often sweetened more. They usually have a sweet filling, such as raisins and peel, which is added before baking.

Bath buns
Makes 12 buns

75 g (3 oz) plus 1 teaspoon sugar
150 ml (5 fl oz) lukewarm milk
15 g (½ oz) fresh yeast
450 g (1 lb) flour
½ teaspoon salt
125 g (4 oz) butter
2 eggs, lightly beaten
125 g (4 oz) currants
50 g (2 oz) candied peel
GLAZE
½ egg, lightly beaten with 1 tablespoon milk and sweetened with 1 tablespoon sugar
50 g (2 oz) sugar

In a small mixing bowl, dissolve 1 tea-

Bath buns, warming, spicy teabreads made from yeast dough.

spoon of sugar in the warm milk. Crumble the yeast on top and mix well. Leave the milk-and-yeast mixture in a warm place for 15–20 minutes or until it becomes frothy.

Sift the flour and the salt into a warm mixing bowl and mix in the remaining sugar. With your fingertips, rub the butter into the flour mixture. Make a well in the centre of the flour mixture and pour in the frothy yeast and the beaten eggs. Mix in with a fork and then, using well-floured hands, knead lightly to make a soft dough.

Put the dough in a greased bowl, cover with a cloth or a plastic bag and place in a warm place for 1 hour, or until the dough has doubled in size. Turn the dough on to a floured board and knead in the currants and candied peel.

Preheat the oven to hot 190°C (Gas Mark 5, 375°F). Lightly grease a baking sheet.

Divide the dough into 12 pieces and shape into buns. Place the buns on the baking sheet, well spaced to leave room used for yellow and other light colour fruits; redcurrant for red and other dark coloured fruits.

Jam Glaze

125 g (4 oz) apricot jam or redcurrant jelly
1 tablespoon water
1 teaspoon lemon juice

With a wooden spoon, press the apricot jam or redcurrant jelly through a sieve into a saucepan.

Add the water and lemon juice. Cook, stirring constantly for 2–3 minutes, or until the glaze is thick and sticky. Remove the pan from the heat and use the glaze while it is still hot.

Icings

Firm icings are still warm when they are put on cakes; they harden as they cool. An uncooked glacé icing calls for 175–225 grams (6–8 ounces) icing sugar mixed with 2 tablespoons of very hot water, plus flavourings and colouring (if used). Cooked glacé icing is more interesting.

Glacé Icing

Glacé icing is the simplest, quickest type of cooked icing to make and is ideal for topping a plain sponge cake. If you like, add ¼ teaspoon of vanilla or coffee essence to the icing sugar at the same time as the syrup. Orange or lemon icing can be made by adding the grated rinds of 2 oranges or lemons to the sugar syrup before it comes to the boil.
Makes about 600 millilitres (1 pint)

450 g (1 lb) sugar
300 ml (10 fl oz) water
225 g (8 oz) icing sugar

In a medium-sized saucepan, dissolve the sugar in the water over low heat, stirring constantly. Increase the heat to moderate, cover the pan and bring the syrup to the boil. Continue boiling until the syrup registers 102°C (215°F) to 104°C (220°F) on a sugar thermometer (about 1 minute), or until a small amount removed from the pan and cooled will form a short thread between your thumb and index finger. Remove the pan from the heat and allow the syrup to cool slightly.

Place the icing sugar in a medium-sized bowl. With a wooden spoon, gradually beat in the syrup. Continue beating until the icing is thick and smooth. Place the bowl over a pan of simmering water and stir until the icing is warm and of a spreading consistency.

Pour the icing on to the centre of the cake and spread it out quickly with a knife dipped in hot water.

Chocolate glacé icing can be made by replacing 25 grams (1 ounce) of the icing sugar with cocoa powder.

Chocolate Icing

Makes enough for one 23 centimetre (9 inch) cake, top and sides

225 g (8 oz) dark cooking chocolate, broken into pieces
125 ml (4 fl oz) double cream
350 g (12 oz) icing sugar

In a heatproof bowl set over a pan of simmering water, melt the chocolate over low heat. Remove the pan from the heat and remove the bowl from the pan. Set aside to cool for 10 minutes. Beat in the cream and icing sugar, beating until the mixture is smooth. Spread the icing over the top

and sides of the cake using a palette knife. Be sure that the icing is smooth.

Set the cake aside in a cool place for 2 hours, or until the icing has set.

Buttercream Icing

Buttercream icing is probably the most versatile of the soft icings, since numerous flavours can be added.
Makes enough to fill and ice one 23 centimetre (9 inch) cake

75 g (3 oz) unsalted butter, at room temperature
350 g (12 oz) icing sugar, sifted
⅛ teaspoon salt
1½ teaspoons vanilla essence
2 tablespoons double cream or milk

Place the butter in a large mixing bowl and, with the back of a wooden spoon or an electric mixer, cream it. When it is smooth, gradually add half of the sugar and the salt. Cream the butter and sugar together until the mixture is pale and

To make glacé icing, sift the icing sugar through a fine sieve into a bowl.

Gradually beat in warm water or any flavouring or colour to be added.

Beat the mixture vigorously for 3 minutes until it is shiny and smooth.

Now pour the icing on top of the cake and spread evenly with a palette knife.

To make icing sugar decoration on a cake, place a doily on top and sift on the sugar.

Gently lift the doily off the cake with the tips of your fingers.

fluffy. Mix in the vanilla essence and cream or milk and beat in the remaining sugar.

Variations: **Chocolate Buttercream Icing:** See page 135. Or add 50 grams (2 ounces) of melted dark cooking chocolate with the cream and vanilla essence to the basic Butter-cream Icing. Alternatively, replace 25 grams (1 ounce) of the icing sugar with cocoa powder.

Orange or Lemon Buttercream Icing: Substitute the grated rind of ½ orange or lemon and 3 tablespoons of orange or lemon juice for the cream in the basic Buttercream Icing.

Fillings

In addition to jam and flavoured whipped cream which need no further description, pastry cream (a type of custard) and lemon curd can also be used as cake fillings.

138

Pastry Cream
Makes 350 millilitres (12 fluid ounces)

2 egg yolks
4 tablespoons sugar
1 tablespoon cornflour
1 tablespoon plus 1 teaspoon flour
300 ml (10 fl oz) milk
½ teaspoon vanilla essence
1 egg white

In a medium-sized bowl, lightly beat the egg yolks with a fork. Add the sugar and beat the mixture until it is creamy. Sift in the cornflour and flour a little at a time, beating constantly, then gradually mix in about one-quarter of the milk and the vanilla essence.

In a medium-sized saucepan, scald the remaining milk over high heat. Pour the hot milk into the egg-and-sugar mixture, beating well with a wire whisk. Return the mixture to the pan and, stirring constantly, bring it back to the boil. Remove the pan from the heat and beat the mixture until it is smooth. Set aside and allow it to cool.

In a small bowl, whisk the egg white with a wire whisk until it forms stiff peaks. Transfer about one-quarter of the warm cream mixture to a medium-sized bowl. Carefully fold the egg white into the mixture. Fold the egg-white mixture into the remaining cream in the saucepan. Return the saucepan to the stove and cook the mixture over low heat for 2 minutes, stirring occasionally.

Cool before using the cream.

Lemon Curd
Makes about 2 kilograms (4 pounds)

350 g (12 oz) butter, cut into small pieces
900 g (2 lb) castor sugar
thinly pared rind and juice of 6 large lemons
8 eggs, well beaten

Place a large heatproof mixing bowl over a pan half filled with hot water. Put the butter, sugar, lemon rind and juice in the bowl. Set the pan over moderately low heat. Cook the mixture, stirring constantly with a wooden spoon, until the sugar has dissolved.

Using a wire whisk or rotary beater, whisk in the eggs. Continue cooking, stirring constantly, for 35–40 minutes or until the lemon curd thickens.

Remove the pan from the heat. Lift the bowl out of the pan. With a slotted spoon, remove and discard the rind.

Ladle the lemon curd into clean, dry jam jars. Lightly press a circle of grease-proof or waxed paper on to the surface of the curd in each jar.

Cover the jars with jam covers and secure them with rubber bands. Label the jars and store them in a cool, dark, dry place. Eat within 1 month.

Sauces

Sauces are the most frequent type of topping. They can be served hot or cold to enhance ice-cream, pancakes and puddings. Thin custard, which is too frequently made with custard powder, tastes infinitely better when made fresh.

Vanilla Custard
Makes about 600 millilitres (1 pint)

450 ml (15 fl oz) milk
1 vanilla pod
4 egg yolks
50 g (2 oz) sugar

Place the milk and vanilla pod in the top of a double boiler or in a heatproof bowl placed over a saucepan of water and heat to just below boiling point over moderate heat. When bubbles form at the edge of the pan, remove the milk from the heat. Cover the pan or bowl and set it aside for 10 minutes. Remove the vanilla pod with a slotted spoon.

In a large bowl, beat the egg yolks and sugar together with a wire whisk until they are smooth and creamy. Gradually strain in the milk, stirring constantly. Pour the custard back into the top of the double boiler or bowl and cook over hot (not boiling) water for 3–5 minutes, or until the custard begins to thicken, stirring constantly with a wooden spoon. Care should be taken not to overcook the custard or it will curdle. The custard should be thick enough to coat the back of the spoon. Remove the pan or bowl from the heat and pour the custard into a bowl or jug. Serve warm or chilled.

Fruit sauces

Fruit sauces can be made with fresh fruit, canned fruit, or jam. Fresh fruit sauces can be frozen. Soft fruits such as raspberries, strawberries, plums, peaches and apricots are best for fruit sauces.

To make a fresh fruit sauce, the fruit must be ripe and firm. Place the chosen fruit in a saucepan with just enough water to cover the bottom of the pan. Cook the

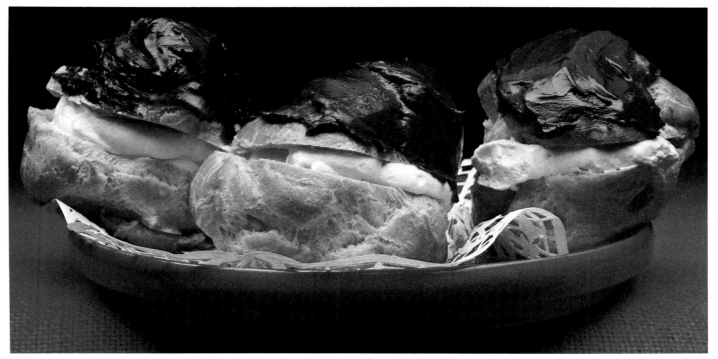

fruit over moderate heat for 10–15 minutes, or until it is tender. Transfer it to a sieve placed over a bowl. With a wooden spoon, press the fruit through the sieve into the bowl. Add at least a tablespoon of sugar or more to your taste. The juice of half a lemon will sharpen up the flavour if it is weak.

Pour the sauce back into the saucepan if it is to be served hot and cook over moderate heat, stirring frequently, for 2 minutes, or until it is heated through. Place the strained sauce in the refrigerator to chill for 30 minutes if it is to be served cold.

Canned fruit sauce

This can be made with any sort of small canned fruit – berries, cherries, blackcurrants. Serve as an accompaniment to ice-cream, or filled choux puffs.
6 servings

1 kg (2¼ lb) can of fruit
Peel and juice of 1 lemon
1 dessertspoon arrowroot
2 tablespoons water

Drain the fruit and put it aside. Put the juice and lemon peel into a saucepan and bring slowly to the boil. Mix the arrowroot with the water until it has dissolved and add it to the boiling syrup. Stir vigorously until the mixture thickens slightly. Remove from the heat and extract the lemon peel. Add the reserved fruit. Serve hot or cold, but not chilled.

Jam sauce
Makes about 350 millilitres (12 fl oz)

4 tablespoons jam
Grated rind and juice of 1 lemon
4 tablespoons sugar
300 ml (10 fl oz) water
2 teaspoons cornflour dissolved in 1 tablespoon water

In a small saucepan, melt the jam with the lemon rind and juice, sugar and water over moderate heat, stirring with a wooden spoon until the sugar has completely dissolved. Remove the saucepan from the heat and set it aside for 10 minutes.

Add the cornflour mixture to the jam mixture and stir well. Return the saucepan to the heat. Bring the sauce to the boil, stirring constantly. Remove from the heat and pour into a warmed sauce boat. Serve hot.

Chocolate Sauce

This is a semi-sweet sauce, suitable for using on ice-creams, sorbets, puddings, meringues and cakes.
Makes 600 millilitres (1 pint)

175 g (6 oz) dark cooking chocolate, broken into pieces
425 ml (14 fl oz) canned evaporated milk
1 teaspoon vanilla essence
2 drops almond essence

In a double-saucepan, or in a heatproof bowl placed over a pan of hot water, melt

Finished, luscious choux puffs, filled with a rich pastry cream mixture and topped with chocolate sauce.

the chocolate with the milk, stirring occasionally. As soon as the chocolate has melted, remove the bowl or pan from the heat. Beat the vanilla and almond essences into the chocolate mixture. Continue heating until the sauce is smooth. Serve warm.

Meringue topping

Meringue topping can be either the soft, melt-in-the-month type or crunchy depending on how long it is cooked and at what temperature. For either type of meringue use from 25–50 grams (1–2 ounces) of sugar for each egg white, depending on how sweet you want it to be. Two egg whites are sufficient for a 20 centimetre (8 inch) flan, three for 23 centimetre (9 inch) one. In a medium-sized mixing bowl, using a wire whisk or rotary beater, beat the egg whites until they are frothy. Gradually beat in the sugar and continue beating until the meringue mixture forms stiff peaks. Pile the meringue on top of the filling to cover it completely. For a soft meringue bake at 200°C (Gas Mark 6, 400°C), for 6–10 minutes, that is until just the peaks of the meringue are brown. For a crunchy meringue bake at 180°C (Gas Mark 4, 350°F) for 20–25 minutes, or until the meringue has set and is golden brown on top.

Chapter Seven

Preparing tasty food is the core of a good meal, but it is not the whole story. For dietary balance and attractive presentation are of almost equal importance. All meals, whether for single people, families, or guests, should contain variety in colour, texture and nutrients.

Finishing touches are of three sorts, those that are built into the menu planning, those that are part of the table arrangement and general ambience, and those that garnish the food to enhance its attractiveness. Thus planning the finishing touches begins as soon as you think about a meal.

Meal Planning

When planning your meal, remember colour—no fish served in white sauce, mashed potatoes with cauliflower, or gammon accompanied by turnip and carrots. Texture, too, should be important. Have contrasts within the same course and between courses. For example, crunchy raw vegetables with a smooth cheese flan and a beef casserole followed by a crisp lettuce salad. Flavours should offer contrasts: a bland pudding after a spicy main course; a succulent roast followed by tangy citrus fruits.

By serving a variety of foods at a meal and in the course of a day, you ensure a balanced diet. But understanding the principles of nutrition is equally important.

Nutrition

As either menu planner or cook, you should know the basics of good nutrition, which should be observed in all meal planning. This will ensure good health and reduce the likelihood of obesity. It should also reduce your food budget, because the foods that are best for you are often less expensive than those that provide little benefit.

Most foods contain three substances, carbohydrates, fats and proteins. Only a few foods are pure: sugar (100 per cent carbohydrate); oil and lard (100 per cent fat). Foods also contain minerals and vitamins and trace elements, all of which are essential to good health, appearance and general well being.

Carbohydrates are the general name given to the starches and sugars in our diet. Virtually your entire intake is of vegetable origin, especially grains, with only traces found in meat, poultry and fish.

Fats are of both animal and plant origin, and everybody should have some of each kind daily. But since much of the fat in our diet is hidden, you should use a minimum of animal fats in cooking. It is important, however, to include some vegetable fats daily. Fats of mainly animal origin cause a build up of fatty substances, called cholesterol, which is dangerous to health (see page 48). Thus as menu planner and cook you should work to keep total fat intake down, while ensuring an adequate intake of vegetable fats.

Your body uses carbohydrates to supply energy, and when the carbohydrates are used up it turns to the fats, converting them first to carbohydrates and then to energy. Conversely, excess carbohydrates are changed into fats for storage for future needs. Gaining weight means your food intake is greater than your energy needs, and your body is storing the rest as fat.

Proteins, which are of both animal and vegetable origin, form the building blocks for our bodies. They are made up of many different amino acids, of which eight are essential for adults and ten for children. Animal protein contains all the essential amino acids, whereas no vegetable protein contains all eight. Thus vegetarians need to consume a wide range of protein foods to ensure adequate amounts of all the essential amino acids.

About 11 per cent of an adult's food intake and 14 per cent of a child's or adolescent's should be protein. If your protein intake is greater than your body needs, the excess is converted into carbohydrates for energy (and from carbohydrates into fat for storage once energy needs are fulfilled).

Minerals are required for strong bones and teeth, for maintaining the correct composition of body fluids (blood, lymph, perspiration), and for cell development.

The most important minerals are calcium, magnesium and phosphorus for teeth and bones; iron, phosphorus, potassium and sulphur for body cells, and sodium, chlorine and potassium for body fluids. Other minerals and trace elements needed in minute amounts are supplied in a normal diet. In some inland parts of the world, however, iodine is lacking in the soil and hence is not found in vegetables. Goitre, the swelling and malfunctioning of the thyroid gland, can result from insufficient iodine in the daily diet. Eat salt-water fish or use iodised or sea salt if you have reason to believe your diet lacks sufficient iodine.

Vitamins are organic substances found in foods. They are also essential for maintaining a healthy body. If you follow a diet based on the seven food groups discussed below, you should get enough of all vitamins. Sometimes, however, your diet does become deficient, and in this case vitamin tablets are recommended.

Some vitamins, such as A, D and E are often found in food with a high proportion of fat, whereas others, especially C and some of the B complex, are water soluble, which means they are lost when food is overcooked and decrease in amount when food is stored too long or exposed to air. A variety of diseases are caused by severe vitamin deficiency; most

noteworthy is scurvy caused by a lack of vitamin C.

Calorie is the unit used to measure the energy output of food (soon to be replaced by an EEC-wide unit called the *joule*). Pure protein and pure carbohydrate supply 4 calories per gram (or 116 calories per ounce), while pure fat supplies 9 calories per gram (or 263 per ounce). Calorie counts for foods differ greatly because few foods are pure.

Nutritionists recommend that adults obtain no more than 25 per cent of their calorie intake from fats and the rest from carbohydrates and proteins. The problem for most people is to keep fat consumption down. The cook can help here by frying fewer foods, draining it well on paper towels, and by using less butter in cooking and on bread. And remember that those favourite snack foods chocolate, crisps and salted nuts are high in fats.

The number of calories needed depends on age, weight, height and amount of activity. Thus an 11 stone man requires 2600–2800 calories per day whereas a 9 stone woman needs 1850–2000. Children and adolescents require more calories in relation to their size, with a 4 stone child needing as much as an adult woman.

In order to fulfil all the nutritional needs described above, a variety of foods must be eaten daily. To help people choose these foods, some nutritionists have placed foods in seven categories and recommend the number of servings of each daily. Thus without counting calories or proteins, minerals or vitamins you are able to achieve a daily balance. You will notice that alcoholic beverages and snack foods are not included; these supply calories without giving nutritive benefit.

Family Meal Planning

When you are planning meals, you must take into account foods eaten outside the home, both in terms of calories and of balanced diet. If foods from categories 1, 2, 5 and 7 predominate, you should emphasize the other groups at breakfast and the evening meal.

Unless you are lucky or have only one to feed, you are going to have to balance the likes and dislikes of several prople, while trying to maintain daily and weekly variety. If you plan your menus in advance (see Chapter Two pages 22-25

Daily nutritional requirements

Category	Minimum quantity daily
1. Bread, cereals, flour	2 servings daily
2. Milk, milk products, including cheese	2 servings daily
3. Meat, poultry, fish, eggs, dried beans	1 or more servings daily
4. Leafy, green and yellow vegetables	2 servings daily
5. Potatoes, root and other vegetables not in 4, fruits	2 servings daily
6. Citrus fruits, tomatoes, strawberries, raw cabbage	1 or more servings daily
7. Butter, margarine, fats oils	25 grams (1 ounce) daily

and Chapter Five pages 72-95), obtaining variety will be easier. Try to include a new recipe weekly and introduce new foods occasionally.

If you are starting out with a new partner, you will have a little time at the beginning in which to broaden a fussy eater's horizons. Do not waste it by being overly solicitous at menu planning time. Quietly serve the food and see what happens. A grudging 'it was OK' means you should try it again next month. Even an outright (no) should not be taken to mean 'never again', especially if your partner's food horizons are broadening.

Try not to serve the same combinations every time—chicken and peas, sausage and carrots—which can become tiresome and predictable. Also do not always serve the same meal on the same day of the week; every Monday should not be Sunday's leftovers, nor every Wednesday boiled mince. In addition to your regular favourites, include things you enjoy less frequently or which are seasonal: ox tongue, scallops, game, asparagus, to name only a few.

A well-planned and calculated meal should not have small amounts of leftovers like a tablespoon of potato and a half piece of meat. But on occasions you should plan to have enough leftovers for another meal, since large joints are more economical and more succulent than small-sized pieces. Also you save time and energy (both fuel and personal) in the cooking.

Above all keep the dinner atmosphere pleasant and relaxed. Meals offer a superb opportunity to come together for enjoyable, lively conversation and good nourishing food.

Cooking for Guests

Party cooking should not differ greatly from family cooking, although you do have more details to think about. These comprise the menu, and also include perhaps the wine, and the table setting. What you prepare need not be complicated or expensive, though it should be carefully garnished and served up nicely. For smell, presentation and taste in that order determine the pleasure of the diners.

The success of a party is based on a combination of a well-planned menu, good cooking, and a relaxed host and/or hostess, who is with the guests most of the time. The last is more important than the food, because people have come to enjoy good talk and cameraderie, and the food is only an adjunct, albeit an important one, to this. A nervous, fussing host or hostess presenting an excellent meal will be less well thought of than one who can combine good food with a relaxed lively atmosphere.

In menu planning follow the same family-meal rules for achieving a balanced diet, choosing food from a larger number of categories. Additionally, keep calories down by not adding fatty enrichments to

all the courses. If you use cream in your main course sauce, avoid serving them with the dessert no matter how customary.

You should also know the dietary needs of your guests (low calorie, low fat, allergic, diabetic, delicate digestion) and unostentatiously cater for it by serving diet-approved foods. (In serious cases consult with the person in advance to make sure.) The following menu would fit many diets. Grilled stuffed mushroom or tomato, followed by baked fish, one or two vegetables, plain potatoes and a lightly dressed green salad, and ending with a fresh fruit salad with a meringue topping. It is festive, low in fat and calories, and filling. Those without special diets would be satisfied too.

The traditional menu calls for a starter which can be soup, fruit, meat, fish or vegetables. It should be relatively small, to whet the appetite not satisify it, and contrast in colour, texture and content with the main course. Often starters are served already composed on individual plates—they can be put on the table before the guests come to it and will then form part of the table decor.

The starter is followed by the main course which combines a protein dish (usually hot and meat, poultry or fish) with vegetables and probably a sauce. Everything should be served from warmed platters and dished on to warmed plates. Garnishing, which need not be fancy, is important (see below), because appearance counts for a lot. Servings need not be large, when you are offering many courses. A green or mixed salad could follow the main course using the same plates.

Next comes either the dessert or the cheese, though both are not necessary. If you are serving both, keep the sweet light. Which you decide to have first is a matter of personal preference. When you are changing wines for the cheese course, it might, but does not have to, follow the dessert to give a break between the different wines.

Sometimes instead of, or in addition to, cheese and dessert, a savoury is served, following the old English custom. A savoury is a small, highly seasoned dish, generally hot, which is used to end a dinner. The original objective was to clear the palate before the port or liqueur.

Non-traditional dinners need not be divided so strictly into courses and in fact it is sometimes pleasant to serve a number of courses together, buffet style. The starter can become healthy finger foods—raw vegetables, marinated mushrooms, prawns and a dipping sauce, to name only a few—to be eaten with pre-dinner drinks.

Organize preparations for a dinner party in the same way as for any other meal, though it is advisable to write out a full timetable (see Chapter Five page 73). In addition to the food you should probably decide on setting the table in advance.

Table setting: When you are laying a table the rule is to place the cutlery you are going to use first at the outside. Knives and spoons go on the right, forks on the left. If your starter calls for a fork and knife put them farthest from the centre; closer to the plate put the knife and fork for the main course. The dessert spoon plus fork go across the top of the plate with the spoon closer to the plate with its bowl at the left; the fork goes above the spoon with the tines at the right.

The wine glass (or glasses) go at the top right hand corner of the setting with the glass you are using first on the right (outside). The bread and butter plate, possibly with a napkin on it, is placed to the left of the fork.

Traditionally, you serve from the left and clear from the right. However, convenience should be the main aim – and the easiest way to pass the plates around the table the method adopted.

At a dinner party you and your guests spend a large part of the evening sitting round the table, so how it looks is important. You can create a mood by the type of table you lay. Crisp white linen or a lace cloth and napkins are perfect with sparkling glasses and fine china for a formal meal, gingham or printed cotton sets off bright coloured plain china or chunky pottery to advantage.

Colour is a mood maker too: for light summer meals plain pale colours or fresh floral cottons are attractive; in winter a richly coloured cloth and napkins look warming and welcoming. Have mats or trivets to put the hot serving dishes on; these can either match or contrast with your place mats.

Candles and flowers always make a table look festive, but remember that your guests would probably like to see one another without looking through or around the centrepiece. Even if a large centrepiece is on the table when the guests arrive, remove it to a mantlepiece or sideboard before the meal is served if possible. A low centrepiece, perhaps with candles in it, may not interfere with the sight lines and can stay throughout the meal. Use non-drip candles, which are more expensive, to save your table and tablecloth from dripping wax.

Garnishes: Garnishes are any edible decorations that are added just before serving to improve the appearance of food. They are used with every part of the meal from starter to dessert, though not necessarily with every course. It would be unwise, for instance, to provide beautiful complex garnishes with several courses, because you would be overdressing the meal. One outstanding garnish, however, can be accompanied during a meal by several simple ones.

Simple garnishes frequently supply contrasts in colour, texture or flavour. Hence the popularity of parsley, chopped or as a sprig, and watercress with meats and non-green vegetables, and of whipped cream and flaked almonds on desserts. Other simple garnishes include diced or grated cheese, sliced or whole olives, onion rings (raw or marinated), chopped fresh herbs, sieved hard-boiled eggs, toasted sesame seeds and shredded coconut. And remember aspic and coloured jellies. Citrus fruits, cut into slices or wedges, are used both for colour and flavour.

Soup garnishes sometimes indicate what is being served. For example, asparagus tips are floated on a cream of asparagus soup or mushroom slices on a mushroom soup. At other times minced herbs or croûtons (small fried bread cubes) are used to supply contrasting flavour and texture.

Simple dessert garnishes include clustered fresh berries or glacéed fruits, chocolate caraque, tiny meringues and chopped nuts. On fresh fruit, shredded coconut or mint leaves may be used.

Garnishes can also be complex, requiring considerable cutting and combining or using a piping bag and nozzle. In most cases these decorations go better with canapés, starters, simple luncheon dishes and cold buffets rather than with a hot main dinner course. One exception is mashed potato piped around a serving platter or individual dishes with the main course, usually in a sauce, piled in the centre and reheated under the grill. Cakes, too, can be magnificently decorated using a piping bag and the various nozzles available.

While garnishes are important for appearance, you must not use too many at once, for simple elegance is the better style. No food should be completely hidden by its garnish. In general, no more than two should be used at a time and except for the sweet course one of these should be green (parsley, fresh herbs, watercress). Thus garnish a fish with lemon slices and finely chopped parsley spread in a single line rather than randomly scattered, or chops with tomato wedges and watercress. For dessert, a trifle piped with cream and a few chocolate curls is more appealing than one heaped with cream, chopped jelly, nuts and fruit.

Beverages

Beverages comprise all drinking liquids, including alcoholic ones. Coffee and tea are the most complex to deal with because of the wide range of choice and the numerous methods of brewing. Milk, which is a relatively simple beverage, is discussed elsewhere (see page 52).

Tea

If tea were simple to make more people would drink a well-made cup. It is made from the leaves of the plant *camellia sinensis*, which is widely cultivated in many tropical and sub-tropical regions of the world.

There are three principal classifications: Black, Green, and Oolong.

Black tea is the most common and still most popular tea in the western world. Its leaves are fully fermented in the process of manufacture, which makes them black.

Green tea is mainly produced in China and Japan, and for that reason is frequently referred to as China tea. The particular characteristic of green tea is that the leaf is dried immediately and does not undergo fermentation, which preserves the green colour of the leaves. Green tea is more astringent in flavour than black tea and tends to be an acquired taste.

Oolong tea is only partly fermented before drying and is manufactured in

Taiwan and China. The leaves are brown in colour and, when brewed, produce a pale brown tea with a characteristic aroma and flavour.

How to make tea
In order to make perfect tea every time follow this method.

Fill the kettle with freshly-drawn water from the cold tap and place over moderate heat. Just before the water boils, pour a little of it into the teapot to warm the pot and then discard the water. (This enables the tea to infuse better.) Place one teaspoon of tea per person and one 'for the pot' in the teapot. As soon as the water boils bring the teapot to the kettle and pour in the water. Place the lid on the pot and allow to stand for 3–5 minutes before using. Serve with milk, sugar or lemon to taste.

Iced tea has barely made its way east across the Atlantic, but when summer days are hot, it can be a refreshing change. Ideally, strong, freshly brewed tea is poured over many ice cubes that melt and cool the drink. But this method is extravagant and impractical when the supply of ice is limited. Instead pour the leftover morning brew into a jar and chill it, or make a second strong pot to strain and refrigerate.

To serve, place three or four ice cubes in a tall glass, pour the tea over them slowly, and serve. Pass sugar and lemon separately. Sometimes a sprig of mint is added as well. Tea that is cloudy has been made with hard water; sometimes it clears when ice is added.

Tea leaves should be stored in airtight containers to retain freshness and full flavour. Also buy often and in small amounts. Experiment with unfamiliar teas and vary them with the time of day and occasion. Tea is far more exciting than the traditional 'cuppa' suggests.

Coffee

The flavour of coffee, like that of wine, depends greatly on where it has been grown because climate, soil, elevation, aspect and age of tree all affect the final product.

Most packaged coffee consists of a blend from several sources chosen to complement one another and to give a distinctive, uniform flavour. Some coffees, however, come from a single area. Most Brazilian coffee, for instance, is

144

blended because it is somewhat harsh, but the finest quality is sold unblended as Brazilian. Other names found on special coffees are Colombia, Kenya, Blue Mountain (Jamaica) and moka (Yemen). Each has unique, subtle differences in flavour.

The different coffee-making methods discussed below require grinds of different degrees of fineness. Infused and percolated coffees call for a medium grind; the filtered and Cona methods for a fine grind.

How to make coffee
Some basic principles apply to coffee-making no matter what type of coffee you make. The best coffee, for instance, is made from freshly roasted beans ground just before you make the coffee. Ideally, coffee should not be allowed to boil, and although 1–2 minutes of boiling is not detrimental to the taste and flavour of the finished coffee, continued boiling will certainly impair its quality.

Basically, western-style coffee-making consists of passing boiling water through coffee grounds, carrying with it the colour and flavour but leaving the grounds behind, usually in a separate section of the coffee pot.

Infused coffee: Pour boiling water on to freshly ground coffee in a warmed jug (about 1 tablespoon of coffee per person). Stir the coffee and leave the jug in a warm place for about 10 minutes. Pour the coffee through a strainer into a heated coffee pot, or straight into coffee cups.

Percolated coffee: Methods vary widely according to the type of percolator used, and it is, therefore, wise to follow the instructions given with your percolator. The principle involved, however, is that the water circulates through the coffee grounds, extracting the flavour and colour and then drips through a strainer, leaving the grounds behind.

Filtered coffee: This is a great favourite in France, and can be produced by placing a perforated filter over a cup or jug and filling the filter with about 1 tablespoon of coffee per person. Then pour boiling water through the filter, to extract flavour and colour as it drips into the cup or jug below.

Cona or suction method: Fill the lower container with water and the upper with coffee grounds. On heating, the water is sucked up the funnel between the

two containers, remaining there for about 3 minutes. When it is removed from the heat, the coffee filters down into the lower container, leaving the grounds in the funnel.

Espresso or Italian coffee: This is strong, dark, slightly bitter and is made under pressure in a machine. It can also be made in a drip pot, or *napoletana*, the basket of the inner cylinder being filled with very finely ground coffee and the outer cylinder with water. The spouted vessel is then placed on top of the drip pot, with the spout facing downwards. Over low heat, the water is brought to the boil. The *napoletana* is then reversed so that the spout points upwards and lets the water drip through.

Arabic, Turkish or Greek coffee: This is more complicated—and more wasteful in terms of the amount of coffee grounds used. It is, nevertheless, a most attractive beverage and one that is becoming increasingly popular in western countries. To make Arabic coffee, boil water in an Arabic coffee-maker over moderate heat. Add sugar to taste (usually about 1 teaspoon per cup) and $2\frac{1}{2}$ teaspoons of very finely pulverized coffee grounds to the pot, allowing the coffee grounds to remain on the surface of the water. Bring to the boil again, then remove from the heat to allow the froth to die down. Boil again, then remove from the heat. As the froth dies down, stir the coffee grounds into the liquid. Pour the coffee immediately into small demi-tasse cups, allowing 1–2 minutes before drinking to let the sediment sink to the bottom of the cup.

Instant coffee: Although not up to the standard of good freshly brewed coffee, instant coffee is used in most homes. And with a little care its quality can be improved. Most important, use enough powder. Next, instead of pouring boiling water directly on to the powder (which scorches and gives it a bitter taste) pour it into the bowl of a metal spoon and let it run into the cup or pot. This cools the water just enough to ensure maximum flavour.

Storage
Once roasted, coffee does not keep fresh for long. Therefore buy it in small amounts and keep it in airtight jars in a cool place.

Gaelic coffee and a plunger coffee pot.

Beer

Beer is a brewed and fermented beverage made from malted barley or other cereal grains. It is flavoured with hops, the tiny blossoms of the hop vine. Since the making of beer dates back to the beginnings of history, it is not surprising that many types of beer, with different flavours and consistencies, have developed. The two major divisions are light beer, the more popular in most of the western world, and dark beer. The differences depend on how the grain has been treated before fermentation and on the particular type of yeast used for the fermentation. In general, beer contains about 3–7 per cent alcohol, though a few types have a higher alcohol content.

In the western world light beers are favoured today, and lager has probably become the most widely popular. The famous beers of Denmark, Holland, and Germany are all lagers, and most other countries have home-brewed lagers as well. In England, bitter, slightly darker and less carbonated than lager, is popular. The term ale encompasses all the light brews that are not lagers.

Stout and porter are in most places only known as names found in old books, but both remain popular in some areas. Ireland, for instance, is famed for its stout. Both these beers are dark, or black, made from roasted malt, sometimes with the addition of burnt sugar.

Beer may be served at any time. Its characteristic sharp tang complements highly flavoured or spicy dishes and such foods as hamburgers, steaks, corned beef and cabbage, Irish stews, sausages, cold meats, all pork dishes and fried dishes. All the sharper cheeses go well with beer or ale.

Wine

Wine is the fermented juice of grapes. One species of vine, *vitis vinifera*, produces almost all the grapes used in wine-making (the only exception being some hardy vines native to the north-eastern United States which, on the whole, produce rather inferior wines).

Wine is an alcoholic drink, ranging from about 7–13 per cent alcoholic strength for table wines and around 20 per cent for fortified wines. It can be red, white or rosé, still or sparkling, sweet or dry.

Wine is made wherever grapes are grown, that is, in most non-tropical areas without extremely harsh winters. Major producing areas lie along the northern shore of the Mediterranean from Cyprus and Greece to Spain and also in north Africa. Italy has the largest wine output, but arguably the greatest wines are produced in France, in areas north of the Mediterranean shore and in Germany, around the Rhine and Moselle valleys. Other superb wine areas include around Lake Balaton in Hungary and in the Balkans, particularly northern Yugoslavia. Outside Europe, California produces the most outstanding wines, with others of good quality coming from Australia, South Africa, Chile and Argentina. Wines from less well-known areas often give better quality for money, especially in the lower price range.

Wine and Food

Wine is in the happy position of being inextricably bound up with the pleasant ritual of eating good food. Whether a simple cheese and bread snack or a full gourmet *haute cuisine* dinner, wine can and does add to its lustre and enjoyment.

There are some general guidelines as to which wines best accompany different foods, but they are all necessarily subjective and need not be followed slavishly —if you prefer a red wine with fish or a light white wine with a rich meat casserole, the choice is yours. The wine and food chart on page 148 is intended to serve as a guide for the inexperienced wine drinker who is uncertain about what to purchase and/or wishes to try something different. But, in addition, remember these general 'natural' rules— mainly based on common sense rather than on a refined palate!

1. National cuisines and wines (if the country produces them) usually complement each other and whenever possible should be served together—a Château Lafite, beautiful though it is, will do relatively little for a rich Spaghetti Bolognese while a good rustic Chianti Classico will, and by the same token, that same Chianti will not enhance the delicate flavour of Beef Wellington in the same way as a Château Lafite.

2. If you are serving more than one wine with a meal, the general—and sensible—thing to do is to serve white before red, young wines before mature, dry before sweet.

Buying Wines

Most of us most of the time buy 'vin ordinaire' or plonk as some derisively call it. Some such wines can be awful, but many are surprisingly good. And the only way to discover which you like is by tasting. Make a point of remembering the name and the shipper of wines you have enjoyed. If you find you like several wines from the same source, it can be worth trying other wines blended by the same company.

In shops, examine the labels, noting how specific the information is. Something called 'dry red table wine' can come from any source and is likely to be a blend of wines from many different places, probably even from several different countries. Other labels may indicate a single country of origin— Spanish Burgundy—but it, too, is likely to be a blend. And blends can vary astonishingly from shipper to shipper.

Look for wines from a specific area. In Spain, for instance, Rioja and Valdepeñas reds have both body and character. Hungarian Bull's Blood (Egri Bikavér) and French regional wines (Côtes du Rhône, Côtes de Provence) are other examples of regional wines which can be of good quality for the price. At the expensive end of the market are the château-bottled wines of France, the village-named wines of the Rhine and Moselle. Many have specific identifiable names, almost all will be subject to the *appellation controlee* laws of their region. They are almost always expensive, many should not be drunk until 8–12 years after the date on the bottle, and for a special occasion there is absolutely nothing to beat them.

Wine continues to grow and develop even after it is bottled, therefore you are dealing with a living substance which must be handled gently. No wine should be bought and drunk on the same day. This is because it has been shaken up in transit, which makes it bitter and unpleasant. Even an inexpensive wine will improve by resting quietly for a few days; for expensive wines the resting period should be longer.

Red wines should be opened in advance. With fine wines the timing depends on age and variety; with more ordinary ones an hour or so is plenty. Decanting red wine helps to aerate it, bringing out its full flavour. With old, expensive wines, decanting is also done in order to leave any deposit behind. Pour gently and slowly in either case so as not to disturb the wine. A wine basket is unnecessary with young wines.

White wines and rosés are not normally uncorked in advance.

Red wines should be served at a cool room temperature of about 18°C (65°F). White wine, rosé and champagne are all served chilled. The sweeter the wine the colder it should be. Thus a dry wine should be refrigerated about 2 hours before serving, a sweet one up to 5 hours in advance. Wine that is too cold lacks full flavour. Since wine loses its flavour soon after opening, if you use only a small quantity from a bottle it is advisable to transfer the remaining wine into a smaller bottle and re-cork it. Ideally the wine should be used within a week of opening the bottle.

The best all-purpose glass for most wines should be clear, to show the true colour of the wine, a tulip shape, so that the bouquet of the wine isn't lost and, most important, the right size. Glasses should never be filled more than half-full; therefore a general all-purpose glass for wine should be about 250–300 millilitres (8–10 fluid ounces) in size. Champagne should not be served in the old fashioned shallow shape as these allow the sparkling bubbles to evaporate too quickly.

Storing Wine

Not everyone has or needs a wine cellar. All you need is a dark place with a uniform temperature preferably between 10°–18°C (50°–65°F), though uniformity is more important than coolness.

Bottles must rest on their sides; never stand upright, for the cork will dry out and let air in and air can ruin wine. Thus you will need either wine racks (bought or home-made) or a sturdy wine box or two. (Sherry cartons are often more durable than wine cartons.) Always remove the bottles gently to disturb them as little as possible.

Some final tips

Having done all the work, you face the question of what to wear. Naturally style is personal and clothing should suit the occasion, but beyond this give some thought to practical considerations. First, wear clothes you can work in comfortably

Moselle wine with grape name (riesling) on the label and an AP quality mark.

and easily. They should not be too tight or too warm. You are going to have to move around a lot as well as bend often. Wear comfortable shoes for the same reason. And for women especially, watch out for your sleeves. Long or three-quarter length sleeves have a nasty way of scooping up gravy, catching cooking-spoon handles and knocking off soft icings and meringues as you reach across to do something. The best advice is don't wear such sleeves; second best advice is to fold them up out of harm's way.

Wear a big coverall apron while dishing up and carving. If you do not have one, tuck one tea towel in at your neck and a second at your waist. Spots are annoying and difficult to get out of clothes and cleaning bills are high.

Ultimately the recipe for any dinner or party boils down to plan ahead, cook ahead, do your best, stay flexible, and enjoy the meal, your family and your guests. Take occasional disaster in your stride, neither making a great fuss over it or letting it cause depression. These things happen to everyone. If unexpected people turn up, add another vegetable or another course or even another type of meat. One successful party that increased from six to ten without warning was eked out by serving a pound of sausages, each halved, along with the small joint. A simple savoury of grilled cheese on small bread squares served with a good sprinkling of freshly ground pepper followed the pudding. Nobody left hungry and all enjoyed the evening—including the host and hostess!

The label of a blended light Italian wine, with the Italian equivalent of appellation côntrolée.

A label with all the signs of a medium-quality white Brugundy, including 'mise en bouteilles'.

Wine and food chart

Hors d'oeuvre

Pate, quiche, etc

Fairly strong dry white, such as Traminer, a Rhine wine such as Rüdesheimer, rosé such as Rosé d'Anjou or light red, such as Beaujolais

Salad or cold hors d'oeuvre

Dry white, such as Alsatian Sylvaner or Yugoslavian Zilavka or Riesling

Soups

Dry sherry or a light Madeira is served with consommés, otherwise wine is not usually served with soup

Fish

Grilled or lightly poached fish

Light wine, such as Chablis, Pouilly Fuissé or Moselle

Fish in rich cream sauce

Heavy white, such as white Burgundy (Meursault, Montrachet) or Rhine wine, such as Niersteiner

Shellfish

Light white (Chablis is traditional with oysters), Muscadet, Italian Soave or a slightly flinty Loire, such as Sancerre or Vouvray

Shellfish served as a risotto or with rich sauce

Rosé, such as Tavel, a white Loire wine, such as Pouilly Fumé or a white Burgundy, such as Puligny Montrachet

Smoked Fish

Heavy white, such as white Burgundy, Alsatian Traminer or a spicy Rhine spätlese wine

Dark meat

Beef, roasted or grilled

Bordeaux, such as Château Montrose or St. Emilion. (Any good Bordeaux is perfect with a roast)

Beef casseroles and stews

Sturdy red Burgundy, such as Beaune, a Rhône wine, such as Châteauneuf-du-Pape, a heavier Italian red, such as Barolo or a Hungarian Egri Bikaver

Steaks

Bordeaux, such as St. Estephe, a medium red Burgundy, such as Nuits St. Georges, or a Californian Cabernet Sauvignon

Lamb, roasted or grilled

Bordeaux, such as a Margaux, a light Burgundy, such as Beaujolais or Macon or a light Italian wine, such as Bardolino or Valpolicella or a Californian Cabernet Sauvignon

Lamb casseroles, stews and risottos

Bordeaux, such as a Medoc, Cabernet Sauvignon, an Italian wine such as Chianti or Valpolicella

Game (grouse, partridge, pheasant)

Bordeaux, such as St. Emilion or Château Haut-Brion

Hare, venison

Strong red, such as Côtes du Rhône or a heavy Burgundy, such as Chambertin

White meat

Pork

Medium-sweet white, such as Graves or Orvieto or a rosé, such as Côtes de Provence or Mateus

Veal

Strong white, such as Montrachet, Pinot Chardonnay or a light red, such as Valpolicella, Zinfandel or Beaujolais

Ham

Rosé, such as Tavel or Rosé d'Anjou or a light red, such as Macon

Poultry

Chicken, cooked simply

Heavier white, such as Hungarian Riesling or a white Burgundy

Chicken cooked with red wine or in a very rich vegetable-type stew

Light red, such as Beaujolais or Fleurie

Duck

Heavy white Burgundy, such as Meurseult or a rosé, such as Tavel

Goose

White, such as Rhine wine or an Alsatian or Hungarian Riesling

Turkey

Heavy white, such as Traminer, a Rhine wine or a rosé, such as Côtes de Provence

Cheese

Soft (Brie, Camembert, etc)

Medium red Burgundy, such as Beaune or a Bordeaux, such as St. Julien

Medium (Port-Salut, Cheddar, etc)

Light, fruity red, such as Fleurie or Beaujolais, or a spicy white, such as Alsatian Gewürztraminer or a Tavel

Cream or Goat's

Medium white, such as Graves, an Alsatian Traminer or a Rhine wine

Blue cheese (Stilton, etc)

Light red such as Bardolino, a medium Burgundy such as Brouilly or a Cabernet Sauvignon

Desserts

Sauternes or Barsac are the traditional dessert wines, but any German wine marked spätlese or auslese would also be suitable. For an extra rich dessert, try a Hungarian Tokay

After-dinner

Port, the heavier Madeiras or, for a change, a mature Hungarian Tokay or the 'queen of Sauternes', Château d'Yquem

Index

Numbers in italics denote
illustrations.

Picture Credits
Bryce Attwell 55;
Barnaby's Picture Library
22/3;
Camera Press/Photo by
H. von Sterneck 149;
Alan Duns 4/5, 16, 47, 49, 53,
59, 65, 72, 84, 88, 93, 94, 120,
127, 128, 129, 131, 145;
Eddie Ely 30, 116t;
Melvin Grey 24;
Graeme Harris 62/3;
John Hovell 32, 36;
Courtesy of Hygena 2000 11;
Paul Kemp 13b, 109, 136, 137,
138;
Don Last 80;
David Levin 13t, 109, 137,
138;
David Meldrum 33, 90, 91, 119;
Roger Phillips 2/3, 12, 19, 27,
43, 45, 50/1, 57, 60, 77, 81, 82,
83, 86, 87, 113, 116b, 118,
123, 124, 125, 132, 139, 147;
Courtesy of Thorn Electrical
Appliances 28;
Transworld Feature
Syndicate 141;
Jerry Tubby 35;
Courtesy of W. F. Rational
Kitchens 6.